# REFLECTIONS ON CRIME

# REFLECTIONS ON CRIME

## An Introduction to Criminology and Criminal Justice

James A. Inciardi
*University of Delaware*

Holt, Rinehart and Winston

New York   Chicago   San Francisco   Dallas
Montreal   Toronto   London   Sydney

To
James A. Inciardi,
My Father;
and
Marie C. Inciardi,
My Mother.

© 1978 by Holt, Rinehart and Winston

**Library of Congress Cataloging in Publication Data**

Inciardi, James A
   Reflections on crime.
   Includes index.
   1. Crime and criminals.  2. Criminal justice,
Administration of.   3. Crime and criminals—
United States.   I. Title.
HV6025.I45        364        76-17253

ISBN 0-03-036261-X pbk.

 90   090   98765432

Printed in the United States of America

# PREFACE

*Reflections on Crime,* as the subtitle suggests, is an introduction to both criminology and criminal justice. Some may find this a bit peculiar since the two have traditionally been approached as separate disciplines with alternative fields of concentration. Criminology, in its broadest definition, has been interpreted as the scientific study of crime and criminals, with its specific concerns generally focusing on the causes of crime, the characteristics of offenders, the magnitude and trends of crimes, the conditions under which behavior becomes defined as criminal, the prevention and control of crime, and the rehabilitation of offenders. Criminal justice, on the other hand, has typically concentrated on the structure, functions, and decision processes of those agencies which deal with the management of crime—the police, the courts, and the correctional process.

This suggests that criminology and criminal justice are indeed separate disciplines, but, interestingly, they approach essentially the same subject matter—crime and criminals—but from differing perspectives. Criminologists have been associated more often with theory and research, while those in criminal justice have been identified with the actual processes utilized to administer and control crime and offenders. Criminology has endured in academic and research environments while criminal justice emerges on the front lines of the administration of justice.

Yet the distinction is not quite that simple, for both disciplines tend to overlap one another in many areas, primarily because the boundaries of criminology have been drawn from many fields—physical science, biology, medicine, economics, anthropology, law, religion, psychology, sociology, social work, education, political science, public administration, *and* criminal justice. For example, "corrections," which has generally been considered a subfield or branch of criminology, includes such topics as prisons, jails, juvenile training schools, probation and parole machinery, and the procedures and programs implemented within these institutions and agencies for the purposes of rehabilitating the offender and protecting the community. But corrections as such is also a part of the institutional arrangements, activities, and processes that are collectively referred to as the "criminal justice system"; along with law enforcement and the judicial process, it is a subsystem of the criminal justice process. Similarly, the mechanisms developed for the measurement of crime, the control of crime, and the prevention of crime, while often and clearly functions of various agencies in the criminal justice system, have been examined at length by criminology. Furthermore, almost every aspect of the criminal justice process has been the subject of criminologic research.

From an alternative perspective, the criminal justice discipline has also ventured into the traditional territory of criminology. Practitioners in this field have examined the causes of crime, trends of crime, and the characteristics and categories of offenders. Textbooks in criminal justice, furthermore, often begin with an extended discussion of the same topics found in criminology books—the definition of crime, the nature of law, the extent of crime, the theories of causation, and the history of punishment.

In sum, the issue is that both criminology and criminal justice have the same base—crime. This is not to suggest that the two disciplines should be combined, for criminology has theory and research as its primary concerns while criminal justice is more operational, dealing mainly with administrative matters. Yet one cannot be fully understood without a knowledge of the other, and the preliminary concerns of both—crime and the criminal—are the same. And it is within this perspective that *Reflections on Crime* serves as an introduction to both criminology and criminal justice.

In developing this volume, my interest and purpose was to provide the reader with a simple introduction to the issues and concepts which relate to the study of crime and offenders. On numerous occasions, students from both criminology and criminal justice as well as practitioners from other fields have asked for direction in locating some overview of the phenomenon of crime—a starting point from which they might further venture into the more comprehensive texts or other volumes which concentrate on more focused topics. As such, this commentary on crime has been structured to serve only as an introduction. The basic ideas, concepts, and issues are offered, and sources for the study of more explicit and detailed aspects of criminal phenomena are suggested.

Finally, in an effort to engender a useful perspective on the nature of crime, I have frequently drawn from other disciplines. Throughout the volume, for example, there is much that might be called history. A sometimes historical approach often seemed appropriate since many contemporary concerns can be more fully appreciated when viewed within the contexts of both the past and the present. In addition, several chapters examine the content and impact of both myth and popular culture, for these have significantly influenced many of our images of crime and criminals. After reading this book, it is hoped that students will not only develop a more rounded understanding of crime, but in addition, that they begin to reevaluate their current conceptions of the problem of crime, for this was the primary purpose of my efforts.

J. A. I.

# CONTENTS

Chapter 1   **INTRODUCTION: CONCEPTS AND CONCEPTIONS OF CRIME AND CRIMINALS**   **1**

*Toward a Definition of Crime   2*
*Conceptions of Crime in American Culture   12*
*Suggested Readings   25*

Chapter 2   **SOME PERSPECTIVES ON THE HISTORY OF CRIME IN AMERICA**   **26**

*Crime and Vice in Colonial America   28*
*The Rise of Criminal Districts and Street Gangs   32*
*Political Corruption and the Commercialization of Vice   37*
*Crime on the Western Frontier   41*
*Early Twentieth-Century Gangsterism   42*
*Prohibition and the Genesis of Organized Crime   45*
*Violence in the Streets   49*
*Suggested Readings   53*

Chapter 3   **ASSESSING THE MAGNITUDE AND TRENDS OF CRIME**   **54**

*The Evolution of Criminal Statistics in the United States   55*
*The Uniform Crime Reports   59*
*The Extent of Crime   66*
*The Unreliability of Criminal Statistics   76*

*Victim Survey Research   80*
*Self-Reported Criminal Behavior   86*
*Epilogue   88*
*Suggested Readings   89*

Chapter 4      **THE SEARCH FOR CAUSES: A LOST**
               **CAUSE IN CRIMINOLOGY**                      **90**

*Early Theories of Crime   92*
*The Emergence of Scientific Criminology   97*
*Twentieth-Century Biological Determinism   98*
*From Eclectic Theory of Sociological Theory   101*
*Changing Perspectives on Crime Causation   109*
*Postscript—Lombroso Rides Again   113*
*Suggested Readings   114*

Chapter 5      **FROM BONNIE AND CLYDE TO**
               **WATERGATE: AN OBSERVATION OF**
               **BEHAVIOR SYSTEMS IN CRIME**                 **116**

*Criminal Types and Typologies   118*
*Behavior Systems in Crime   126*
*Criminal Behavior Systems and Social Control   147*
*Suggested Readings   154*

Chapter 6      **THE DISCOVERY OF CRIMINAL**
               **JUSTICE IN AMERICA**                        **155**

*The Emergence of "Criminal Justice"   158*
*Criminal Justice as a "System"   161*
*The Rise of Criminal Justice   176*
*Suggested Readings   178*

Postscript     **THE PURSUIT OF KNOWLEDGE IN**
               **CRIMINOLOGY AND CRIMINAL**
               **JUSTICE**                                   **179**

**Bibliographical References**                               **181**

**Index**                                                    **205**

# 1

# Introduction:
# Concepts and Conceptions
# of Crime and Criminals

Most of us feel that we have a reasonable understanding of what crime is all about. We are confronted with it almost daily as part of mass media entertainment and news presentations, and we see commentaries on it in our local newspapers. We are also conscious of the fear of crime. We lock our homes and automobiles to protect our property, and we avoid places and circumstances not considered "safe" in order to protect our lives. Furthermore, given the 104.5 million crimes of homicide, forcible rape, robbery, aggravated assault, burglary, larceny, and motor vehicle theft reported to police agencies across the country from 1960 through 1975, a significant number of us have also been direct victims of crime.

When thinking about crime, many of us feel that there is a given range of behaviors that are deemed acceptable, and what falls beyond those limits constitutes crime. We realize, for example, that the taking of a human life, or sexual assault, or the theft of property are designated as "crimes," and when we reflect on "crime in the streets"—murder, rape, and robbery—we may think of crime as something alien, something that exists outside of organized society.

Yet crime is very much a part of our contemporary social world. In spite of the many shared understandings, few Americans tend to think analytically about crime, and most have a limited, patchy, and distorted view of it. "Crime" is a broad term of both variable and uncritical usages. The range of behaviors it circumscribes is not only widely diffused, but it is also constantly changing. Given the complex nature of crime, the first inquiry here will focus on achieving a useful definition of the phenomenon, followed by a discussion of the relative character of crime, how certain behaviors become defined as criminal, where some of our distorted views of crime have descended from, and sources for a more analytical perspective on crime.

## TOWARD A DEFINITION OF CRIME

Crime reflects a range of phenomena that have been subject to the interpretation of specialists from numerous fields, including sociology, criminology, psychology, law, medicine, social work, anthropology, and criminal justice. Each of these reflects differing perspectives on social behavior, and as a result, there is necessarily little agreement as to the explicit nature and meaning of crime. The various conceptions differ from one another primarily according to the extent to which they take cognizance of natural law, criminal law, and the relativity of social norms.

Among the earliest meanings applied to crime was that drawn from *natural law.* Natural law referred to a body of principles and rules that were believed to be uniquely fitting for and binding upon any community of rational beings. Any violation of these rules and principles was deemed to be "criminal." In this notion, natural law comes from a source higher than man; it is a "higher law" understood to be binding even in the absence of man-made law. The idea of natural law was incorporated into the Code of Hammurabi, the first known written legal document, which dates back to perhaps 1900 B.C. It was adopted by the ancient Romans and played a key role in the formulation and spread of Roman law, which persisted for more than a millennium throughout most of the civilized world. The concept of natural law can also be found underlying a portion of Anglo-American law. In addition to the "natural right" to life and property, the laws that are based on the idealized morals of a society descend from the natural law concept.

Interestingly, since natural law has generally referred to that which determines what is right and wrong and has its power made valid by nature, it would follow that its precepts would have some universality. On this point, during the latter part of the nineteenth century, Baron Raffaele Garofalo, a judge of the Court of Criminal Appeal of Naples, made an elaborate study to determine whether there might be a "natural crime," that is, an act or group of acts which had been considered criminal by all persons everywhere. Garofalo indicated:

The sole point of inquiry is whether, among the crimes and offenses recognized by existing laws, there are any which at all times and in all places had been recognized as punishable acts. When we think of certain hideous crimes such as parricide (the murdering of a parent or close relative), assassination, murder for the sake of robbery, murder from sheer brutality, ... the question would seem to require an affirmative answer. But a slight investigation seems to dispel this idea.[1]

More recently, criminologist Hermann Mannheim has undertaken a complex examination of the natural law movement throughout the Western world, and found that it was subject to widely varying interpretations:

There is no single and unchanging concept of natural law. While its underlying idea is the longing of mankind for an absolute yardstick to measure the goodness or badness of human actions and the law of the State and to define their relations to religion and morality, the final lesson is that no such yardstick can be found.[2]

Within the fields of sociology and criminology where the natural law concept has had only limited importance, two alternative definitional frames of reference currently prevail—a legal perspective and a social perspective. Among the theorists and practitioners who rely on the criminal law for an interpretation of the scope and meaning of crime, many have adopted the definition of crime offered by lawyer/sociologist, Paul W. Tappan, who suggested that crime is "... an intentional act or omission in violation of criminal law (statutory and case law), committed without defense of justification, and sanctioned by the state as a felony or misdemeanor."[3]

Tappan's definition of crime embodies a variety of concepts. As an "intentional act or omission," this notion of crime reflects the central philosophy of the American system of law—that an *act,* or the *omission of an act,* must be committed, and that persons cannot be punished for their thoughts. This suggests that some action must take place, or that there must be some failure to act when there is a legal duty to do so. To be a crime, there must also be *criminal intent* and the actor must have no legally recognized defense or justification for the act. And finally, the act must involve what has been defined as crime by the criminal law.

By way of explanation, Tappan's conceptualization of crime, although framed in legal terms, is clearly specific. It requires an act, as in the case of robbery or theft or some other behavior that is prohibited by the criminal law, or the omission of an act that is legally required, as in the case of an air controller who deliberately fails to warn a pilot of heavy airport traffic, thus causing an accident. The notion of criminal intent suggests the actor's awareness of what is right and wrong under the law with an intention to violate the law, as contrasted with the retarded, the insane, or the young who may not have their full use of reason. Defense or justification refers to actions precipitated by victims or observers who are attempting to protect their own or other's lives and property from a law violator.

While this definition of crime may be specific, it is in some ways narrow since it includes only those violations of the law that are "sanctioned by the state as a felony or misdemeanor." The issue here is the distinction between a felony and a misdemeanor, as contrasted with other possible violations of the criminal law, and requires a brief examination of some basic legal terms.

*Statutory law,* as embodied in Tappan's definition, descends from the legislature; it is law created by statute. *Case law* emerges from court interpretations of statutory law and from court decisions where rules have not been codified. *Common law* refers to the customs, traditions, judicial decisions, and other materials that guide courts in their decision-making but which have not been enacted into statutes or embodied into the Constitution.[4] The common law developed in England during the eleventh century and is the basis of Anglo-American law. It emerged on a case-by-case basis as opposed to written or statutory law, and currently, the terms common law and case law are often used interchangeably.

Historically, a *felony,* under common law, was a crime punishable by death or forfeiture of property, and included such offenses as murder, manslaughter, forcible rape, sodomy, larceny, robbery, arson, and burglary. A *misdemeanor* was a lesser offense considered as lacking the moral reprehensibility of a felony. Since the early days of the common law, other felonies, such as statutory rape, have been added to the law by statute.

Currently, the distinction between felony and misdemeanor is similar. Felony is now a generic term for serious offenses punishable by death or by imprisonment in a state or federal prison. A misdemeanor is generally a minor offense that is punishable by no more than a $1,000 fine and/or one year of imprisonment, typically in a local institution.

While Tappen's definition of crime includes felonies and misdemeanors, it fails to comment on classifications deemed neither felony nor misdemeanor. In some jurisdictions there are infractions designated as "offenses" and "violations" which are subject to prosecution by the state. These may vary from one place to another, but have included such crimes as prostitution and possession of marijuana for personal use.[5]

A more inclusive definition of crime within the legal framework that has been accepted by many has been proposed by criminologist Edwin H. Sutherland; it suggests that an act is a crime when it is in violation of the law:

> The essential characteristic of crime is that it is behavior which is prohibited by the State and against which the State may react, at least as a last resort, by punishment. The two abstract criteria generally regarded by legal scholars as necessary elements in a definition of crime are legal description of an act as socially harmful and legal provision of a penalty for the act.[6]

## The Relativity of Crime

In defining crime in terms of felonies and misdemeanors, or as actions prohibited by law, difficulties can emerge since the content of criminal codes is constantly changing in both time and place. Sutherland has pointed out that during the age of the Vikings, it was a crime in Iceland to compose verses about another if they exceeded four stanzas, even if the sentiment was complimentary; the fourteenth-century English serf was not permitted to send his son to school, and those of status lower than a landowner were forbidden by law to keep a dog; and a Prussian law of 1784 prohibited mothers and nurses from taking children under two years of age into their beds.[7] Furthermore, legal codes at different times have defined as crime such activities as printing a book, professing the medical doctrine of circulation of the blood, driving with reins, selling coins to foreigners, having gold in the house, purchasing goods at a market for the purpose of selling them at a higher price, and writing a check for less than $1.00.

More currently, what is legal in some jurisdictions in the United States is criminal in others. The state of Georgia has a $1,000 fine or six months incarceration as the maximum for adultery, while in Louisiana, adultery does not fall within the proscriptions of the law.[8] And in Topeka, Kansas, it is illegal for a waiter to serve wine in a tea cup; in

Riverside, California, a citizen may not carry a lunch pail on a public thoroughfare; a Lynn, Massachusetts, ordinance states that babies may not be given coffee to drink; and in Oklahoma, it is illegal to take a bite of another person's hamburger. Even more widespread are the disparities in how various crimes are defined. Depending on the jurisdiction, for example, the possession of marijuana for personal use may be defined as an offense, a misdemeanor, or a felony.

Legal mandates for punishment of given crimes in the United States also reflect the issue of relativity in that they have manifested wide variations from the colonial period through the present. In early Pennsylvania, for example, the capital offenses found within the English or Puritan Criminal Code of 1676 included homicide, bestiality (sexual relations between a human and an animal), homosexual relations, kidnapping, perjury for the purpose of convicting the innocent of a capital offense, revolution, heresy, and assault of a parent by a child above the age of sixteen.[9] The Criminal Code of 1676 endured until 1682 when it was replaced by the Quaker Criminal Codes, which called for the death penalty only in cases of premeditated murder. The harsher Puritan codes were then reestablished in 1718 and remained in force until after the close of the Revolutionary War.

More recently, capital statutes in America have varied widely from one jurisdiction to another. As of June 1972, when the U.S. Supreme Court's *Furman* decision effectively, although temporarily, blocked the death penalty, capital statutes existed in 44 states.[10] The death penalty had been repealed in Iowa and West Virginia in 1965, in Oregon in 1964, in Alaska and Hawaii in 1957, and in Maine as early as 1887. By contrast, as of 1972, there were 10 capital statutes in Virginia, 11 in Kentucky, 13 in Arkansas, and as many as 17 in Alabama.* Furthermore, while the majority of states included first degree murder and kidnapping among the offenses punishable by death, crimes such as rape, attempted rape, and statutory rape were of a capital nature only in southern and border states. Finally, the more common crime of burglary was deemed a capital offense as recently as 1972 in North Carolina and Alabama.[11] Although the *Furman* decision may have blocked the death penalty in

*The capital offenses in Alabama include kidnapping for ransom, attempted kidnapping for ransom, first-degree arson with loss of life or maiming, second-degree arson with loss of life or maiming, assault on a prison guard or any murder by a life-term prisoner, burglary, sabotage, dynamiting under or near an inhabited area, killing in a duel, killing with a concealed weapon, murder, lynching, rape, carnal knowledge, robbery, and treason.

1972, the execution of Gary Gilmore on January 17, 1977, at the Utah State Penitentiary has served to reestablish the issue of relativity among capital offenses.

This relativity of crime, concerning the jurisdictional variances in both definitions and sanctions, has led many sociologists and criminologists to examine crime and deviant behavior in a more social perspective that goes beyond the content of criminal codes. This trend of recent decades has been built upon the work of Emile Durkheim, the nineteenth-century French sociologist who argued that criminal behavior was that which offended the *conscience collective*—the values held in common by the members of any relatively well-integrated social system.[12]

This more sociological view of crime, often referred to as "labeling theory," is circumscribed by the notion of *nominalism*—that realities are achieved only when they can be imagined and labeled. Nominalism is characterized by a conception of misconduct, or deviance, or crime, as having no meaning until it is given meaning.[13] Deviance or crime, then, does not exist until it is given a name and defined in nominal terms. Inquiries are directed at the processes of social interaction that define behaviors as deviant or criminal. More specifically, the approach views crime as one of the many forms of deviant behavior and examines the genesis and definition of deviance as an interactive process, following three major themes: the definition of deviance, the labeling of deviants, and the reactions to deviation. According to this point of view, crime is a human construction, and the definition of behavior as criminal involves a process, a status transformation that develops over a period of time. Howard S. Becker has suggested that "social groups create deviance by making rules whose infraction constitute deviance." As such, in contrast with the natural law concept:

> ... deviance is *not* a quality of an act the person commits, but rather a consequence of the application by others of rules and sanctions to an "offender." The deviant is one to whom that label has successfully been applied; deviant behavior is behavior that people so label.[14]

But rules that might be violated do not occur automatically, nor are they brought to bear on specific actions without some reason. Rules are directed toward behaviors that are perceived to be "harmful" to a group, for as Kai T. Erikson offered, "the term, deviance, refers to conduct which the people of a group consider so dangerous or embarrassing or irritating that they bring special sanctions to bear against the persons who exhibit it."[15] What may be harmful to a group, or "dangerous or embarrassing or irritating," is of a relative nature, and must be discovered and pointed out. Becker suggested that this process of discovery and designation is the enterprise of some crusading reformer.[16] Such a crusader, or "moral entrepreneur," is "fervent and righteous" and operates with an absolute ethic. The crusader views certain elements in society as truly, totally, and unconditionally evil and feels that nothing can be right in the world until rules are made to remove or correct such wickedness. The crusader's mission is a holy war, for the perfidy that has been observed is perceived as a potential breach in the stability of society, and only its eradication can insure a better way of life. The crusader's role involes bringing the "evil" to the attention of the public at large, to the opinion makers, and ultimately to the law makers.

Following this line of reasoning, a variety of sociologists and criminologists examined historical data descriptive of processes which served to define certain behaviors as criminal, and found that in any variety of circumstances, the efforts of many crusading reformers and their supporters were not necessarily or entirely humanitarian. In this respect, Richard Quinney has suggested that criminal definitions are descriptive of behaviors that are in conflict not with the conscience collective, but with the interests of those segments of society that have the power to shape public policy.[17] Modern society, he argued, is characterized by an organization of differences, with varied interests distributed among the socially differentiated positions. These interests, furthermore, are organized around the activities pursued by each segment, usually of a political, economic, religious, kinship, educational, or civic nature. Since there is a structured inequality in society characterized by an unequal distribution of power and conflict among its various divisions, combined with a differentiated interest structure (as determined by the respective classes, statuses, sexes, ages, occupations, races, religions, political orientations, and general attitudinal and value systems), the segments tend to compete with one another in terms of the priority of their respective interests.

The creation of crime as the product of a crusade can be observed to some degree in the Prohibition movement, where the "interest structures" of numerous reformers and their supporters were threatened. The movement, in part, was seemingly an assertion of a rural Protestant mind against that of the emerging urban culture, and this rural-urban cleft had its roots in the earliest chapters of American history:

> The first American colonists brought over the doctrine that country and village life were good, while city life was wicked. The sturdy yeoman farmer was considered to be the backbone of England, the essential fodder of her army. The creeping enclosures which displaced the farmers from the earth of England were evil, as were the land speculators and absentee owners, corrupted by the luxuries of the Court and of the great wen, London. The city was the home of vice, and the royal palace hid covert Popery. It was to flee these persecuting enemies that the *Mayflower* crossed the first frontier, the Atlantic Ocean.[18]

The eulogy of rural virtue, brought to the colonies early in the seventeenth century, served as the foundation for an antiurban movement that would culminate three centuries later. The agrarian life was considered pure, sacred, and wholesome, and the farmers were the stock of the earth, the backbone of the American democracy, the incarnation of a wholesomeness that could never be attained by those surrounded by the depravity of the cities. Designated as the "agrarian myth," this ideology so permeated the thinking of frontier America that it tended to shape much of its perception of reality.[19] Having been formulated in part by the classical writers and promulgated by the upper classes and landed gentry,[20] the agrarian myth found many of its earliest supporters in the American presidency. Jefferson had been a spokesman for the small farmer and saw commerce and industrial capitalism as parasitic; Jackson had been a strong opponent of commercialism while favoring an agrarian democracy; Tyler had condemned the liquid wealth of the urban aristocrat; and Polk had advanced the notion that national prosperity could be based only on an agrarian economy.

In the new country the cities began to grow. Drinking and the liquor trade were seen as symbols of an urban morality and of urbanism in general, and were seen as directly opposed to the more fundamental rural creeds of Methodism, Congregationalism, Presbyterianism, and the Baptists which emphasized individual human toil, a profound faith in the Bible, and total abstinence. The new urban centers with their commercialization and specialization were destroying the self-sufficiency of the farm and village, creating a situation of unwanted dependence.[21] Urbanism was perceived as the real sin in society, and the reform movement was an organization of rural interests against the "wicked city" and its impending dominance.

In general, the reform group was typically composed of, and for the most part dominated by, persons of middle and upper social position, and their efforts were directed at providing "salvation" for the less

privileged. But this provision of the means of salvation was a legitima-
tion of the reformers' own moral posture—a segment of their complex
interests—and of the power they derived from their superior position
in society. More specific interests were also at stake. Frances E. Willard
of the Woman's Christian Temperance Union (WCTU), for example,
saw the movement as a mechanism for uplifting the position of women
in American society. Conscious of the censure that women had received for their general lack of esprit de corps, she used the WCTU as
a way of developing feelings of mutuality and consensus among
women.[22] Similarly, it has been suggested that numerous industrialists
supported the Prohibition movement as a function of their interests,
feeling that the abolition of liquor might provide a more manageable
and productive labor force.[23]

In retrospect, the nature of crime can be variable. The natural law
concept suggests that crime is objectively given in society, while a
more sociological focus views crime to be subjectively problematic.
Similarly, definitions of crime are also variable. Legal definitions are
specific, and are based on the criminal law. Yet the varying content of
the law across jurisdictions confounds any attempt to fully understand
the content of what we might refer to as "crime." This has resulted in
efforts to widen the definition of crime to include types of socially
deviant behavior which are not necessarily punishable as offenses in
a court of law. In counterpoint, however, while a less specific perspective enhances our understanding of how some deviance and crime can
come into being, it fails to account for the full spectrum of criminal
definitions. The fact that some crimes "come into being" by moral
enterprise, or that criminal behavior may emerge as the result of criminal definitions suddenly applied to acts previously regarded as noncriminal, explains little about many long-standing criminal definitions
regarding crimes against person and property. And further, it is within
a totally legal structure that crime is currently defined and measured,
and within which the American system of justice and crime control
operates. And finally, the importance of the legal structure to a definition of crime was stressed more than four decades ago by Jerome Michael and Mortimer J. Adler, who argued that without the criminal law
there would be no crime:

> If crime is merely an instance of conduct which is proscribed by the
> criminal code it follows that the criminal law is the formal cause of crime.
> That does not mean that the law produces the behavior which it prohibits

... it means only that the criminal law gives behavior its quality of criminality.[24]

## Criminals and Criminality

While the concept of crime can be variable, the situation becomes even more complex when attempting to consider who may be the "criminal." The law finds the criminal to be "one who has been defined as such by the criminal law,"[25] but this designation is not fully clear. Robert G. Caldwell suggests that the term is appropriate only for those who have been convicted of a particular offense in a criminal court.[26] If this be the case, what of those who have committed crimes but have not been judged guilty, or even apprehended?

Legal definitions of the criminal, while in many ways specific, do not always specify when the status of criminal actually begins, and more importantly, when it ends. If a man maliciously takes the life of his brother, but the crime never becomes known, is he a criminal? If the crime does become known, does he then become a criminal? If he is arrested and confesses his act, but his case is dismissed on a legal technicality, is he a criminal? In this behalf lawyer-criminologist, Sue Titus Reid has recounted some perplexing cases:

> Dr. Samuel Sheppard, an Ohio osteopathic surgeon, served ten years in prison for the murder of his wife before the conviction was reversed because of the prejudicial publicity in the case. When he left the United States to begin a new life in France, he said that he was sick of being continually on trial in America. Too many people made him feel like an outcast—the staring, the finger-pointing and the hard time they gave him. Legally innocent of the crime for which he was tried, Sheppard was, nevertheless, considered by many to be a criminal. But apparently he did not find a new life in France, for he subsequently committed suicide.
>
> In 1969 a 60-year-old man was released from prison after serving 34 years for stealing $5 worth of chocolate bars and marshmallows. The officials said he was mentally deficient. Is he a criminal?
>
> In 1969 a young man, convicted of rape, was released after three years in prison, when his "double" confessed the crime. Is the first man a criminal?[27]

Importantly, were these people indeed criminals? And further, when, if ever, did their statuses as criminals end?

This definitional dilemma seemingly has no ultimate solution, for society prohibits a criminal from ever renouncing that status once the legal label has been applied. Furthermore, the criminal label is also applied to many without the benefit of the legal processes which serve to formalize the label. This would suggest that in many ways, the criminal label is a social definition, and the criminal is simply the person to whom the society assigns the label or status. This assignment, finally, emerges from society's knowledge of crime and criminal justice, from its conceptions of crime and criminal justice as learned through both personal and mass communication, and from the myths and folklore about crime which have pervaded our social thinking for more than a century.

## CONCEPTIONS OF CRIME IN AMERICAN CULTURE

American society has a generalized *criminal mythology,* a complex of conceptions of crime and criminals generated by history, cultural traditions, the arts, mass communication media, governmental structures, and interest groups. When thinking about crime, most of us give almost immediate consideration to "crime in the streets" or "organized crime," for these are the more popular, or most feared, categories of crime that are given attention in the press, television, and popular culture. But these represent only a small portion of the crime in America. White-collar crime involves billions of dollars annually through tax evasion, price fixing, embezzlement, swindling, and consumer fraud. Conduct once deemed immoral and made criminal—gambling, prostitution, alcohol, and drug abuse—reflects a face of crime that has resulted in placing criminal definitions on millions of persons. There are criminal regulatory violations in the areas of traffic control, building codes, fire ordinances, standards of quality, safety precautions, and misrepresentation that result in more deaths each year than criminal homicide. There is corruption in public office through bribes, payoffs, fixes, and conflicts of interest that occur in every branch of government at every level. And there is police crime in the form of wrongful arrest, brutality, and blackmail. Furthermore, the way that crime is depicted both through mechanisms of communication and in our imaginations is often vastly different from the manner in which it develops in its natural environment.

Similarly, our criminal mythology also includes a series of stereotyped conceptions as to the nature and composition of the criminal. This mythology offers set characterizations for murderers, rapists, robbers, racketeers, addicts, burglars, and prostitutes. The more typical conception of the rapist, for example, involves a deranged and un-shaven stranger who brutally attacks and ravages a young woman in her home, her car, or on a dark corner of her neighborhood. This notion emerges in sharp contrast to many rape situations in which the victim and offender are clearly known to one another. Or consider the prosti-tute. Our image is always of a woman, in spite of the fact that male prostitution is a concrete reality in urban America. The female prosti-tute is typically imagined as young, her clothing brief and gaudy, her makeup generously applied. She either walks the streets with her pimp close by—a well-dressed black man sporting a wide brimmed hat and leaning against his over-customized Cadillac—or she works in a brothel, owned and operated by a lusty and busty woman who has retired from the streets and has moved up in her profession. While this may be the image of the female prostitute, it reflects only part of the *flat-backing* industry. There are the high status, independent call girls who cater to upper levels of the business and social world; there are the urban and suburban housewives who operate in the safety of the day-light hours; there are drug users who hustle to secure funds for a fix; there are the rural entrepreneurs who flock to the nation's truck stops; there are the teenage runaways who seek out prostitution as a means of survival; and there are the aged for whom prostitution serves as a supplement to their limited welfare or social security checks.[28]

Criminal mythology does not limit itself only to the nature of crime and criminals, but in addition, as we will see in later chapters, it has impacted on our perceptions concerning the extent of crime, where crime is most likely to occur, and why crime occurs. And given the extent to which criminal mythology has seemingly influenced many of our perceptions about crime, it is important at this point to examine myth, its content, and some of the ways that it has contributed to our images of crime.

## Myth, Mythology, and Crime

Myth, like crime, has been variously described. To the classical scholar, the ethnologist, or the anthropologist, myth is a story, reported as having actually occurred sometime in the past, in a previous age, which explains the cosmological and supernatural traditions of a peo-ple, their gods, heroes, cultural traits, and religious beliefs.[29] Within this conception, myth has a religious background with the principal actor or actors as deities. They tell of the creation of man, of animals, of landmarks, why certain natural phenomena came to be (e.g. why a rainbow appears), why some animals have certain characteristics (e.g. why the bat is blind or flies only at night), and how and why rituals and ceremonies began or why they continue.[30] Popular conceptions of myth often relate to this classical perspective, and references to myth may conjure up thoughts of the ancient Greeks, the tale of Odysseus and the Cyclops, Hermes and Apollo, or Jason and the Argonauts. Conversely, to those unacquainted with the study of myth, the term can suggest the idea of popular misconceptions and false beliefs.[31] Yet while this usage may seem trivial and the more scholarly view narrow, neither conception should be rejected. Together, they focus on the content of myth. For as G. S. Kirk, Professor of Classics at the University of Bristol, has suggested, myth implies no more than a traditional story, and its restriction to particular kinds of tale or ritual is precarious and misleading.[32]

Myth, more specifically, implies collective fantasy, drawing its fabulous plots from a sanctuary of notions based more on traditions and convenience than on fact. *Myth is a body of lore regarded as "roughly true" on some plane of universalized experience; it serves as an instrument, a functioning device and controlling image that tenders philosophical meaning to the data of subjective reality.*[33]

Mythology, like myth, can also be a confusing term. It comes from *muthos,* which, for the Greeks, meant a tale, a statement, a story, or the plot of a play;[34] and from *muthologia,* a term first used by Plato to reflect the telling of stories.[35] It can be a confusing label, for it denotes the study of myths, the content of myths, or a particular set of myths.[36]

Criminal mythology or myths of crime and criminals warrants examination since much of our understanding and belief systems about the phenomenon of crime is based on misconception, stereotype, or events and images from an earlier frame of time. Such images and misconceptions, as noted earlier, touch upon the full spectrum of criminological phenomena: the nature of crime and criminals, the causes of crime, the extent of crime, the history of crime, and the management and control of crime. And the myths of crime can derive from any variety of sources. They emerge, for example, from historical events, from the misrepresentation of history, from distorted images presented in mass media and popular culture forms, from inadequate reporting procedures, from political and social movements, or from the deliberate efforts of a group to protect or foster their interests.

Typically, however, a criminal myth cannot be traced to one particular source, but instead originates from the convergence of a variety of events and processes. Consider, for example, a selection of our contemporary drug myths.[37] It is generally believed that all drug users are degenerate and dependent individuals, despite current data which suggest that perhaps fewer than 10 percent become dysfunctional as a result of drug-taking; that drug addicts are products of the urban ghetto, when by contrast, contemporary research has isolated populations of drug-dependent persons at all levels of the social complex; that all drug users are criminally involved, in spite of current findings which suggest that significant proportions are economically independent. Similarly, contemporary drug mythology has tended to support the notions that drug users are "dope fiends," that there is an "addiction-prone personality," that drug addiction is responsible for as much as 80 percent of all "street crime," that the use of marijuana will lead to heroin addiction, that severe punishment of drug users will prevent others from using drugs, that life sentences for "pushers" will curtail drug selling, that "scare tactics" in educational programs will prevent drug use.[38]

While these represent but a sampling of the mythical images that intersect the continuity of our contemporary drug awareness, they have galvanized many of our perceptions and responses to "the drug problem." And they descended from the reciprocal actions of political, social, economic, legislative, intellectual, scientific, religious, and moral postures that have endured in this country. As I have noted in an earlier publication, they emerged:

—from the more rural creeds of nineteenth-century Methodism, Presbyterianism, Congregationalism, and the Baptists, which emphasized individual human toil and self-sufficiency while designating the use of intoxicating substances as an unwholesome surrender to the evils of an urban morality;

—from the medical literature of the late 1800s which arbitrarily designated the use of morphine and opium as a vice, a habit, an appetite, and a disease;

—from the early association of opium smoking with the Chinese—a cultural and racial group which has been legally defined as alien until 1943 and even today is perceived as odd and mysterious;

—from the direct effects of American narcotics legislation which served to define all addicts as criminal offenders;

—from nineteenth- and twentieth-century police literature which stressed the involvement of professional and habitual criminals with the use of drugs;

—from the initiative of moral entrepreneurs and moral crusaders who defined drug use as evil, and, hence, influenced and directed the perceptions of both local and national opinion makers and rule creators;

—from the publicized findings of misguided research efforts, those contaminated by the use of limited and biased samples, impressionistic data, methodological imbalances, and inexperienced practitioners;

—from the sacred repository of intellectual and cultural lag—the gap which persists between the generation and publication of new data and the ultimate dismissal of earlier proclamations;

—from the suppression of controversial or disquieting knowledge by the cohorts of private, public, and corporate bodies whose internal interest structures are more effectively supported by alternative and distorted conceptions of reality.[39]

Becker has examined how much of the myth and hysteria about marijuana use was produced by an enterprise coordinated by the Federal Bureau of Narcotics during the 1930s.[40] He suggested that the Bureau perceived marijuana use as an area of wrongdoing, and had a personal interest in successfully putting such drug use under its strict control. The Bureau's efforts involved the development of legislation affecting the use of marijuana and providing "facts" and "figures" for journalistic accounts of the "problem." One of the Bureau's major strategies was an "educational" program which melodramatically presented the public with descriptions of the "evil effects" of the drug. They were often atrocity stories, and in an article published in *American Magazine,* the Commissioner of Narcotics himself, Harry J. Anslinger, related:

> An entire family was murdered by a youthful [marihuana] addict in Florida. When officers arrived at the home they found the youth staggering about in a human slaughterhouse. With an ax he had killed his father, mother, two brothers, and a sister. He seemed to be in a daze. He had no recollection of having committed the multiple crime. The officers knew him ordinarily as a sane, rather quiet young man; now he was pitifully crazed. They sought the reason. The boy said he had been in the habit of smoking something which youthful friends called "muggles," a childish name for marihuana.[41]

## Crime and Popular Culture

A variety of our distorted images of crime descend from the content of American popular culture. Popular culture is the culture of the masses, the pseudocultural amusements that occupy the nation's leisure time—that which reflects the styles, interests, manners, and tastes of the large, heterogeneous, and bewilderingly diverse audience. It includes the popular arts—the movies, the stage, television and radio broadcasts, music, journalism, fictional writings, and the poetry, painting, and sculpture that appeal to the majority and do not require a high level of intellectual or cultural refinement. It includes fads and fashions in dress and speech, sports, styles of interaction, and modes of entertainment. It has been suggested that while popular culture includes many diverse forms and can intersect many avenues of cultural activity, its boundaries are limited. Such works as James Joyce's *Ulysses* and T. S. Eliot's *The Waste Land,* much contemporary symphonic music and abstract art have a rather restricted audience and are not of mass appeal.[42] On the other hand, a brief sampling of the popular arts would necessarily include the majority of our current novelists, rock, soul, jazz, country and western music, the Broadway show, and such printed matter as the comic strip, the true experience magazine, and science fiction, suspense, and love stories.

The notion of mass or popular culture is a relatively recent phenomenon in western civilization, having appeared only subsequent to widespread industrialization. The primary condition for the emergence of popular culture was the massive population growth in Europe and the Americas, and the consequent concentration of people into cohesive urban and near-urban units with common social, economic, and cultural characteristics.[43] To this was added the expansion of leisure time, an outgrowth of machine civilization, as well as changes in the basic social structure which allowed for the identification and recognition of a mass public:

> After revolution broke the domination of cultural standards by the upper classes, the spread of education and literacy through the great middle class and below created a new audience which represented the tastes of the population at large. Control of the means of cultural production and transmission passed from a previously privileged elite to the urbanized, democratized middle classes. By the middle of the nineteenth century nearly everyone in the United States (except slaves and Indians) was minimally literate; by the middle of the twentieth, three-quarters of American adults possessed a high school education or better. This mass society had much more leisure time, much more disposable income, and it needed a new art —neither folk nor elite—to use the one and fill the other.[44]

Popular culture in American was aided by advances in technology. During the nineteenth century, machines widened and cheapened the public's access to the printed page—high speed presses, inexpensive paper, new ways of graphic representation, and more efficient methods of production and distribution. During the twentieth century, the spectrum was further broadened through film, radio, and television. Each of these forms has its own unique history, and each has affected our images of crime with varying levels of impact.[45]

Pulp fiction, an early example of a popular form, depicted crime in a very special way. The first pulpwood fiction magazine, *Golden Argosy, Freighted with Treasures for Boys and Girls,* came into being on December 2, 1882, published by Frank Andrew Munsey.[46] Munsey had been a telegraph operator for Western Union in his home town in southern Maine before he ventured into the publishing business with $300 in borrowed capital. His *Golden Argosy* was intended as a cheap fiction weekly of inspirational stories for children, but after some years of struggling, he converted it into *Argosy,* specializing in adventure stories.[47] *Argosy* included all the categories of pulp fiction—love stories, science fiction, westerns, jungle heroes, and crime and detectives. It was an all-fiction magazine, printed on a rough wood-pulp paper, and its eligibility for second-class postal rates helped to launch it as a new form of mass fiction. The success of *Argosy* spirited other publishers to imitate the Munsey product—Street & Smith, Doubleday, Dell, and Butterick; by the close of World War I, there were some two dozen pulp magazines, and by the 1930s there were more than two hundred.[48]

Conspicuous among the pulps were such titles as *Detective Fiction Weekly, Detective Story, Dime Detective, Hollywood Detective, Clues Detective Stories, Spicy Detective, The Phantom Detective, Mystery, Crimebusters, The Shadow,* and *Black Mask.* The world of crime in pulp fiction revolved around the detective, primarily the "private eye." And all private eyes were strikingly similar:

> The new private detectives of the pulps, while varied individuals, shared certain attitudes and qualifications. They usually stayed away from small towns, most of them working for detective agencies or on their own in large cities. New York, Chicago, Detroit, Miami and Los Angeles, which *Black Mask* called the New Wild West. They shared, many of the private eyes, a distrust of police and politicians. They could patiently collect evidence, but they could also cut corners the way the law couldn't. They were sometimes drunk, often times broke. A private eye would always help somebody in trouble, though he would downplay his compassion.[49]

This portrait fashioned an image of the private detective which has endured through many generations. The image is one of an aggressive, straight-shooting hero, fighting crime on the mean and jaded streets of the urban colossus. And the world of crime it presented was both limited and distorted. It was, at best, a nightmare projection of the real world of the '20s, '30s, and '40s. It was primarily a night world, filled with speakeasies, gambling joints, rundown hotels, and roadhouses. Criminals were cold and sinister. They drove long black cars and carried machine guns and .45 automatics. People were shot, kidnapped, and tortured.

While the pulp detective story offered one contorted view of crime for some three decades, the comic strip stepped even further from reality. Comics began with Richard Outcault's *The Yellow Kid,* published in Joseph Pulitzer's *New York World* on May 5, 1895.[50] *The Yellow Kid*'s world was that of the tough immigrant. It was one of sadness and hopelessness. The locus was Hogan's Alley, a squalid slum, and the characters were essentially children who reveled in the world of the poor, rejecting Horatio Alger's American dream. *The Yellow Kid* was short lived, disappearing in 1898 when its creator returned to his former profession of freelance illustrating, but its success and popularity was responsible for what has now become a dominant form of popular art and entertainment.[51]

The crime comics began some decades after the days of *The Yellow Kid,* and appeared in both strip and book form. They generally reflected the struggle of "good" against "evil," and their central theme was frequently projected in their titles—*Crime Does Not Pay, Crime Smasher, Crime Stopper, Crimebusters.*[52] Chester Gould's *Dick Tracy,* begun in 1931, has represented perhaps the most popular genre for more than four decades. Tracy has endured as a symbol of goodness, and his stance is unshakable; if he cannot destroy crime whenever it comes to his attention, the whole moral fiber of American culture becomes threatened.[53] The narrowness and distortion that characterized crime in the pulps was even more celebrated in *Dick Tracy.* It projected a demonic character of crime through the use of grotesque figures. They were either unusually ugly, physically distorted, part animal, or otherwise strongly sinister human beings: "the Blank," who hid his face behind a featureless mask; Jerome Trohs, a midget with a giant ego and a criminal brain; "the Brow," a master spy whose forehead was a mass of creases and wrinkles; "Shaky," who must kill in order to steady his shattered nerves; "Mr. Bribery," collector of roses and shrunken heads; as well as "Pruneface," "Flattop," "Shoulders," "Flyface," "the Mole," "Rhodent," "Piggy," "Spots," "the Pouch," and "Ugly Christine," to name only a few.[54]

*Dick Tracy* has been called "the first realistic police strip,"[55] but it is hardly realistic. The characters are either "good" or "bad," and are readily identified as such. The "bad" are not only physically ugly, but morally ugly as well; they were one-dimensional, grim and brutal, and performed distorted varieties of activity. Tracy himself was an artificial image. He is depicted as absolutely honest and incorruptible, an iron-willed man who never lost his nerve but relentlessly pursued his villain through every possible procedure of crime detection. And finally, the "crime-does-not-pay" ethos was carried to absurdity. The "evil" not only paid for their crimes, but they usually did so in what appeared as some grisly circus of horrors—they were shot through the head, impaled on flag poles, buried alive, scalded, hanged, or frozen to death.[56]

For several decades, the gangster film also reflected a series of images of crime and criminals that were unlike the world at large. Among the first was Josef von Sternberg's silent film, *Underworld,* produced by Paramount in 1927, but the era of the gangster film did not begin until Warner Brothers' *Little Caesar* in 1930. Since that time almost a half century ago, virtually hundreds of films have been produced that fall into that general category.[57]

For several decades, the criminal was depicted as one who felt that "might" made "right." He cared little for other people, and lived by a code so narrowly in his own interest that it didn't limit his behavior. His business included bootlegging, gambling, prostitution, drugs, and armed robbery, and nothing was allowed to hinder his operations. He was violent, brutal, ruthless, often mentally unbalanced, always evil, and living outside of society, he decisively preyed upon it.

In the early cycle of films, the "crime-does-not-pay" theme was as apparent as in the pulp stories and comic strips. Yet at the same time, gangsters were also tragic heroes. They were shown beginning their lives poor and powerless, escaping the ghetto by savagely fighting their way up through the mob, and ultimately paying for their crimes with violent death.[58] The first of this genre was *Little Caesar* in 1930, followed by more than a hundred films during the next three years, including *The Public Enemy, Blonde Crazy, City Streets,* and *The Secret Six* in 1931, *Scarface* and *The Hatchet Man* in 1932, and *Blondie Johnson* in 1933.[59] Again, crime as witnessed by the mass audience was suffering from the same limitations and distortions that were apparent in popular print. This was carried even further with the enforcement in 1934 of the Motion Picture Producers and Distributors of America production code which had been enacted a few years earlier in response to growing concerns over the films' presentation of violence and disrespect for law enforcement. Under the code, there were two major interests:

1. Crime Against the Law. These shall never be presented in such a way as to show sympathy with the crime as against law and justice or to inspire others with a desire for imitation.
2. Methods of crime should not be explicitly presented.[60]

The second cycle of films began with the enforcement of the MPP-DA Code, and the central characters were FBI or narcotics agents rather than criminals. Again, the myth of crime and criminals continued. The "crime" presented was that of street gangsterism, organized crime, and mob violence. Agents of the law were restricted to G-men, crusading cops, and special prosecutors—a breed quite different from the majority of the nation's law enforcement personnel. Furthermore, many of those who had played criminal roles during the first cycle—Edward G. Robinson, James Cagney, Humphrey Bogart—were the agents of law and justice in the second cycle, and exhibited essentially the same type of behavior in both. The more popular films of the period included *G-Men* in 1935, *Bullets or Ballots* and *Public Enemy's Wife* in 1936, and *Racket Busters, Crime School, Angels with Dirty Faces,* and *I Am the Law* in 1938.

Beginning with the early 1940s, crime films began to highlight the heroes of the pulps—the private eye—presenting essentially the same images that were evident in their printed counterparts. Subsequent fads emerged, portraying those types of criminal activity that were front page news in the nation's daily presses. Later decades saw the resurrection of the previous interest in gangland, combined with films that presented brutal and unrestrained violence. This was especially the case during the late '60s and early '70s. And while some recent films have focused on a more realistic view of crime, one factor seems to have characterized crime in the cinema over the last half century. Rarely is anything ever said about the society that continually created the criminal. We have been led to believe that he is a mutation of some sort, and that if we can get rid of him, there will be law and order.[61]

Radio, like pulp fiction, the comic strip, and the gangster film, typically offered the harsher world of crime where murder was always presented. It was a world limited to the fringes of society, to the slums and their inhabitants on the one hand and to high society on the other. It was a world of hoodlums, prostitutes, hitmen, and the violence that might occur in a Beverly Hills mansion or a Manhattan penthouse.

Furthermore, radio borrowed many of its characters and story lines from the other media—*The Shadow, Sam Spade, Dick Tracy.* And the themes were conspicuously the same as those seen elsewhere. *Crime Does Not Pay* was a syndicated show heard on WMGM that was patterned after the comic strip of the same name. *Crime Fighters* was a 30-minute series which depicted stories of the "master manhunters" who matched wits with "master criminals."[62] The images of the world of crime and police were again far removed from that of the full spectrum of crime and criminality.

While television has offered us a repetition of what already appeared in the older media, it also introduced us to several new approaches to crime. It provided views of the world of the traditional private eye, but at the same time it gave us "detectives" of a sort who occupied a high position in society and who reflected prevailing cultural attitudes. Erle Stanley Gardner's *Perry Mason* was this type; the series began in 1957, and some two decades later it is still being repeated on the nation's local and independent television stations.

What currently dominates television's portrayal of crime is as unrealistic as its predecessors, yet at the same time, it does give us glimpses of a world we might identify with. It combines the appeal of a somewhat rebellious or eccentric or in other ways "different" figure with the authoritative morality of the police and the day-to-day concerns of the common people.[63] Each "star" or personality brings a different view and attitude to the nature of crime. The absurdity, however, lies in the unrealistic nature of the characters presented—ones that rarely exist in the real world. There is "McMillan," a police commissioner who operates as a totally autonomous detective (and at one time even with the aid of his wife as a detective assistant); there is "McCloud," a transplanted western hero; there is "Columbo," a bumbling, sloppy, good-natured super-sleuth; there are "The Rookies," a small group of special police officers who have strong moral impulses toward helping people; and at one time there was "Ironside," a former chief of police paralyzed from the waist down by a sniper's bullet who led a special investigation team from his wheelchair.

It should be added here that television, as well as film, radio and printed fiction of every sort, did, and still do, often present figures and characterizations that sometimes populate a realistic world. Television and contemporary film, more so than other popular media, often do tend to focus on problems related directly to those of the audience. But in general, when crime is portrayed, the issues examined are generally limited to those far removed from our world of experience. And more importantly, when they do enter our own spectrum of understanding, they do so in a rather oblique way, with only the more violent forms of behavior offered as the central subject matter.

## Folklore, History, and Crime

It has been suggested that radio and TV, the movies, and fictional literature have presented a series of slanted and biased images of crime to a wide audience. It has also been suggested that distorted notions of crime and criminals have been spirited into our imaginations through the crusading efforts of governmental agencies and officials, and through contemporary mechanisms of crime reporting. These images and notions intersect the continuity of our awareness of crime and help to construct our criminal mythology. Yet there are additional items that become part of this complex of ideas. There can be a point at which a segment of the folklore and traditions of our culture become part of this mythology.

Folklore is a term that has often been interpreted as a synonym for error, fallacy, or historical inaccuracy.[64] But more appropriately, it covers a whole range of communicative events structured and transmitted according to traditional practices.[65] Folklore is a communicative process that produces and utilizes objects, ideas, and expressive devices that have meaning for the group and its individual members. It can include beliefs and superstitutions; riddles, rhymes, and proverbs, tales, hoaxes, and jokes; ballads and songs, literature and anecdotes, cultural traditions, traits, tales and legends.[66] Folklore can reflect much about social relations, and the attitudes and values of a group, and it can elaborate the dimensions of various social phenomena.

The content of folklore, on the other hand, can involve certain distortions of history, and this has often been the case with culturally transmitted images of crime. The widespread interpretation of the outlaw or bandit as "folk hero" is a typical example. The bandit-hero has been typified as a noble robber, a victim of injustice who takes only from the rich to give to the poor, who kills only in self-defense or for revenge, and in so doing, is admired and supported by his people. The bandit-hero or noble robber was first depicted in the fourteenth-century English ballads and poetry which described the adventures of such outlaws as Robin Hood and Fulk FitzWaren. And while Robin Hood was a mythical hero created by minstrals and storytellers, his characterization reflected the prototype from which later outlaws were understood as folk heroes—Jack Shepherd and Dick Turpin of England; Angelo Duca of Italy; Diego Corrientes of Spain; Pancho Villa of Mexico; and in America, Jesse James, Sam Bass, Joaquín Murieta, Billy the Kid, Clyde Barrow, and Bonnie Parker.[67]

While bandits may be folk heroes and represent symbols for the cultures from which they emerged, much of what folklore transmits concerning them can be false. This "dehistorization" process was especially apparent with Billy the Kid, Jesse James and other "heroes" of the American west. It resulted in part from the fashions in writing, publishing, and marketing of books that were a segment of late nineteenth-century mass culture. Of importance here were the "dime novels," collections of fiction and "true adventure" stories written by popular authors and published in cheap paperback editions. The dime novels that depicted events of the American west were highly sensationalized, and only limited attempts at accurate reporting were ever undertaken.[68] Perhaps the most popular of the writers of the "wild west" was Edward Z. C. Judson, who wrote under the name of Ned Buntline. He was a prolific writer of dime novels, a genre that he is erroneously credited with having originated, and it has been reported that he wrote as many as four hundred of these works.[69] Much of what Buntline wrote replaced historical data with pure fiction.

While Ned Buntline never wrote about Jesse James, Billy the Kid, or the other well-known bandit-heroes, he established a style that was to persist in the writings of many of his peers and successors. The works of Clarence E. Ray, for example, inexpensive illustrated volumes prepared for sale aboard passenger trains around the turn of the century, offered sensationalized "histories" describing the lives of Frank and Jesse James, the Dalton brothers, and the Oklahoma bandits that were considerably far from reality.[70] The series of outlaw stories that appeared in the *Police Gazette* contained numerous falsehoods and errors that were later repeated, sometimes word for word, in the writings of others.[71] Walter Noble Burns, with his style of heroic narrative, fashioned his *The Saga of Billy the Kid* into so romantic a piece of folklore that popular demand has kept it in continuous publication on two continents for more than 50 years.[72] Burns's story of Joaquín Murieta, the famous outlaw of California's age of gold, perpetuated fiction that occurred some 80 years before his writing.[73]

A folklore, similar to that surrounding the western outlaw, has also occurred with respect to twentieth-century crime. Many of our conceptions about organized crime have come from Sicilian folklore, combined with the inaccurate reporting by the press and the sensationalism of many contemporary authors.[74] And as we will observe in later chapters, the problem prevades much of our information about crime and criminals. The immediate issue to be addressed, however, is not the accuracy of a specific criminal event, but the lack of historical analysis in the study of crime. Many of our distorted images of crime, whether they be from literature, film, or journalism, tend to persist due to a lack of historical and analytical thinking on the part of those who have the task of presenting us with reliable information. History can place criminological phenomena within the frame of time; it is the very essence of detached inquiry. The historical view provides a laboratory for a more complete analysis of the scope, persistence, and change in crime. And as we continue into a further study and analysis of crime in contemporary society, our task will be considered within the wider issues of historical relevance and conceptual reliability.[75]

## SUGGESTED READINGS

BECKER, HOWARD S., *Outsiders: Studies in the Sociology of Deviance* (New York: Free Press, 1963).

BERGER, ARTHUR ASA, *The Comic-Stripped American* (Baltimore: Penguin Books, 1974).

BRUNVAND, JAN HAROLD, *Folklore: A Study and Research Guide* (New York: St. Martin's Press, 1976).

DURKHEIM, EMILE, *The Division of Labor in Society* (New York: Free Press, 1947).

ERIKSON, KAI T., *Wayward Puritans: A Study in the Sociology of Deviance* (New York: Wiley, 1966).

INCIARDI, JAMES A., BLOCK, ALAN A., and HALLOWELL, LYLE, *Historical Approaches to Crime: Research Strategies and Issues* (Beverly Hills: Sage, 1977).

MANNHEIM, HERMANN, *Comparative Criminology* (Boston: Houghton Mifflin, 1965).

MICHAEL, JEROME, and ADLER, MORTIMER J., *Crime, Law and Social Science* (New York: Harcourt, Brace, 1933).

QUINNEY, RICHARD, *The Social Reality of Crime* (Boston: Little, Brown, 1970).

SUTHERLAND, EDWIN H., *White Collar Crime* (New York: Holt, Rinehart and Winston, 1949).

# 2

# Some Perspectives on the History of Crime in America

To my knowledge there is no concise history of crime in the United States, and this curious situation has occurred for any variety of reasons. Criminology, for example, has been compelled by other concerns. As a comparatively new science and scholarly discipline, the search for the causes of crime emerged as its primary task. This endeavor has occupied a significant part of its short history. Beyond the issue of crime causation, other avenues of inquiry have focused on the nature and meaning of crime, the concept of law, the identification of criminals, the control and treatment of offenders, and methods for assessing the extent and impact of crime. Similarly, history has been concerned with other matters. Unlike criminology, history is an ancient discipline, yet in contrast with the more limited scope of crime and criminals, the area of inquiry to be traversed by history is abysmal. Historians have been charged with the tasks of reconstructing and interpreting the origins and flow of all human events since their beginning, and to do so not only with the materials of their own collection, but with those offered by other fields of knowledge as well. Furthermore, those who have chosen the complexities of American life and culture as the focus of their historical inquiry have begun their task with the analysis of the more macro issues, abandoning crime as a matter yet to be dealt with.

Going beyond the traditional interests and concerns of criminology and history, the phenomenon of crime is one that can easily elude any general historical inquiry. First, by its very nature, crime is subject to concealment by both offenders and victims, and hence, it does not routinely come to the attention of those who record human events.

Second, and as we will observe more clearly in the following chapter, standard mechanisms for recording the incidence and prevalence of crime are of fairly recent vintage, and even these current avenues of compilation are at best, incomplete. Third, much of the historical data on crime which do exist are indeed widely scattered, and a significant portion of information which was available at one time is now buried in antiquity. The data on crime and criminals are generally restricted to four sources: early court or other legal records, newspaper reports, personal memoirs, and the chronicles of individual observers and recorders in specific places and periods. Regarding court and other legal materials, the vast majority have become lost, destroyed, or otherwise inaccessible, and what remains is scattered throughout the forgotten archives of many hundreds of communities. The memoirs and reports from the press and other observers have also suffered their losses. And what has not been destroyed or buried through time often reflects only that which may have been considered sensational, unusual, or of peculiar or personal interest to the given observer. Finally, as we have noted earlier, "crime" covers a wide range of phenomena that have been subject to varying definitions and interpretations. There are currently hundreds of behaviors which became defined as crime only recently, and were perhaps ignored by former observers. Furthermore, due to various social and technological changes which have emerged during recent centuries, events which are currently deemed "crime" might not have occurred in previous epochs.

Yet this should not suggest that we are totally barren of historical data on crime, or that historians, criminologists, or representatives of other fields of inquiry have fully ignored the subject. For while we may be lacking a concise "history" of crime in America, we, nevertheless, have a wealth of descriptive information on particular occurrences, crises, personages, and fashions in crime. From these sources, combined with some of the less obscure materials gathered from ancient archives, many criminological phenomena have been reconstructed while others have been partially analyzed. This historical repository allows us to at least generate some understanding of early perceptions of crime, how criminal patterns may have emerged and persisted, and how previous styles in human behavior and crime may have impacted on contemporary social patterns.

Within this context, a concise history of crime in America is not being offered here. Rather, for the sake of providing a broad, and however partial, overview of some of the persistent and changing issues, a series of perspectives are presented on those particular events, styles, and trends in crime which seem to be more conspicuous in American history. Viewed within an historical perspective, many of the problems of crime facing us today can be better realized and understood. It might also be noted here that this brief overview of crime generally targets those events and locations for which data are the most readily available. Our discussion of urban crime, for example, focuses primarily on New York. This position has been taken not only because New York has been the nation's largest city for the better part of its history, but given its position as a seaport, a point of immigration, an industrial complex, and a publishing capital, more data on crime has been generated there than for any other urban complex.

## CRIME AND VICE IN COLONIAL AMERICA

In 1620, the colonial population was estimated at only 2,302 persons; by 1650 the figure barely exceeded 50,000; and in 1750 there were slightly more than 1,000,000 persons distributed throughout the 13 original colonies.[1] Given such a limited population base during our first century, crime as we understand it today hardly existed. The few settlers were scattered from New England to the Carolinas in a series of small villages and remote outposts where the communal bonds were strong and where opportunities for crime were scarce. Theft, for example, was quite uncommon, for there was little to steal. The colonists had only small houses, few personal belongings, and only the necessities of clothing.[2] Early court records suggest that in the larger settlements of Newport, Philadelphia, and Charlestown, crime was similarly almost nonexistent through the first half of the seventeenth century.[3]

The early Massachusetts colony of Charlestown was relatively free of crime, at least until 1640 when the community initiated trade with the West Indies. As commerce increased, the population expanded, and the records of Boston's Suffolk County Court during the 30 years following contained an ever growing level of assault, arson, breaking and entering, embezzlement, fighting and brawling, manslaughter, theft, receiving stolen goods, pickpocketing, robbery, and confidence games.[4] The Puritan colony of Massachusetts Bay, in spite of its strong religious bonds, was also not without its problems. During the period 1641 through 1682, the records of the Essex County Court included the conviction of 1,369 persons for some 2,382 offenses.[5] In comparison with contemporary standards, the "crime rate" in this small colony was relatively high. As reflected by Table 2–1, rates of crime are interpreted in terms of both convictions and offenders. The number of convictions per 100 population ranged from 4.22 in the 1651–1655 period to a high of 6.46 in 1661–1665, declining to 4.15 in 1676–1680. The rate by offender remained relatively stable during this period, and was at a lower level since any individual offender convicted for more than one crime during each five-year period was counted only once. A further interpretation of the Puritan data on crime reflects much about that community's conception of crime. An analysis of the rates for specific offenses suggests that almost half involved crimes against the church or contempt of authority, almost 15 percent involved fornication, with about half as many being for breaches of peace, and slightly less than 20 percent were crimes against persons or property. The exact nature of the crime in the balance of the offenses was not noted in the early court records from which these data were drawn, and as Erikson has noted, these vintage records had numerous omissions.[6]

TABLE 2–1.  Crime Rates by Convictions and Offenders, Essex County Court, 1651–1680

|                | 1651–1655 | 1656–1660 | 1661–1665 | 1666–1670 | 1671–1675 | 1676–1680 |
|----------------|-----------|-----------|-----------|-----------|-----------|-----------|
| Population     | 4500      | 5200      | 6100      | 7300      | 8900      | 7500      |
| Convictions    | 190       | 275       | 394       | 393       | 391       | 311       |
| Rate/100 pop.  | 4.22      | 5.29      | 6.46      | 5.38      | 4.38      | 4.15      |
| Offenders      | 161       | 182       | 222       | 257       | 324       | 269       |
| Rate/100 pop.  | 3.60      | 3.50      | 3.64      | 3.52      | 3.64      | 3.58      |

Source: Kai T. Erikson, *Wayward Puritans: A Study in the Sociology of Deviance* (New York: Wiley, 1966), p. 173.

The challenges of crime facing New Amsterdam, and later New York, from its earliest days through the seventeenth century were limited by the city's youth and modest population. Burglaries and other larcenies were few, and problems of a public nature were confined largely to disorderly behavior in the hard-drinking communities of sailors on shore leave.[7] Yet early New Amsterdam was not conspicuous for its virtue during this period, and cases of prostitution appear as early as the 1660s in the minutes of the Mayor's Court of New York.[8]

Toward the close of the seventeenth century, standards of accepted morality declined significantly as the spectrum of conditions which attended the growth of the city—increasing population levels compounded by the large numbers of foreigners and mariners who peopled the waterfronts—created an atmosphere for crime. Not only did these factors in themselves foster vice, but they, in turn, were intensified by the effects of war. With the coming of the Queen Anne's War in 1702, the American phase of the War of Spanish Succession, cases of adultery and bastardy multiplied, especially among the seafaring class, and prostitution became one of the concomitants of urban life in New York.[9] Perhaps the earliest general rendezvous of Manhattan courtesans was the Battery, for as early as the 1730s both English and Dutch members of this ancient profession plied their trade along its platform or aboard the privateers docked off its western shore.[10]

The other major cities also experienced increases in crime, disorder, and vice during this period. Burglary, street robbery, and highway robbery suddenly became a problem after 1700, and petty thefts and assaults emerged among the growing populations of "disorderly poor" that had flocked to the cities during the war. Pirates were present in all seaport towns, engaging in illicit trade with local businessmen and merchants, and the appearance of paper money at the beginning of the eighteenth century called forth numerous counterfeiting operations throughout the larger settlements.[11]

While prostitution was evident in most towns, organized vice became rooted in New York as soon as it became the depot for the British forces in the French and Indian War. By 1753, formalized houses of prostitution were well established in several parts of the city, and the corporal efforts of the judicial administration failed to alter their traffic.[12] Commercialized prostitution rapidly spread after midcentury, aided by the growing population of the city and the regular patronage of the floating class of sailors and mariners. The Battery, furthermore, especially in the vicinity of St. Paul's Church, continued to have a reputation as a center of dissipations and pleasures. For as elaborated by a contemporary visitor in 1774:

> Above 500 ladies of pleasure keep lodgings contiguous within the consecrated liberties of St. Paul's. This part of the city belongs to the church, and has thence obtained the name of the *Holy Ground.* Here all the prostitutes reside, among whom are many fine well dressed women, and it is remarkable that they live in much greater cordiality one with another than any nests of that kind do in Britain or Ireland.[13]

The Revolutionary War served as an additional stimulus in the development of vice districts in the great metropolis. Characteristic of every war, the presence of soldiers had attracted prostitutes, gamblers and saloon keepers, and near present-day Washington Square they organized and built a tent colony. When the city was finally occupied by the British during the latter part of 1776, bands of English and German soldiers arrived, advancing the armed services population to an excess of 33,000, and encouraging a further influx of prostitutes. Traders contracted to supply women for the troops and brought to New York doxies from England as well as blacks from the West Indies.[14]

The successive periods of city growth and wartime society during the 1700s not only witnessed the developmental aspects of the commercialization of vice, but similarly, criminal predation also became manifest as an emergent problem. By 1749 crime had become a major concern on Manhattan Island. Burglaries, robbery, and crimes of violence had become evident, and were attributed to the infestation of rogues and thieves attracted by the city's war wealth. Less than three decades later, in 1774, when New York politician James Delancey commented that Manhattan had the reputation of the least safe city in the colonies for both property and persons, offenses with notable incidence levels went beyond burglary and street crime to include pocketpicking, shopbreaking and highway robbery.[15] And, too, life in Loyalist New York during the early years following the Revolution was severely imperiled by the prevalence of crime:

> With every dark corner crowded with thieves and bawds, with low dens down on the wharves handing out grog, with drunken sailors and soldiers prowling the streets at night ... women could not venture out after dark ... men were set upon by thieves, robbed and beaten.[16]

In the wake of the French and Indian War, crimes of numerous variety swept through every seaport city. Counterfeiting, petty theft, housebreaking, burglary, highway robbery, assault, rape, and murder were prominent, and the cities and towns had no police to curb them. This period also spawned perhaps the first American criminal syndicate. Operating on an intercolonial scale during the 1760s, a group of organized thieves headquartered in the Carolina back country dealt extensively in the theft and transportation of horses, slaves, and merchandise. What was stolen in the south was transported to New York and Rhode Island for shipment to the French and Dutch West Indies, and goods taken in the north were carried to Georgia and Florida for trade with pirates and smugglers. The group was also relatively successful at avoiding detection and arrest, moving rapidly from one city to the next as their crimes became known.[17]

The eighteenth century also witnessed threats to law and order involving blacks and Indians, both slave and free. Blacks were no more guilty of crime than whites, but driven by fear, townspeople often dealt with them with unreasonable brutality. Furthermore:

> Harsh treatment of Negroes and Indians in all towns resulted in frequent runaways. In South Carolina, where there were estimated to be twenty-eight thousand Negroes to thirty thousand whites, fear of a black uprising was always present. Panic inspired by a projected servile insurrection near Charles Town in 1738 could be satisfied only with the discovery and severe punishment of its instigators. At Newport in 1737 a mulatto woman was executed for twisting the neck of a child and throwing him down a well, and an Indian girl was hanged for killing a fellow servant. Boston authorities suspected Negroes and Indians of instigating the wave of fires during 1721–1723, and the next year passed a most severe code restricting their freedom of action. Nevertheless, cases of robbery and rape by Indians and slaves continued.[18]

## THE RISE OF CRIMINAL DISTRICTS AND STREET GANGS

By the turn of the nineteenth century, the continued growth of the older cities and the establishment of newer ones had become apparent. Accompanying this process of urbanization was the emergence of new areas of vice and crime. Prostitution, vice, and preditory crime had been present to some degree in all cities, but while America was under British rule and during the first few decades after the Revolutionary War, their proportions had never been overwhelming. Small, segregated areas of vice and crime were common in waterfront districts in which brothels, taverns, and saloons catered to seamen on leave, and where the cities' "disorderly poor" created a minor menace to the safety of the streets. Yet as successive wars plagued the colonies, prostitutes followed soldiers as they either occupied or were stationed in the cities, and with them came the war refugees, immigrants, and those who meant to capitalize on the urban war wealth. By the 1840s, criminal gangs, criminal districts, and vice areas began to emerge in the older and more established urban centers.

In New York, the vice, crime, and disorganization that developed prior to the Revolution was less than preeminent when contrasted with the dramatic transformations in the fabric of the city which occurred following the nation's achievement of independence. Initially, New York had always been a city of transients. For, in addition to the superiority of its location for commerce which attracted legions of merchants, mariners, and visitors from other lands during the years of resistance, revolution, and reconstruction, the city had also been a seedbed of rebellion, a patriot bastion, an occupied city, and finally the capital of the newly emerging American nation. And further, it had been growing as a port of entry and haven for mendicant foreigners and war refugees. Pauperism increased, as did a separation of the classes.

The trans-Atlantic migrations, specifically, served to enhance the size and discontinuities of the city's population. Demographic transitions and successive years of famine in Europe spirited the arrival of more than twenty million peasant immigrants to the New World during the ten decades following the turn of the nineteenth century. Fatigue, hardship and destitution prevented most of these displaced migrants from going beyond the ports of entry. And significant proportions, having disembarked through the gates of New York, became reluctant additions to the city's indigent collectivity.[19] To these were added the tens of thousands of American farmers who had been driven from the soil to the factories of lower Manhattan when the Industrial Revolution reduced the value of manual effort in agrarian production.

The newcomers, both native and foreign, crowded into the less desirable sections of the already congested city—to the Five Points, Hell's Kitchen, the Fourth Ward, the Lower East Side and the Upper West Side. The confrontation with the new way of life, the separation and loneliness, the insecurity and uncertainty of employment, and the feelings of insignificance, crisis, and frustration amidst such squalid conditions had their apparent effects:

> Almost resignedly, the immigrants witnessed in themselves a deterioration. All relationships became less binding, all behavior dependent on individual whim. The result was a marked personal decline and a noticeable wavering of standards.[20]

Gambling, drinking, and pauperism became evident, and the atmosphere of unrestraint attracted criminals who were dispersed in other areas of the city and country. Yet the immigrant and displaced farmer were rarely serious lawbreakers. Their offspring, however, were attentive to whatever might increase their standard of living, and it was within this context that criminal gangs and criminal districts emerged and matured in the ever changing city.

The earliest gangs consisted almost entirely of Irishmen. The Irish, emigrating to this country in vast numbers and lacking funds, education, and skills, were met with contempt by native New Yorkers and were forced into the city's worst slum—the Five Points district. This section of lower Manhattan was formed by the intersection of five streets—Anthony, Orange, Cross, Little Water, and Mulberry—and it became the core of what ultimately grew into the largest Irish community outside of Dublin. The housing was composed of clapboard tenements, built on the former site of the old Collect, or Fresh Water Pond, a marshy area of wetland and meadow extending from present day Chambers Street to Canal Street, east of Broadway. The marsh had been poorly drained and filled with garbage, and by 1820 the inadequate foundations of the tenements had begun to slowly sink into the moist soil. The Irish clustered by the thousands in the Five Points, and lacking other means of earning a living, many developed criminal careers.[21]

The first of the city's organized gangs had their genesis in the tenements of the Five Points, yet their actual structuring into working units followed the opening of the *green-grocery speakeasies* which sprang up along those streets which formed the Points.[22] The first of these speakeasies was opened by one Rosanna Peers on Center Street, just south of Anthony. Piles of decaying green vegetables were displayed outside the doors of Rosanna's establishment, but her chief source of revenue came from the potent liquor sold in her back room at prices lower than those in recognized saloons. This speakeasy quickly became the resort of thugs, pickpockets, murderers, and thieves. "The Forty Thieves," which history suggests was the first New York gang with a definite, acknowledged leadership, appears to have been formed in Rosanna's jaded emporium, and her back room was used as the gang's traditional meeting place. The Forty Thieves were predominantly muggers and pickpockets, and operated on the Lower East Side of Manhattan from the early 1820s to just prior to the Civil War. Like many other gangs succeeding them, they encouraged a sub-mob of juveniles, dubbed the "Forty Little Thieves," from which they recruited new talent.

Following the Forty Thieves Gang, the "Kerryonians" were organized in 1825 and were also headquartered at the Rosanna Peers grocery store. The members of the Kerryonians Gang had all been born in County Kerry, Ireland, and much of their time was devoted to mugging Englishmen. Other gangs of note which developed in this area were the "Roach Guards," "Dead Rabbits," "Chickesters," "Plug Uglies," and "Shirt Tails." The Dead Rabbits were originally part of the Roach Guards, organized to honor the name of a Five Points liquor dealer. There was internal dissension within the gang, and at one of their meetings a dead rabbit was thrown into the room. It was accepted as an omen by one of the opposing factions, which withdrew and formed an independent unit under the banner of the maligned animal. The Plug Uglies were formed in the mid-1820s and took their name from the giant plug hats which each member filled with rags and straw to protect their heads during gang battles. The Shirt Tails were so called because they wore their shirts on the outside of their trousers, like Chinamen. Little is known of the origins of the Chickesters, yet their claim to immortality comes from their persistence in outliving all of the original Five Points gangs and in spawning the more murderous gangs of the post-Civil War era.

From the Bowery, directly north of the Five Points, came such gangs as the "American Guards," "Atlantic Guards," "True Blue Americans," and the "Bowery Boys"; and from Hell's Kitchen on New York's middle West Side came the "Hudson Dusters," "Potashes," and "Gophers." These gangs of the Five Points, Bowery, and Hell's Kitchen, which often included hundreds of men and boys, consisted of many small gangs grouped together and led by a supreme chieftain who commanded absolute loyalty. Gangsters were regularly dispatched by their leaders to nearby areas to steal, rob and kill, or to wage street battles against rival gangs. And with violence and theft as patterned activities, the gangs of New York proceeded to terrorize the city for some one hundred years. Furthermore, they represented the first enduring criminal organizations and established the subcultural systems from which later racketeers descended.

While Five Points, Hell's Kitchen, and Bowery gangs were operating within the directives of street crime and with members most frequently thieves and murderers, the criminal groups who settled in the Fourth Ward of New York confined their activities to alternate types of predatory behavior. The Fourth Ward, lying east and south of the Five Points along the East River, had been the finest residential section of New York during the eighteenth century. Its streets were lined with splendid mansions inhabited by the first families of the city, the wealthy merchants, and the political heroes. John Hancock's home was located here, as was George Washington's at the time of his inauguration. But the wave of immigration which broke upon the American continent soon after the Revolution forced the aristocracy northward, and by the 1840s the old mansions had given way to rows of tenements housing a population steeped in poverty and vice.

Gangsterism in the Fourth Ward was initially devoted to theft along the East and Hudson River piers, followed by piracy in the grand manner of Blackbeard and Henry Morgan. The river thieves included the "Charlton Street Gang," the "Hookers," "Daybreak Boys," "Swamp Angels" and the "Old Border Gang," and in all, there were some 500 river pirates organized into more than 50 active gangs.[23] The Charlton Street Gang included a collection of bandits who operated from a small sloop which sailed along the Hudson from the Harlem River as far north as Poughkeepsie, some 70 miles above Manhattan Island. With the Jolly Roger flying from the masthead, they robbed riverside farmhouses and mansions and held men, women, and children for ransom. The Daybreak Boys were the best organized of the gangs. They prowled about the docks and along the rivers in rowboats and became notorious during the 1850s for their success in scuttling ships throughout the New York port. Manhattan waters were also regularly invaded by the gangs of Irishtown, a sparsely settled region between Brooklyn and Williamsburg. Other river bandits were also expert sneak thieves, and as masked burglars they plundered the small towns along both shores of Long Island Sound.[24]

The gangs of youthful and young adult criminals who made war on one another and terrorized the streets of New York were also evident in other cities. Philadelphia had its "Buffaloes," "Blood Tubs," "Rugs," and "Copper Heads"; Baltimore had its "Stringers"; and a group known as the "Crawfish Boys" plagued the streets of Cincinnati. Other urban areas developed later than the large cities in the east, but they, nevertheless, had their exposure to street gangsterism. In 1837 when New York was a major metropolis and its Five Points area had already developed as a center for street crime, Chicago was just a settlement of some 500 buildings with a population of only 4,100. Within a few decades, however, Chicago's underworld had emerged with an active criminal class.[25] Similarly, it was not until 1835 that the first dwelling appeared along the beach of Yerba Buena Cove, the present site of San

Francisco, but with the discovery of gold along the nearby American River in 1848, the Barbary Coast quickly grew as a leading American underworld.[26]

## POLITICAL CORRUPTION AND THE COMMERCIALIZATION OF VICE

The Civil War and its aftermath initiated a variety of changes in many of the larger cities that ultimately had a significant impact on gangland organization and behavior. These troubled years, for example, saw the city of New York transformed into a metropolis. The recession that preceded the war had ended by the fall of 1861, and prosperity grew apace. War-created wealth and the commercial, financial, and industrial developments it cultivated produced a flourishing economy. But the prosperity was selective, wages lagged behind rapidly rising prices, workers were forced into greater poverty, and tensions increased between the rich and poor. The city's social fabric was severely strained. For as the population of destitute refugees and migrants increased, and the local laboring classes became further separated from the "American Dream," hosts of others reveled in easy money and lavish display. Standards of morality deteriorated, corruption fell like a leper's shadow over the city, and New York entered what became known as the Flesh Age.[27]

Before the War the criminal districts and centers of vice had been generally confined to the Five Points, the Bowery, and the waterfront of the Fourth Ward. But almost immediately after the surrender at Appomattox, the houses of prostitution, dance halls, concert saloons, and gambling casinos appeared throughout the city. They operated without molestation, because of regular payments to corrupt police and political overlords. The Tenderloin or Satan's Circus became the most notable of the "wide open" pleasure districts frequented by the cosmopolitan New Yorker. This region embraced the area from Madison Square to Forty-eighth Street, between Fifth and Ninth Avenues. Here were located the more infamous gambling resorts and brothels, the garish saloons, restaurants, and dance halls where prostitutes overtly solicited customers. There were resorts which catered to the wealthy and discreet, and others for the less fashionable clientele.[28]

The political corruption that served to shape the organization and commercialization of vice and crime during the years following the

Civil War was rooted in the bossism and machine politics of Tammany Hall. And this political structure had not only been in control of the city government for many decades prior to the war, but it had also been functionally related to the emergent colonies of Irish immigrants and the mosaic of street gangs which tramped throughout the city.

The Tammany organization, originally a Jeffersonian political club founded in New York City in 1789 as the Society of St. Tammany, was mobilized in army fashion within the city wards during the 1820s and 1830s.[29] It backed issues which were popular among the tenement classes, and distributed fuel, food, and clothing throughout the poverty districts during times of economic crisis. Tammany also gained popularity and power through political patronage. The organization, having grown into an important factor in party politics in New York City, was regularly consulted in the choice of Democratic candidates. Officials who were placed in office through Tammany support, in turn, conferred with the Society regarding the distribution of municipal, state, and federal jobs.

The complex entanglement of machine politics, Irish settlements, street gangs, and organized vice was meshed within a symbiotic network. Tammany politics utilized the Irish immigrants and street gangs to maintain their power base by providing the members of this growing minority sector with opportunities for upward mobility through employment and the spoils of graft. Initially, the pattern of Irish settlement, which was characterized by disembarkation through the New York port without the means for dispersion further into the continent, surrendered to the city some 130,000 Irish-born before mid-century. By 1850 one-fourth of the population of the city was Irish, and a half decade later this minority collective represented one-third of the potential voters. Tammany, in organizing for its own survival, offered hospitality to the newly arriving Irish. Ward politicians rigorously opposed the rising trend of anti-Catholicism and readily accepted the newcomers into the ranks of their influence. Irishmen were naturalized by the thousands with the understanding they would vote Democratic, and scores of others were guaranteed positions within the sectors of public administration.

Tammany entanglements with the Irish dominated gangs of the Bowery, Five Points, and other city wards were also structured into highly functional operations. Gang leaders and line members were dispatched at the polls to serve as bullies. They not only intimidated voters to cast Democratic, but, in addition, they were paid nominal sums to vote three and four times for Tammany candidates. District leaders and ward heelers provided protection for gang henchmen by keeping them out of jail and extended immunities to gang-operated houses of prostitution and gambling establishments. Tammany bosses at all levels of officialdom, given an enduring survival power through patronage and election manipulation, defrauded the city treasury of innumerable sums of cash and property. The more notorious of the machine politicians were William Tweed and Richard Croker. Tweed allegedly swindled the city out of $30 million in cash and an additional $170 million in bribes and other types of graft; Croker, who became perhaps the most powerful figure in the history of New York politics, accumulated some $7 million a year through the extension of police protection to every form of vice and crime.

While organized prostitution and commercialized vice flourished during the postwar era under the protection of a corrupt city administration, the New York gangland continued to expand and reflected levels of structural integration significantly more formal than those characteristic of the early encampments of street predators. Perhaps the greatest of the gangs to come into existence following the Civil War was the "Whyos," a unique collection of thieves, murderers, and street fighters. The Whyos were an outgrowth of the Chichesters of the early Five Points, with members also drawn from the river pirates of the Fourth Ward. They maintained their principal rendezvous in Mulberry Bend, an area slightly north and east of the Five Points district. For a 40 year period the Whyos were dominant in the New York underworld and considered the whole of Manhattan their province. Among their 500 members were bands of organized burglars, sneak thieves, and pickpockets; a number owned gambling saloons, panel houses, and places of prostitution; some regularly accepted murder, stabbing, and blackjacking commissions; and all of their operations were undertaken within the protective hospitality of political corruption.

Numerous other gangs with divergent areas of enterprise evolved during the long career of Whyo preeminence—the "Harley Mob" from Broadway in the vicinity of Houston Street, the "Dutch Mob" from Houston to Fifth Streets east of the Bowery, the "Mackerelville Crowd" from the area bounded by Eleventh and Thirteenth Streets and by First Avenue and Avenue A, and the "Rag Gang" of the Bowery. Along the West Side of Manhattan emerged the "Stable Gang," the "Silver Gang," and the infamous "Hell's Kitchen Gang" from the area north and south of Thirty-fourth Street west of Eighth Avenue. And further, while these and dozens of smaller cohorts of gangsters, almost entirely of Irish membership, organized and plundered delimited kingdoms across the surface of the city, Italian gangs in Little Italy, Jewish gangs on the Lower East Side and the "Tongs" of Chinatown also developed and held forth. Their activities went beyond the more humble terrorism of the pre-War street gangs to include all varieties of larceny, fencing operations, white slavery, and extortion.

As Tammany operations and their entanglements with street gangs developed in New York, they were ultimately copied and established the patterns of growth and structure for other political machines along the eastern seaboard and finally for urban clusters across the nation. Tammany-like mobilization and dynamism were reflected in the activities of Philadelphia's "Republican Gas Ring," and in the bossism of Dr. Albert Ames of Minneapolis, Abe "Curly" Ruef of San Francisco, Martin Behrman of New Orleans, George "Old Boy" Cox of Cincinnati, and "Colonial" Edward Butler of St. Louis. Similarly, those who forged the American political machines that dominated the 1920s and 1930s— Frank Hague, James Curley, Ed Crump, Gene Talmadge, Tom Pendergast, and Huey Long—fashioned themselves after their Tammany predecessors.[30]

The decades following mid-century and the Civil War also witnessed the consolidation of the professional criminal population within the ganglands and vice regions of New York City. The professional criminals, discussed in greater detail in later chapters, were among the elite of the underworld and members of an exclusive fraternity that pursued crime within the context of an occupational career pattern. Their efforts were essentially nonviolent, undertaken with a high degree of skill, for monetary gain, and in a manner that tended to exploit interests for maximizing financial opportunities and minimizing the risks of apprehension. As predatory entrepreneurs, their patterns of specialization and maturation in crime circumscribed an occupational structure and social organization which reflected standardized avenues of recruitment and training, a formalized body of knowledge and skills, status hierarchies, codes of ethics, business maxims and rules, associations, structured lines of communication, and a complex system of in-group linguistic constructions. The more typical forms of professional criminal behavior included bank and house burglary, sneak theft, shoplifting, picking pockets, forgery and counterfeiting, extortion, and confidence swindling.[31]

The professional criminals who occupied New York's submerged regions of vice and crime were a highly mobile population, having migrated from many cities and countries. Significant numbers, however, descended from local frontiers, having been initially socialized into their professional careers from the ranks of the numerous street gangs of the central city. The "Molasses Gang," for example, a contemporary of the Whyos, trained scores of pickpockets, burglars, and sneak thieves; the Old Border Gang contained an elite class of shoplifters and pickpockets; and bank burglars and panel thieves were associated with the many small gangs that infested the districts around Broadway and Houston Streets, the Lower East Side, and the middle West Side.[32] In Chicago, a similar situation was manifest in the newly developed vice districts of Little Cheyenne, The Bad Lands, Satan's Mile, Hell's Half Acre, the Levee, Coon Hollow, Whisky Row, and Dead Man's Alley. The majority of the professional thieves were a highly mobile group, frequenting the underworlds of all the major cities in the east, midwest, and far west.[33]


## CRIME ON THE WESTERN FRONTIER

While the post-Civil War period witnessed the growth of street gangsterism in the cities, it also gave birth to the professional outlaw of America's rural west. Initially, many in this new breed of banditry were drawn from the Union and Confederate veterans who were wandering the country in search of fortune, and their first order of business was the rustling of the herds of cattle in the unbounded ranges in Texas, Oklahoma, and Wyoming.[34] To these were added the soldiers of fortune, prostitutes, and eastern criminals seeking refuge in the 74,000 square mile territory west of Fort Smith, Arkansas, where there were no courts or formal laws under which a fugitive could be extradited.[35] Their efforts quickly went beyond rustling to include the armed robbery of stagecoaches, banks, and trains. Stage robbery had begun in the 1850s, but became most profitable some two decades later when the coach was more frequently used to transport gold dust and wealthy investors through the mountainous and secluded mining regions.[36] Bank robbery on a regular scale also emerged during the 1870s, and has remained as an American criminal institution for some 100 years.[37] Finally, train robbery began on October 6, 1866 when John and Simeon Reno boarded an Ohio and Mississippi Railway express car near Seymour, Indiana, and removed $13,000 from its safe.[38] Similar robberies became common throughout the west during the 1870s and 1880s and have become mythologized in the exploits of Frank and Jesse James, the Younger brothers, the Daltons, Chris Evans, John Sontag, Bill Doolin, Sam Bass, Henry Starr, and Black Bart.[39]

In an attempt to control the violent and predatory behavior of the bandits, the west spawned county and town vigilance committees, which were quasi-public efforts to adapt self-government to the special conditions of the frontier. The vigilante, or watchman, received considerable attention in the pulp journalism which described their activities in post-gold rush California. Similar self-appointed enforcement bodies emerged in the states of Montana, Idaho, Nevada, Nebraska, Wyoming, and North Dakota.[40] Vigilantism had been known in the south a century earlier when it was used as a mechanism for controlling horse thieves and slaves, but its more violent styles appeared later in the frontier west, in the mining camps of the mountain states, and in the cattle country of the Great Plains. Vigilante groups were often quite large, their methods of "justice" were harsh, few rules were observed, their victims were numerous, and to be caught by one of these self-appointed enforcement bodies generally ended in death by violence.[41]

As the nineteenth century drew to a close, the era of the western bandit was nearing its end. Not only had the outlaws been reduced in numbers by vigilantism, but special efforts on the part of railroads, the Texas Rangers, Wells, Fargo and Company, the Pinkerton National Detective Agency, and an expanding body of trained law enforcement personnel had further controlled their predatory behavior.[42] Finally, urbanization was stretching across the nation, and the frontier in which the outlaw and bandit operated was laid waste by new settlements, competing cities, and metropolitan centers:

> The bandits had been born of the wilderness: its thickets and swamps had been the background and its lonely trails the scene of its operations. And now the wilderness itself was vanishing, the scene had shifted, and like actors on a vacant stage, they were left with no background for the consummation of their plotting.[43]

## EARLY TWENTIETH-CENTURY GANGSTERISM

As the nineteenth century passed through its final years and the new century began, the nature and structure of the central city ganglands underwent notable transformations. A series of reform movements effected numerous changes within city administrations, and the level of corruption was reduced within political and criminal justice sectors.[44] Fearful of public sentiment and the relentless castigation of the press, politicians extended decreasing levels of protection to vice resorts and the more violent organizations of gangs while police made concerted gestures against the underworld memberships that had been rooted in such areas as the Five Points district and Hell's Kitchen in New York and Whisky Row in Chicago. Concomitantly, harbor police suppressed the river gangs, and private and public law enforcement agencies directed specialized efforts against segments of the professional criminal population. By the close of the first decade of the twentieth century, many of the more eminent gangland heroes were either demoralized or imprisoned, their predatory organizations had been dispersed, and the most popular and infamous criminal hangouts had either been shut down or were operating as sad relics of their former splendor.

Yet the dispersal of the gangs did not accomplish their complete submission, and new factions rapidly formed around new, ambitious leaders. Furthermore, other gangs escaped political and judicial intimidation, and endured with their traditional leadership and following. With limited police protection, however, combined with the closing of most of the criminal haunts, gambling houses, and larger centers for prostitution, it became necessary for the underworld groups to develop new sources of revenue. Rich harvests were almost immediately found by many in the constant industrial strife which afflicted the needle and allied trades on New York's East Side. Labor unions hired gangland associates to molest or murder strike breakers and intimidate workmen who refused to be organized, while employers engaged other gangsters to assault union pickets and raid union meetings.

The professional criminal underworld, by contrast, was affected only minimally by the efforts of the political, moral, and criminal justice crusades. Because of its unique, more decentralized system of immunities, its members continued almost unhindered in their traditional arenas of predatory behavior.[45] Finally, other underworlds were also rapidly gaining momentum within the Jewish and Italian communities of numerous cities.

The most influential of the Jewish gangs during the pre-Prohibition segment of the twentieth century in New York was directed by Benny Fein, an East Side lushworker, mugger, and pickpocket. Fein commanded numerous small gangs composed of his Jewish contemporaries as well as remnants from the Hudson Dusters, Gophers, and other Irish gangs from Hell's Kitchen. His major contribution involved the districting of the lower half of Manhattan Island, where he assigned one of his vassal gangs to each area. His services were utilized by both factions in the strife-torn encampments of industrial New York, and his efforts were so widely feared that he was offered large sums of money to remain neutral during threatened strikes.[46]

The rise of the Italian underworld represented the most significant phase in criminal organizational development during this period of history. It emerged in the form of *Black Hand* operations committed by Italians and Sicilians against one another. Blackhanding, a uniquely American phenomenon with no direct roots in Italian, Sicilian, or *Mafia* ancestry, was a form of extortion communicated through letters containing threats. Framed in gentle terms but making reference to rape and murder, the letters were anonymously signed "The Black Hand" or "La Mano Nera." And although it was not supported by any organized criminal structure, the Black Hand achieved a high level of effectiveness in many cities. Black Hand extortion was reminiscent of the demands for tribute which had existed in western Sicily, and recollections of the old world Mafia reprisals served to instill fear and cooperation within the new world immigrant colonies.[47]

*L'Unione siciliana*, an association initially active in combatting the festering evil of the Black Hand, ultimately spearheaded the structure and growth of the organized Italian underworld. *L'Unione siciliana* was assembled in late nineteenth-century New York as a fraternal order designed to advance the interests and improve the unfavorable images of those who immigrated from Sicily and the southern portions of the Italian mainland. It provided its members with life insurance and other social benefits and was active in numerous projects aimed at the elimination of street crime within the Sicilian-American communities.[48] As the early decades of the twentieth century witnessed the immigration of millions from Italy and Sicily, additional branches of *L'Unione siciliana* were chartered wherever Sicilians settled in significant numbers. However, the respectability of the society became jaded in the early 1920s as many gangsters infiltrated its membership. As a large and prestigious association, its leadership represented a natural medium for those criminal profiteers who wished to widen their spheres of influence. Ultimately, the most powerful positions were completely controlled by criminal factions and the Union became the object of unyielding struggles for control.

## PROHIBITION AND THE GENESIS OF CONTEMPORARY ORGANIZED CRIME

In retrospect, the underworlds of the nation's largest cities, spanning a period of almost three centuries, had evolved from trifling clusters of vice maidens and miscellaneous orders of disesteemed thieves into a complex mosaic of territories controlled and traversed by organized bands of predators, professional thieves, labor racketeers, and corrupt political officials. Yet even the multitude of gangsterdoms of the early twentieth century were limited in their areas of endeavor and organization. And they were confined to these areas until the onset of Prohibition—the event that brought about the greatest change in the organizational nature of criminal behavior.

Prohibition provided the mechanism through which crime could expand into more diverse areas of activity and over wider geographical ranges. Furthermore, this period in American history, given prominence by the ratification of the Eighteenth Amendment on January 29, 1919, which prohibited the manufacture, distribution, and sale of alcoholic beverages, witnessed the final achievement of an ideological process that had been developing since the early days of the Republic.

Historians generally disagree over the forces that were preeminently responsible for the passage of the new legislation. Explanations have focused upon the long-standing abuses of the saloon, the wartime concern for conserving grain for food, chauvinistic feelings against the German-Americans who were prominent in brewing and distilling, and the political influence of the Anti-Saloon League.[49] Alternatively, and as noted in the previous chapter, the movement toward national prohibition has been interpreted as an assertion of a rural, Protestant mind against the urban culture that was emerging at the close of the nineteenth century; it was a rural victory and an organization of interests against the "wicked" city and its impending dominance.[50] But whatever the ultimate causes of national prohibition, the consequences remain manifest. It presented the greatest opportunity for illegal enterprise in perhaps all modern history. The law's insistence on total abstinence from a pattern of social behavior that had existed for millennia drove millions to direct violation of its mandates; strict enforcement was impossible, and the majority of the liquor traffic fell into the hands of the criminal.

The opportunities presented by the new legislation encouraged the central city gangster in his attempts to transcend the limitations and disorganization of the immigrant colonies. Petty gangsters, individual

and semiorganized bands of sneak thieves, burglars, Black Hand extor-
tionists, amateur racketeers, and other criminal types all began to combine their efforts to mutual advantages. Alliances were formulated for
the manufacture of illicit alcohol, and supply lines and avenues for
retail trade were quickly staked out.

In New York, the primitive kinds of racketeering that had been
characteristic of the Five Pointers, Gophers, and other gangs of the
city's East and West sides and the Brooklyn waterfront were replaced
by liquor syndication. And graduates of these less sophisticated predatory bands included, among others, Lepke Buchalter, Gurrah Shapiro,
Joe Masseria, John Torrio, Lucky Luciano, Jack Diamond, Meyer
Lansky, Bugsy Siegel, Dutch Schultz, Owney Madden, Frank Costello,
Frankie Yale, and Vito Genovese. Johnny Torrio, for example, was the
leader of the Five Pointers from 1903 to 1910 and developed a subgroup
of the Pointers named the "James Street Gang." Serving initially as
runners for the Five Pointers and then as Torrio's youthful minions
were Al Capone, Frankie Yale, and Lucky Luciano. In addition, Owney
Madden had been a member of the Gophers; Jack "Legs" Diamond had
served with the Hudson Dusters; Louis "Lepke" Buchalter and Jacob
"Gurrah" Shapiro as well as Vito Genovese were recruits in Jacob "Little
Augie" Orgen's "Lower East Side Gang," a multi-ethnic clan of young
Jewish, Irish, and Italian mobsters drawn from the numerous Five
Points, Fourth Ward, and Hell's Kitchen gangs; Dutch Schultz (Arthur
Flegenheimer) was a product of the "Bergen Avenue Gang," a group of
Bronx street terrorists similar to the Forty Little Thieves Gang of the
1820s; and Benjamin "Bugsy" Siegel served in a juvenile East Side gang
led by Meyer Lansky.

The role of the Italian underworld in organized crime during the
1920s has been well documented, yet the leadership of *L'Unione
siciliana* in directing their efforts is less manifest. During the '20s,
Italian and Sicilian criminals were active in bootlegging, gambling,
prostitution, and drug distribution, but competitive gangs of different
cultural roots prevented the consolidation of these operations into a
city-wide network. Giuseppe "Joe, the Boss" Masseria, an immigrant
with Mafia connections in western Sicily, was perhaps the most powerful single figure in Italian crime during this period. And in the manner
of the clannish old world Mafiosi, he was firm in the belief that individual groups ought to maintain full control over their own operations at
the cost of anyone who dared to interfere. He was opposed to alliances
among criminal groups, and he refused to cooperate with non-Italian/

Sicilian mobsters and racketeers. Masseria's plan for organizing the city's gangs along feudalistic lines was in sharp conflict with those of American-born Italians and Sicilians who wished to embrace all local operations into a geographically expansive confederation. This newer generation pursued alignments which would coordinate the criminal activities of northern and southern Italians and Sicilians with one another as well as with those of the reigning Jewish and Irish gangs.[51]

*L'Unione siciliana* possessed the influence and power for implementing the designs of those who controlled its leadership. Yet its administration was occupied by gangsters of both generational cohorts. Attempts to gain full control over the Union led to numerous battles and frequent changes in branch leadership.

Masseria's bid for absolute supremacy of *L'Unione siciliana* and the Italian underworld in 1930 initiated what became known as the Castellammarese War.[52] It began with his attempt to eliminate Salvatore Maranzano and other Castellammaresi figures—a contingent of criminal personalities who descended from the Sicilian village of Castellammare del Galfo. During the ensuing conflict, waged in New York, Chicago, and other parts of the nation, many of the old world Mafiosi gang leaders fell from power, and the peace treaty in 1931 ended the influences of the Sicilian Mafia on American soil.[53] The close of the war seemingly destroyed Masseria's concept of an absolute national or even regional ruler—the Mafia styled "Boss of Bosses."

In New York City, a "consigliere of six" was established as an arbitration board and court, and with the purging of the Mafiosi delegates from *L'Unione siciliana*, the organized coordination of efforts among criminal racketeers became possible. The new entity became known as *La Cosa Nostra*. It was comprised of a series of local units or "families" linked together by a "commission" which supervised and monitored the movements of the united whole. Its structure was bureaucratic in nature, with a division of labor and hierarchy of positions, a consistent system of rules, and an ethos and orientation which constrained members to act in ways that furthered organizational objectives.

With the growth of *La Cosa Nostra* and organized crime in the early 1930s, the czars of the new syndicate in New York—Luciano, Genovese, Buchalter, Zwillman, Lansky, and Costello—established an enforcement arm to protect their interests against lone rival mobsters or syndicate renegades. Popularly known as Murder, Inc. and initially commanded by Meyer Lansky and Benjamin "Bugsy" Siegel, its troop of paid assassins were recruited from the tough and gang-ridden East

New York and Brownsville sections of Brooklyn. Murder was undertaken on contract, and the services of Murder, Inc. were made available to other syndicate organizations.[54] The syndicate, although tangibly more organized than the chaotic gangsterdoms of the early decades of the century, was, nevertheless, a loose confederation and mosaic of egocentric mobs.[55]

Although the 1940s opened with the sensational trials of Murder, Inc. "hit men," interest in syndicate operations was soon overshadowed by the coming of World War II. The decade emerged as a tranquil and prosperous period for organized crime. Federal agencies turned their attention to internal security, counterespionage, and antisabotage activities, and local police forces were burdened by the draft and manpower shortages. Meanwhile, the war effected significant rises in personal income. Gambling, narcotics traffic, and black market profiteering flourished, and the cuts in liquor production to meet the needs for industrial alcohol brought the return of the illegal alcohol trade.

By contrast the 1950s opened with the Kefauver Committee hearings which brought organized crime to national public attention.[56] These were followed by the Moreland Commission Crime Hearings in New York State which produced a Waterfront Commission for the Port of New York. The Commission sought to combat Brooklyn and Manhattan waterfront racketeers by eliminating the "shape up" system of hiring at piers and by establishing seniority and other rights that served to guarantee increased incomes to longshoremen. Early in 1957 still another Congressional committee began an investigation of organized crime. Under the chairmanship of Senator McClellan of Arkansas, the committee examined the complexities of labor union finances and probed corrupt ties between crooked union officials and executives in the form of sweetheart contracts. Among the prime targets of the McClellan effort was Teamster Union president, James Hoffa, of New York.[57]

The latter part of the decade was also characterized by a series of violent incidents directed against the leadership of the New York organization. In May 1957 Frank Costello narrowly missed death when a bullet creased his head; some two months later, Frank Scalise, a Cosa Nostra underboss, who had been among the original allies of Joe Masseria, was slain on a Bronx street; and in October of the same year, Albert Anastasia was shot to death while sitting in the barbershop of a midtown Manhattan hotel.

Rather than simple outbreaks of mob violence, the incidents were part of Vito Genovese's efforts to seize control of the Costello empire.

Perhaps in an attempt to discuss this series of shootings, more than 100 prominent underworld figures, chiefly from the New York area, met on a secluded private estate in Apalachin, New York. The meeting was discovered by local police and some 63 members of the group were identified. Subsequent prosecutions secured convictions against 20 of the Apalachin delegates for conspiracy to obstruct justice.

The following decade witnessed continued governmental pressure against organized crime. Yet in addition to these criminal justice probes, the "syndicate" had more serious difficulties to contend with. The years of the 1960s through the early 1970s were marked by warfare among several crime families: the Gallo-Profaci War, 1960–1963; the Bonanno War, 1964–1968; the Colombo-Gallo War, 1971–1973. The conflicts reflected internal power struggles and dissatisfactions at various levels of the hierarchy, leaving the continuity of the organization shattered, overexposed in the media, and under constant police surveillance.

## VIOLENCE IN THE STREETS

John Billington was among the 102 pilgrims aboard the Mayflower to arrive at Plymouth in 1620. He was described as a rather violent individual, prone towards fighting and feuding with his neighbors. In 1630, some ten years after the establishment of the Puritan settlement, Billington shot one of his adversaries at close range, was hanged for the killing, and earned the distinction of becoming the country's first known murderer.[58] Since that time, personal violence, mob violence, and violent predatory crime have become characteristic American social patterns.

Mob or collective violence has been especially conspicuous in American history, and it has repeatedly appeared in any variety of forms during the last three centuries. There has been political violence as reflected by the Pilgrim–Puritan conflicts in 1634, the Boston Massacre in 1770, or the Baltimore Election Riot in 1856; economic violence as in the case of the Boston Bread Riot of 1713, the Pullman Strike in 1894, or the Memorial Day Massacre in 1937; racial violence, evident in the New York Slave Revolt of 1712, the many race riots spanning more than a century from Providence in 1831 to Detroit in 1943, or the ghetto riots of the 1960s in Watts, Detroit, and New York; religious and ethnic violence as indicated by the Quaker persecutions during the seventeenth century or the riots against the Mormons in 1838, the Chinese in 1871, and the Italians in 1891; and antiradical and police violence as was apparent with the freedom riders in 1961 or the massacre at the Democratic convention in Chicago in 1968.[59] To this partial listing might be added the many incidents of personal violence such as homicide, assault, forcible rape, or the violence that often occurs during the course of such predatory crimes as robbery and hijacking, or the numerous cases of terrorism, assassination, and political murder.

Interestingly, while police statistics may clearly indicate that violence and street crime are rapidly increasing throughout the nation, history suggests that earlier periods in America's past may have been exceedingly more violent. Impressionistic analyses indicate that the violence associated with the street gangs of the nineteenth century, the outlaws of the western frontier, and the bootleggers and racketeers of the early 1900s was more evident and widespread than its contemporary counterpart. But this would be a difficult comparison to fully document, given the absence of hard data in historical archives. On the other hand, if homicide rates are any indicators of the level of violence in a society, then the 1970s are indeed less violent times.

As indicated in Table 2–2, which reflects the number and rate of homicides in the United States for the years 1881–1900, the homicide rate per 100,000 population steadily increased from 2.47 in 1881, reaching a peak of 15.22 in 1895. This might be compared with the homicide rate in the United States in 1975—9.6 per 100,000 population.[60] Viewing an alternative set of data, it appears that homicide rates by city may have indeed been higher during previous decades. In Table 2–3, for example, the country's 25 largest cities during 1921–1922 are listed by population rank. Kansas City ranked highest in terms of homicide rates with 30.3 per 100,000 population, followed by New Orleans with 21.3. Also, although not presented in this table, Wichita ranked ninety-sixth by population during this period, with homicide rate of 21.9 per 100,000 population.[61] The high of 30.3 in Kansas City during 1921–1922 can be compared with 1975 homicide rates which indicated the Montgomery, Alabama SMSA (Standard Metropolitan Statistical Area) to have the highest rate of 23.9. Also during 1975, New York City had a homicide rate of 21.7 per 100,000 population and the New York SMSA had a rate of 18.0.[62]

Although there are limitations in drawing conclusions from data based solely on incidents of crime reported to the police, these figures do have some comparative reliability. As will be discussed at length in the following chapter, there is extensive underreporting of crime in

TABLE 2–2.   Homicides in the United States, 1881–1900

| Year | Total Homicides | Rate/100,000 pop. |
|------|-----------------|-------------------|
| 1881 | 1,266 | 2.47 |
| 1882 | 1,467 | 2.79 |
| 1883 | 1,697 | 3.16 |
| 1884 | 1,465 | 2.67 |
| 1885 | 1,808 | 3.22 |
| 1886 | 1,499 | 2.61 |
| 1887 | 2,335 | 3.98 |
| 1888 | 2,184 | 3.64 |
| 1889 | 3,567 | 5.82 |
| 1890 | 4,290 | 6.85 |
| 1891 | 5,906 | 9.24 |
| 1892 | 6,791 | 10.42 |
| 1893 | 6,615 | 9.95 |
| 1894 | 9,800 | 14.47 |
| 1895 | 10,500 | 15.22 |
| 1896 | 10,652 | 15.13 |
| 1897 | 9,520 | 13.28 |
| 1898 | 7,840 | 10.72 |
| 1899 | 6,225 | 8.36 |
| 1900 | 8,275 | 10.87 |

Source: These figures were originally compiled by the *Chicago Tribune*, and reported in Arthur Train, *Courts and Criminals* (New York: Scribner's, 1925), p. 87.

official criminal statistics. Yet it seems logical to assume that there was a higher level of underreporting in the 1881–1900 and 1921–1922 data reported here. Both of these compilations on homicides were gathered at a time prior to the FBI's initiation of a standardized mechanism for recording crime. With greater underreporting the actual homicide rates during these early periods may even be higher. Furthermore, with current investigation procedures undertaken by police agencies, medical examiners, insurance companies, the Social Security Administration, and the Internal Revenue Service, death in contemporary society is fairly well documented. In the case of homicide or suspected homicide, the cause of death is routinely investigated. In addition, the absence of a "body" or a "missing person" report also warrants considerable investigation.

In retrospect, this brief overview has offered some general insights into crime trends during earlier periods in U.S. history. As indicated before, it is by no means complete, but it does suggest how certain

TABLE 2–3.  Homicide Rates in 25 Largest U.S. Cities, Ranked by Population,
1921–1922

| City | Population Rank | Homicides/100,000 pop. |
|------|----------------|------------------------|
| New York | 1 | 6.0 |
| Chicago | 2 | 11.5 |
| Philadelphia | 3 | 6.6 |
| Detroit | 4 | 9.7 |
| Cleveland | 5 | 11.1 |
| St. Louis | 6 | 16.3 |
| Boston | 7 | 4.4 |
| Baltimore | 8 | 9.0 |
| Pittsburgh | 9 | 9.3 |
| Los Angeles | 10 | 13.8 |
| San Francisco | 11 | 8.6 |
| Buffalo | 12 | 6.7 |
| Milwaukee | 13 | 3.4 |
| Washington, D. C. | 14 | 11.4 |
| Newark | 15 | 6.7 |
| Cincinnati | 16 | 15.9 |
| New Orleans | 17 | 21.3 |
| Minneapolis | 18 | 6.8 |
| Kansas City | 19 | 30.3 |
| Seattle | 20 | 6.5 |
| Indianapolis | 21 | 8.2 |
| Jersey City | 22 | 3.1 |
| Rochester | 23 | 4.0 |
| Portland | 24 | 6.9 |
| Denver | 25 | 9.4 |

Source: Missouri Association for Criminal Justice, *The Missouri Crime Survey* (New York:
Macmillan, 1926), p. 20.

forms of contemporary criminal behavior emerged and developed, how
others persisted, and why still others declined. Furthermore, it clearly
suggests that the high levels of crime that are manifest in contemporary society are not necessarily new phenomena.

As a final note, it might be pointed out here that while historical
information about crime in America may be incomplete, the reverse
situation exists with respect to the American system of criminal justice. This situation necessarily emerged since the development of the
criminal justice process has been contained in statutes, legal codes,
court records, case decisions, charters, the Constitution, and other writ-

ten documents that have been preserved and maintained for the purpose of further developing and refining systems of law enforcement, court procedures, correctional processes, and overall standards in the administration of justice.[63]

## SUGGESTED READINGS

ALBINI, JOSEPH L., *The American Mafia: Genesis of a Legend* (New York: Appleton-Century-Crofts, 1971).

CRAPSEY, EDWARD, *The Nether Side of New York* (New York: Sheldon, 1872).

CUTLER, JAMES ELBERT, *Lynch Law: An Investigation into the History of Lynching in the United States* (New York: Longmans, Green, 1905).

ERIKSON, KAI T., *Wayward Puritans: A Study in the Sociology of Deviance* (New York: Wiley, 1966).

HOFSTADTER, RICHARD, and WALLACE, MICHAEL, (eds.), *American Violence: A Documentary History* (New York: Random House, 1970).

LANE, ROGER, "Criminal Violence in America, The First Hundred Years," *The Annals*, 423 (January 1976), pp. 1–13.

NELLI, HUMBERT S., "Italians and Crime in Chicago: The Formative Years, 1890–1920," *American Journal of Sociology*, LXIV (January 1969), pp. 373–91.

RECKLESS, WALTER C., *Vice in Chicago* (Chicago: University of Chicago Press, 1933).

RICHARDSON, JAMES F., *The New York Police: Colonial Times to 1901* (New York: Oxford University Press, 1970).

SEMMES, RAPHAEL, *Crime and Punishment in Early Maryland* (Baltimore: Johns Hopkins Press, 1938).

SETTLE, WILLIAM A., *Jesse James Was His Name* (Columbia: University of Missouri Press, 1966).

SINCLAIR, ANDREW, *Era of Excess: A Social History of the Prohibition Movement* (New York: Harper and Row, 1964).

ZINK, HAROLD, *City Bosses in the U.S.* (Durham, N. C.: Duke University Press, 1930).

# 3

# Assessing the Magnitude
# and Trends of Crime

During the past half century, textbooks in both criminology and criminal justice have persisted in a rather confusing tradition. In their discussions of the extent of crime in the United States, a significant number have begun with a pointed commentary on how limited and useless the data of criminal statistics are. For example, in what has now become a somewhat obscure reference, sociologist Harry Best of the University of Kentucky opened his chapter on the extent of crime with the following statement:

> The amount of crime in the United States, or the size of the criminal population, so far as it may be revealed by statistics, is not possible at present to discover, or even to measure with any fair approximation.[1]

Professor Best indeed had a problem. For although at the time of his writing many individual criminal justice agencies had been routinely collecting statistics on crime, arrests, and convictions, the only national data source on crime was descriptive of prison inmates. By the time Best's comments were finally published in 1930, the Congress of the United States had authorized the Federal Bureau of Investigation to collect, compile, and publish nationwide data on crime. In the almost five decades since that time, his thoughts have been continually echoed.[2]

There is no question that criminal statistics are incomplete, variously unreliable, and fully responsible for many of the persisting myths about crime. And indeed, as in Professor Best's day, we cannot closely

approximate the extent of crime in the United States. Yet in counterpoint, the issue that is repeatedly ignored is that social and behavioral
scientists as well as criminal justice personnel and politicians likely
have more data on crime and criminals than on any other social phenomenon. Consider, for example, the massive labor force who collect
and compile data on crime. During 1975 there were almost 600,000
full-time law enforcement employees in the United States.[3] The majority of these record some type of information about crime and criminals.
To these might be added the tens of thousands of court and correctional
personnel who gather or generate both qualitative and quantitative
information on crimes, victims, defendents, and convicted offenders.
Massive amounts of knowledge about criminological phenomena also
descend from special inquiries, investigations, surveys, analyses, and
other research by government bureaucracies, task and strike forces,
committees, panels, the press, the corporate and business sectors, and
scholars in many academic fields. These combine to represent an im-
posing effort at data collection, data synthesis, and data analysis that has
been enduring for generations.

Decidedly, even with this wide variety of information sources, our
knowledge is incomplete, and a portion of it is either incorrect or
otherwise unreliable. Nevertheless, a vast spectrum of information
exists from which researchers, policy makers, and students can draw
and interpret, and the efforts at expanding and improving this knowledge base are continuous. Given both the positive and negative aspects
of the situation, the important tasks are to develop an understanding of
the data on crime and criminals and to use these materials reliably and
with a consciousness of their limitations. Within this context, it is
intended here to demonstrate where our major sources of information
come from, what they include, how to interpret them, and where they
have been misused. Furthermore, the general problems with criminal
statistics are discussed, followed by a commentary on alternate and
supplementary sources of data.


## THE EVOLUTION OF CRIMINAL STATISTICS
## IN THE UNITED STATES

Historically, the majority of the official criminal statistics in the
United States have been grounded in two independent sources of information—enumerations of crimes known to the police compiled at local

levels, and characteristics of offenders based on arrest, judicial, and correctional records. The first rudimentary statistics of this kind were drawn from the records of city and county jails and district or county courts, but as noted in previous chapters, much of this is buried in ancient court and municipal archives while a portion has been permanently lost.

The organization of a formal police department in New York City on July 15, 1845 initiated one of the earliest uniform bases for the collection and compilation of criminal statistics at regular intervals. Although these data were limited to arrests, they, nevertheless, provided the New York Chief of Police and Board of Aldermen with the relative indices of crime deemed appropriate for budgetary allocations and manpower deployment. From an historical perspective, segments of these data tend to reflect the concerns of that community during the middle of the previous century. As indicated in Table 3–1, there were a total of 257,738 arrests in New York City during the period July 15, 1845 through December 31, 1853. Interestingly, crimes against public order and morality accounted for the vast majority of police activity in that the crimes of bigamy, bastardy, disorderly conduct, street fighting, gambling, intoxication, insulting females, disorderly houses, and vagrancy represented 68 percent of all arrests. "Victimless crime" continues to have a significant position in contemporary police activity, but not to the degree indicated in these data. The differences in the types of behaviors recognized as criminal might also be noted here. "Insulting females on the street," "insanity," and the "runaway apprentice" categories do not appear in current criminal codes, while the contemporary drug law violations are noticeably missing in these early arrest statistics.

New York was only one among many American cities that had developed a program of criminal statistics during the nineteenth century. The city of Boston, for example, compiled arrest reports as early as 1849, and their ready availability resulted in a unique study of criminal patterns in that city for a one hundred year period.[4] The first states to develop statistics on crime and criminals were New York, Massachusetts, and Maine, and it is likely that the stimulus for their compilation came from European scholars. These states had turned their attention to statistics almost simultaneously with the publication of Lambert-Adolphe-Jacques Quetelet's *Recherches statistiques sur le Royaume de Pays-Bas* in 1829, his *Physique sociale, ou essai sur le développement des facultés de l'homme* in 1835, and André-Michel Guerry's *Essai sur la statistique morale de la France* in 1833. France was the first country in the world to give birth to criminal statistics in the modern sense, with the first volume of the *Compte général de l'administration de la justice criminelle en France* (General account of the administration of criminal justice in France) issued in 1827.[5] Both Quetelet and Guerry were quick to seize upon the records of crime newly available in their country as the raw material for an analytical exploration into the distribution of crime in society and an assessment of its significance. Quetelet's "social physics" and Guerry's "moral statistical analysis" explored the incidence of crime in relation to age, sex, profession, education, climate, and ethnicity.

State criminal statistics were those drawn from reports forwarded by states' attorneys or clerks of criminal courts to a governor, attorney general, or secretary of state.[6] In New York, the *Revised Statutes of 1829* made it the duty of the court clerks of records to enter judgment of any conviction in the transcript of the minutes they forwarded to the secretary of state.[7] The purpose of filing these transcripts was to furnish evidence of previous convictions when an old offender was committed for trial on a new charge. Similar compilations were initiated in Massachusetts in 1832 when it became the duty of the attorney general to present a report to the legislature concerning the prosecutions attended by himself and his district attorneys.[8] In 1839, the Maine legislature required that county attorneys annually report to the attorney general the number of persons prosecuted, the offenses involved, and the results of the prosecutions, including punishments.[9] Beginning in 1834, the state statistics in many jurisdictions also included information on prisoners detained—their numbers, location, and characteristics.[10]

Although federal criminal statistics historically began with the census of 1880, enumerations of criminals referred to as "statistics of crime" appeared in the census volumes for the years 1850, 1860, and 1870. With few exceptions, the figures reported from 1850 through the turn of the century were prison statistics, relating to individuals found in prison on a certain day of the year or to those committed during the year preceding the census inquiries. These data were first collected by United States marshals, and later by the regular Bureau of Census enumerators.[11]

The uniform collection of criminal statistics on a national basis received its initial stimulus from the International Association of Chiefs of Police. At the 1927 annual meeting of the Association, a "Committee on Uniform Crime Records" was appointed, commissioned to prepare a manual on "Uniform Crime Reporting" for use by police depart-

TABLE 3-1. Total Arrests by New York City Police Department from its First Organization on July 15, 1845, to December 31, 1850, and from July 15, 1845, to December 31, 1853

| Offense at Arrest | 1845–1850 | | 1845–1853 | |
|---|---|---|---|---|
| Arson | 87 | <.1% | 147 | <.1% |
| Assault with intent to kill | 490 | .3% | 1,061 | .4% |
| Assault and battery | 13,896 | 9.6% | 27,904 | 10.8% |
| Assault/interfering with policemen | 733 | .5% | 1,321 | .5% |
| Attempt at rape | 82 | <.1% | 194 | <.1% |
| Attempt to steal | 545 | .4% | 1,218 | .5% |
| Attempt at burglary | 157 | .1% | 371 | .1% |
| Aiding and assisting to escape | 212 | .1% | 420 | .2% |
| Abandonment | 336 | .2% | 899 | .3% |
| Burglary | 751 | .5% | 1,308 | .5% |
| Bigamy | 66 | <.1% | 112 | <.1% |
| Bastardy | 187 | .1% | 644 | .2% |
| Constructive larceny | 171 | .1% | 108 | ——* |
| Disorderly conduct | 20,252 | 14.0% | 34,735 | 13.5% |
| Deserters | 316 | .2% | 428 | .2% |
| Driving without license | 184 | .1% | 361 | .1% |
| Embezzlement | 75 | <.1% | 169 | <.1% |
| Escaped convicts | 303 | .2% | 429 | .2% |
| Forgery | 89 | <.1% | 195 | <.1% |
| Felony | 159 | .1% | 279 | .1% |
| Fraud | 101 | <.1% | 264 | .1% |
| Fighting in the street | 1,987 | 1.4% | 4,131 | 1.6% |
| Gambling | 435 | .3% | 735 | .3% |
| Grand larceny | 2,055 | 1.4% | 4,196 | 1.6% |
| Insanity | 1,484 | 1.0% | 2,873 | 1.1% |
| Intoxication | 36,675 | 25.4% | 63,944 | 24.8% |
| Intoxication/disorderly conduct | 29,190 | 20.2% | 48,217 | 18.7% |
| Indecent exposure | 351 | .2% | 550 | .2% |
| Insulting females on the street | 138 | .1% | 270 | .1% |
| Keeping disorderly houses | 228 | .2% | 592 | .2% |
| Misc. misdemeanors and felonies | 4,039 | 2.8% | 6,983 | 2.7% |
| Murder | 64 | <.1% | 160 | <.1% |
| Obtaining goods by fake pretenses | 240 | .2% | 526 | .2% |
| Petit larceny | 14,454 | 10.0% | 24,298 | 9.4% |
| Pickpockets | 215 | .1% | 687 | .3% |
| Passing counterfeit money | 425 | .2% | 829 | .3% |
| Perjury | 29 | <.1% | 60 | <.1% |
| Rape | 68 | <.1% | 136 | <.1% |
| Robbery in first degree | 169 | .1% | 415 | .1% |
| Receiving stolen goods | 183 | .1% | 377 | .1% |

TABLE 3-1.    (Continued)

| Offense at Arrest | 1845–1850 | | 1845–1853 | |
|---|---|---|---|---|
| Runaway apprentices | 175 | .1% | 344 | .1% |
| Selling liquor without license | 39 | <.1% | 718 | .3% |
| Threatening life | 189 | .1% | 293 | .1% |
| Vagrancy | 11,347 | 7.9% | 21,155 | 8.2% |
| Violation of corporation ordinances | 1,093 | .8% | 2,700 | 1.0% |
| Total | 144,364 | 100.0% | 257,738 | 100.0% |

*The 108 cases of constructive larceny during the 1845–1853 period is presumed to be an error since a larger number were reported for the 1845–1850 period.
Source: A.E. Costello, *Our Police Protectors. History of the New York Police From the Earliest Period to the Present Time* (New York: Author's Edition, 1885), pp. 116, 131.

ments. Based on the efforts of the committee, on June 11, 1930, Congress authorized the Federal Bureau of Investigation (FBI) to collect and compile nationwide data on crime. Pursuant to the Congressional order, the FBI assumed responsibility for directing the voluntary recording of data by police departments on standarized forms provided by the FBI and for receiving, compiling, and publishing the data received. Known as the *Uniform Crime Reports,* they were issued monthly at first, quarterly until 1941, semi-annually through 1957, and annually since 1958.[12]

## THE UNIFORM CRIME REPORTS

The FBI's *Uniform Crime Reports* (*UCR*) offers a nationwide view of crime based on the submission of statistics by city, county, and state law enforcement agencies throughout the country. The *UCR* represents a major source of data on crime in the United States, and it is generally the primary document from which public pronouncements about the extent of crime are drawn. Although it is incomplete and consequently unreliable in some respects, it does offer a relative view of the magnitude and trends of crime across the nation, thus warranting a comprehensive understanding of its contents.

The *UCR* dichotomizes its compilations into two categories— "crimes known to the police" and "arrests." Crimes known to the police include all those events either reported to or observed by the police in those "serious" categories of crime which the FBI designates as Part I offenses, and includes:

*1. Criminal homicide.* (a) Murder and non-negligent manslaughter: All willful felonious homicides as distinguished from deaths caused by negligence. Excludes attempts to kill, assaults to kill, suicides, accidental deaths, or justifiable homicides. Justifiable homicides are limited to: (1) The killing of a person by a law enforcement officer in line of duty; and (2) The killing of a person in the act of committing a felony by a private citizen. (b) Manslaughter by negligence: Any death which the police investigation established was primarily attributable to gross negligence of some individual other than the victim.

*2. Forcible rape.* The carnal knowledge of a female, forcibly and against her will in the categories of rape by force, assault to rape, and attempted rape. Excludes statutory offenses (no force used—victim under age of consent).

*3. Robbery.* Stealing or taking anything of value from the care, custody, or control of a person by force or by violence or by putting in fear, such as strong-arm robbery, stickups, armed robbery, assaults to rob, and attempts to rob.

*4. Aggravated assault.* Assault with intent to kill or for the purpose of inflicting severe bodily injury by shooting, cutting, stabbing, maiming, poisoning, scalding, or by the use of acids, explosives, or other means. Excludes simple assaults.

*5. Burglary—breaking or entering.* Burglary, housebreaking, safecracking, or any breaking or unlawful entry of a structure with the intent to commit a felony or a theft. Includes attempted forcible entry.

*6. Larceny—theft* (except motor vehicle theft). The unlawful taking, carrying, leading, or riding away of property from the possession or constructive possession of another. Thefts of bicycles, automobile accessories, shoplifting, pocket-picking, or any stealing of property or article which is not taken by force and violence or by fraud. Excludes embezzlement, "con" games, forgery, worthless checks, etc.

*7. Motor vehicle theft.* Unlawful taking or stealing or attempted theft of a motor vehicle. A motor vehicle is a self-propelled vehicle that travels on the surface but not on rails. Specifically excluded from this category are motor boats, construction equipment, airplanes, and farming equipment.[13]

Arrests include compilations of arrest reports for the seven Part I offenses combined with those of 22 additional categories which are considered the "less serious" crimes, and which the FBI designates as Part II offenses:

*8. Other assaults (simple).* Assaults which are not of an aggravated nature.

*9. Arson.* Willful or malicious burning with or without intent to defraud. Includes attempts.

*10. Forgery and counterfeiting.* Making, altering, uttering or possessing, with intent to defraud, anything false which is made to appear true. Includes attempts.

*11. Fraud.* Fraudulent conversion and obtaining money or property by false pretenses. Includes bad checks except forgeries and counterfeiting. Also includes larceny by bailee.

*12. Embezzlement.* Misappropriation or misapplication of money or property entrusted to one's care, custody, or control.

*13. Stolen property; buying, receiving, possessing.* Buying, receiving, and possessing stolen property and attempts.

*14. Vandalism.* Willful or malicious destruction, injury, disfigurement, or defacement of property without consent of the owner or person having custody or control.

*15. Weapons; carrying, possessing, etc.* All violations of regulations or statutes controlling the carrying, using, possessing, furnishing, and manufacturing of deadly weapons or silencers. Includes attempts.

*16. Prostitution and commercialized vice.* Sex offenses of a commercialized nature and attempts, such as prostitution, keeping a bawdy house, procuring or transporting women for immoral purposes.

*17. Sex offenses (except forcible rape, prostitution, and commercialized vice).* Statutory rape, offenses against chastity, common decency, morals, and the like. Includes attempts.

*18. Narcotic drug laws.* Offenses relating to narcotic drugs, such as unlawful possession, sale, use, growing and manufacturing of narcotic drugs.

*19. Gambling.* Promoting, permitting, or engaging in illegal gambling.

*20. Offenses against the family and children.* Nonsupport, neglect, desertion, or abuse of family and children.

*21. Driving under the influence.* Driving or operating any motor vehicle or common carrier while drunk or under the influence of liquor or narcotics.

*22. Liquor laws.* State or local liquor law violations, except "drunkenness" (class 23) and "driving under the influence" (class 21). Excludes Federal violations.

*23. Drunkenness.* Drunkenness or intoxication.

*24. Disorderly conduct.* Breach of the peace.

*25. Vagrancy.* Vagabondage, begging, loitering, etc.

*26. All other offenses.* All violations of state or local laws, except classes 1–25 and traffic.

*27. Suspicion.* Arrests for no specific offense and released without formal charges being placed.

*28. Curfew and loitering laws (juveniles).* Offenses relating to violation of local curfew or loitering ordinances where such laws exist.

*29. Runaway (juveniles).* Limited to juveniles taken into protective custody under provisions of local statutes as runaways.[14]

The data on Part I offenses are grouped by city, metropolitan area, state, region, and the nation as a whole to reflect an "Index of Crime" or "Crime Index" for the given year. Furthermore, it is the Crime Index data that are generally relied upon for estimating the incidence and rates of crime. The seven Part I offenses, furthermore, have come to be known as "index crimes," although many lay commentators simply refer to them as "serious crimes."

A sample of the *UCR* data appears in Table 3–2, and a number of things must be kept in mind when reading and interpreting criminal statistics of this type. A total of ten classifications of crime are described in terms of absolute numbers, rates, and percent changes. These labels should be understood as follows:

*Total Crime Index.* The sum of all Part I offenses reported to the police during a given period of time in a given place; in this instance, during 1974 and 1975 in the total United States.

*Violent Crime.* The sum of all Part I violent offenses (homicide, forcible rape, robbery, and aggravated assault).

*Property Crime.* The sum of all Part I property offenses (burglary, larceny-theft, motor vehicle theft).

*Rate/100,000 inhabitants.* The number of offenses that occurred in a given area for every 100,000 inhabitants resident in that area, calculated as follows:

$$\frac{\text{Total Crime Index}}{\text{Population}} \times 100,000 = \text{Rate}$$

Drawing on Table 2, the crime rate in the United States during 1974 was 4,850.4 per 100,000 inhabitants; that is, 4,850.4 Part I offenses were reported to the police for every 100,000 inhabitants in the nation. As such:

$$\frac{1974 \text{ Crime Index}}{1974 \text{ Population}} \times 100,000 = \text{Rate}$$

$$\frac{10,253,400}{211,392,000} \times 100,000 = 4850.4$$

*Percent Change.* The percentage of increase or decrease in the crime index or crime rate over the previous year, calculated as follows:

$$\frac{\text{current total} - \text{previous total}}{\text{previous total}} = \text{percent change}$$

TABLE 3–2.  Index of Crime, United States, 1974–1975

| | Total U.S. Population | Total Crime Index | Violent Crime | Property Crime | Homicide | Forcible Rape | Robbery | Aggravated Assault | Burglary | Larceny Theft | Motor Vehicle Theft |
|---|---|---|---|---|---|---|---|---|---|---|---|
| 1974 | 211,392,000 | 10,253,400 | 974,720 | 9,278,700 | 20,710 | 55,400 | 442,400 | 456,210 | 3,039,200 | 5,262,500 | 977,100 |
| Rate/100,000 inhabitants | — | 4,850.4 | 461.1 | 4,389.3 | 9.8 | 26.2 | 209.3 | 215.8 | 1,437.7 | 2,489.5 | 462.2 |
| 1975 | 213,124,000 | 11,256,600 | 1,026,280 | 10,230,300 | 20,510 | 56,090 | 464,970 | 484,710 | 3,252,100 | 5,977,700 | 1,000,500 |
| Rate/100,000 inhabitants | — | 5,281.7 | 481.5 | 4,800.2 | 9.6 | 26.3 | 218.2 | 227.4 | 1,525.9 | 2,804.8 | 469.4 |
| Percent Change | | | | | | | | | | | |
| a) by crimes | — | +9.8% | +5.3% | +10.3% | -1.0% | +1.2% | +5.1% | +6.2% | +7.0% | +13.6% | +2.4% |
| b) by rate | — | +8.9% | +4.4% | +9.4% | -2.0% | +0.4% | +4.3% | +5.4% | +6.1% | +12.7% | +1.6% |

Source: Uniform Crime Reports, 1975, p. 49.

Drawing again on Table 2, the total crime index increased by some 9.8% from 1974 to 1975. This percentage increase would be calculated as follows:

$$\frac{1975\ \text{Index Crime} - 1974\ \text{Index Crime}}{1974\ \text{Index Crime}} = \text{percent change}$$

$$\frac{11,256,600 - 10,253,400}{10,253,400} = \text{percent change}$$

$$\frac{1,003,200}{10,253,400} = +.098 = +9.8\%$$

A closer examination of Table 2 can provide us with some preliminary insights as to the extent and rate of crime in the United States, at least in terms of those Part I offenses known to the police and reported to the FBI. These data suggest that during 1975 there were a total of 11,256,600 "index" crimes in the country, reflecting an increase of 9.8 percent and a rate of 5,281.7 crimes per 100,000 inhabitants. Noticeably, there were ten times more property crimes than violent crimes (10,-230,200 vs. 1,026,280), and the rates of property crimes have increased to a greater degree since 1974 than those of violent crimes. It should also be observed here that the crime rates are additive and do not operate independently of the total crime rate. That is, since the total crime index represents the sum of each particular offense category, the total crime rate also represents the sum of the individual crime rates.

Although the *UCR* figures are relatively straightforward, they have been subject to selective interpretation and distorted analysis, and this has resulted in many of the myths and misunderstandings we have about the rate and prevalence of various crimes. Mass-media journalism and fiction, for example, would lead one to believe that homicide is an offense that is not only quite frequent, but that it is also rapidly increasing. These notions would be supported by *UCR* figures which indicate that more than 20,000 murders occurred across the nation during 1975, and that the number of homicides had increased by 125 percent since 1960. Although these figures may have been accurately drawn from the *UCR,* they represent an instance of selective reporting. A closer examination of the data quickly suggests that homicide is a comparatively infrequent event. As indicated in Table 3–3, of the estimated 11,256,600 Part I offenses known to the police during 1975, homicide accounted for .18 percent or less than 2/10 of 1 percent. It might also be recalled from Table 2 that both the rate and number of homicides actually declined since 1974. Table 3 also reflects the relative

TABLE 3–3.   Frequency Distribution of Part I and Part II Crimes, United States, 1975

| | | | |
|---|---|---|---|
| *Part I Offenses* | *11,256,600* | *100.0%* | *62.3%* |
| Homicide | 20,510 | .2% | .1% |
| Forcible rape | 56,090 | .5% | .3% |
| Robbery | 464,970 | 4.1% | 2.6% |
| Aggravated assault | 484,710 | 4.3% | 2.7% |
| Burglary | 3,252,100 | 28.9% | 18.0% |
| Larceny-theft | 5,977,700 | 53.1% | 33.1% |
| Motor vehicle theft | 1,000,500 | 8.9% | 5.5% |
| *Part II Offenses* | *6,803,500* | *100.0%* | *37.7%* |
| Other assaults | 422,700 | 6.2% | 2.3% |
| Arson | 18,600 | .3% | .1% |
| Forgery/counterfeiting | 67,100 | 1.0% | .4% |
| Embezzlement | 12,200 | .2% | <.1% |
| Stolen property | 122,000 | 1.8% | .7% |
| Vandalism | 230,700 | 3.4% | 1.3% |
| Weapons | 166,400 | 2.5% | .9% |
| Prostitution/vice | 68,200 | 1.0% | .4% |
| Sex offenses | 64,400 | 1.0% | .4% |
| Narcotic drug laws | 601,400 | 8.8% | 3.3% |
| Gambling | 62,600 | 1.0% | .4% |
| Offenses/family | 68,900 | 1.0% | .4% |
| Driving under influence | 947,100 | 13.9% | 5.3% |
| Liquor laws | 340,100 | 5.0% | 1.9% |
| Drunkenness | 1,217,000 | 17.9% | 6.7% |
| Disorderly conduct | 748,400 | 11.0% | 4.2% |
| Vagrancy | 40,000 | .6% | .2% |
| All other (except traffic) | 1,209,200 | 17.8% | 6.7% |
| Curfew violations | 146,400 | 2.2% | .8% |
| Runaways | 250,100 | 3.7% | 1.4% |
| Total Part I and II Offenses | 18,060,100 | | |

Source: *Uniform Crime Reports, 1975.*

frequency of homicide in terms of "all crime." Part I "offenses known" combined with Part II arrests amount to some 18 million crimes nationwide of which homicide accounted for 1/10 of 1 percent. The relative proportion of homicides becomes even smaller when we consider that only a limited number of the Part II offenses which actually occur are represented in *UCR* arrest figures.

# THE EXTENT OF CRIME

It was indicated earlier that "serious crime" in the United States, as defined by the FBI Part I offenses, amounted to some 11.3 million with a rate of 5281.7 per 100,000 population. This can have little meaning, however, unless the national figures are contrasted with those of individual areas and focus on changes that may have taken place during the past few years. Among the more useful parts of the *Uniform Crime Reports* is a presentation of crime and crime rates in the Standard Metropolitan Statistical Areas (SMSA) across the nation.* Unfortunately, however, the *UCR* only presents these data alphabetically by area, and a typical reading fails to yield any notion as to the relative rankings of each SMSA or any change from previous years. Yet in a recent reanalysis of *UCR* figures by SMSA, city, and state, some interesting insights were offered regarding the distribution and density of crime.[15]

Table 3-4 lists the top twenty SMSA's across the country with the highest rates of total index crime, and contrary to popular beliefs, few of the country's largest cities are included.** Las Vegas, Nevada, ranked as the SMSA with the highest crime rate—10,286.4 per 100,000 population. This SMSA ranked third in 1974, fourth in 1973, twelfth in 1972, and not among the top 20 during 1971, which would suggest that this metropolitan region has been experiencing a rapidly increasing crime rate. Furthermore, the core city of Las Vegas had a crime rate of 18,588.8 per 100,000 population during 1975, the highest core city crime rate in the United States and three and one-half times that of the nation as a

*The SMSA is a U.S. Bureau of Census designation for urban regions with high population density. An SMSA usually contains a core city and the surrounding areas that are socially and economically integrated. The New York SMSA, for example, has a population of 9.6 million and includes New York City (pop. 7.6 million) as well as the counties of Putnam, Rockland, and Westchester just north of the city and Bergen County, New Jersey. The Miami SMSA includes all of Dade County, Florida, an area of 27 contiguous incorporated areas including Miami, Miami Beach, South Miami, and Coral Gables.

**It should be noted here that the *Uniform Crime Reports* lists 232 SMSA's which accounted for 73.3 percent of the population of the United States during 1975. In this analysis only one SMSA—Nassau/Suffolk, New York—was excluded. Nassau/Suffolk are the two counties which make up Long Island and represent a series of small cities and suburban communities of high population density but *without* any central core city. The Nassau/Suffolk SMSA, however, was not among the highest crime areas, and its absence does not affect the rankings reported. Population data for both SMSA's and core cities are based on U.S. Bureau of Census 1975 population estimates.

TABLE 3–4.   Crime Rates Among 20 Highest Ranking Standard Metropolitan
Statistical Areas, 1975

| SMSA | Population | Total Crime | Rate |
|---|---|---|---|
| 1.  Las Vegas | 317,370 | 32,646 | 10,286.4 |
| 2.  Daytona | 209,207 | 21,038 | 10,056.1 |
| 3.  Phoenix | 1,217,949 | 115,488 | 9,482.2 |
| 4.  Miami | 1,416,263 | 134,291 | 9,482.1 |
| 5.  Tucson | 448,981 | 41,417 | 9,224.7 |
| 6.  Ft. Laud-Hollywood | 863,053 | 79,004 | 9,154.0 |
| 7.  W. Palm-Boca Raton | 470,531 | 40,680 | 8,645.6 |
| 8.  Gainesville | 128,861 | 11,052 | 8,576.7 |
| 9.  Bakersfield (Calif.) | 343,969 | 29,264 | 8,507.7 |
| 10.  Little Rock-N. Little Rock | 360,074 | 30,399 | 8,442.4 |
| 11.  Fresno | 448,625 | 37,756 | 8,415.9 |
| 12.  Orlando | 588,639 | 49,014 | 8,326.7 |
| 13.  Stockton (Calif.) | 303,030 | 25,039 | 8,262.9 |
| 14.  Lakeland/Winter Haven | 271,802 | 22,194 | 8,165.5 |
| 15.  San Fran.-Oakland | 3,134,755 | 252,418 | 8,052.2 |
| 16.  Sacramento | 882,098 | 70,801 | 8,026.4 |
| 17.  Modesto | 213,124 | 17,066 | 8,007.5 |
| 18.  Pensacola | 267,677 | 21,222 | 7,928.2 |
| 19.  Detroit | 4,464,076 | 353,369 | 7,915.8 |
| 20.  Albuquerque | 386,320 | 30,369 | 7,861.1 |
| Total U. S. | 213,124,000 | 11,256,566 | 5,281.7 |

Source:  Based on *Uniform Crime Reports, 1975*.

whole. Second in the ranking was Daytona Beach, Florida, with a rate
of 10,056.1 in the SMSA and 17,769.1 in the core city. Interestingly, of
these 20 metropolitan areas with the highest crime rates, 80 percent
were in the states of Florida and California. Arizona, on the other hand,
had the highest statewide crime rate, as follows:

| State | Total Crime | Crime Rate | Rank |
|---|---|---|---|
| Arizona | 185,515 | 8,341.5 | 1 |
| Nevada | 48,265 | 8,152.9 | 2 |
| Florida | 645,263 | 7,721.2 | 3 |
| California | 1,526,293 | 7,204.6 | 4 |
| Michigan | 622,707 | 6,800.3 | 5 |

Since most discussions of crime typically center around the large metropolitan regions in the country, the balance of the tabular analyses here will focus on the ten largest SMSA's in the United States: New York, Chicago, Los Angeles, Philadelphia, Detroit, Boston, San Francisco-Oakland, Washington, D.C., Dallas-Ft. Worth, and St. Louis. As indicated in Table 3–5, the San Francisco-Oakland SMSA ranked the highest with a rate of 8,052.2, suggesting that the highest crime rates do not necessarily appear within the largest urban areas. Contrary to popular mythology, New York ranked sixth among the ten largest metropolitan areas with a rate of 6,967.3. The core area of New York City had a rate of 6,777.1 during 1975, approximately one-third of the rate in the Las Vegas central city.

Some significant changes begin to emerge when the rates of the individual Part I offenses are viewed. As noted earlier, there were 20,510 homicides in the United States during 1975, reflecting a rate of 9.6 per 100,000 inhabitants. Of these 20,510 homicides, 80 percent occurred within metropolitan areas, and the highest rates of homicide were overwhelmingly in the south. On a statewide base, Alabama ranked highest with 16.0 homicides per 100,000 population:

| | | |
|---|---|---|
| 1. | Alabama | 16.0 |
| 2. | South Carolina | 14.7 |
| 3. | Georgia | 14.4 |
| 4. | Mississippi | 13.9 |
| 5. | Florida | 13.5 |

TABLE 3–5.  Crime Rates Among Ten Largest Standard Metropolitan Statistical Areas, 1975

| City | Population | Total Crime | Rate |
|---|---|---|---|
| 1. San Francisco | 3,134,755 | 252,418 | 8,052.2 |
| 2. Detroit | 4,464,076 | 353,369 | 7,915.8 |
| 3. Dallas | 2,535,486 | 190,931 | 7,530.4 |
| 4. Los Angeles | 6,993,768 | 503,656 | 7,201.5 |
| 5. St. Louis | 2,392,543 | 169,943 | 7,103.0 |
| 6. New York | 9,566,994 | 666,565 | 6,967.3 |
| 7. Boston | 3,403,326 | 219,691 | 6,455.2 |
| 8. Washington, D. C. | 3,029,599 | 190,174 | 6,277.2 |
| 9. Chicago | 7,036,930 | 432,257 | 6,142.7 |
| 10. Philadelphia | 4,933,433 | 211,633 | 4,289.8 |

Source:  Based on *Uniform Crime Reports, 1975.*

As indicated below, the highest homicide rate for a metropolitan area was in Montgomery, Alabama—23.9 per 100,000 population:

| | |
|---|---|
| 1. Montgomery | 23.9 |
| 2. Lubbock (Tex.) | 21.8 |
| 3. Savannah | 21.1 |
| 4. Saginaw (Mich.) | 20.5 |
| 5. Tyler (Tex.) | 19.6 |

Among the ten largest metropolitan areas in the United States, as indicated below, New York ranked the highest with a rate of 18.0. The rate in New York City itself was 22.1, yet this was significantly lower than the Montgomery, Alabama core city rate of 34.4 per 100,000 inhabitants.

| | |
|---|---|
| 1. New York | 18.0 |
| 2. Detroit | 17.9 |
| 3. St. Louis | 16.1 |
| 4. Dallas-Ft. Worth | 15.3 |
| 5. Los Angeles | 14.3 |
| 6. Chicago | 13.9 |
| 7. San Francisco-Oakland | 12.4 |
| 8. Washington, D.C. | 12.0 |
| 9. Philadelphia | 12.0 |
| 10. Boston | 5.3 |

During the period 1971–1975, the distribution of homicides has been fairly consistent. The highest rates were typically in the south, and the states of South Carolina, Georgia, Alabama, and Mississippi were invariably among the top five. The metropolitan area with the highest homicide rate seems to fluctuate from year to year, but it generally falls within the southeast part of the country. For example:

| | | |
|---|---|---|
| 1970 | Charlotte (N.C.) | 24.7 |
| 1971 | Wilmington (N.C.) | 21.8 |
| 1972 | Atlanta | 23.0 |
| 1973 | Atlanta | 21.8 |
| 1974 | Jacksonville | 23.0 |
| 1975 | Montgomery | 23.9 |

Among the ten largest SMSA's, the pattern has been more consistent, with New York and Detroit ranking either first or second, and Boston ranking tenth.

While the highest rates of homicide cluster in the south, those of forcible rape appear more scattered. During 1975 there were some 56,090 forcible rapes known to the police, with a rate of 26.3 per 100,000 population and 87.2 percent occurring in metropolitan areas. Contrasted with this national rate of 26.3, Nevada ranked highest among the states with 47.1, Alaska ranked second with a rate of 44.6, and interestingly, this state has ranked either first or second during the five year period under study. Furthermore, Nevada and California have consistently ranked among the top four states during the same period.

The highest rates of forcible rape by SMSA during 1975 reflected a somewhat different distribution, ranked as follows:

| | | |
|---|---|---|
| 1. | Lawton (Okla.) | 77.8 |
| 2. | Little Rock | 73.9 |
| 3. | Memphis | 65.1 |
| 4. | Albuquerque | 58.5 |
| 5. | Orlando | 58.3 |

The majority of these metropolitan areas had consistently high rates of forcible rape during the 1971–1975 period. The Lawton, Oklahoma SMSA reflected the highest rate of 77.8 during 1975, and it ranked fourth in 1974 and second in 1971. Little Rock, ranking second in 1975, also ranked second in 1974, fourth in 1973, eighth in 1972, and ninth in 1971. Memphis, third in 1975, was first in 1974 and 1973.

Among the ten largest metropolitan areas, the pattern was relatively stable over time. As indicated in Table 3–6, the Los Angeles SMSA ranked highest in 1975 with a forcible rape rate of 51.2 per 100,000 population, and it has maintained this first rank position throughout the five year period. By contrast, Chicago, Philadelphia, and Boston have been consistently lowest among the ten SMSA's.

Unlike homicide and forcible rape, high robbery rates have a relationship to high levels of population density. During 1975 there were a total of 464,970 robberies reported in the United States with a rate of 218.2 per 100,000 population. Of these 464,970 robberies, 95.4 percent occurred in metropolitan areas, 61.5 percent occurred in cities over 250,000 in population, and 50.0 percent occurred in the ten largest metropolitan areas. As suggested by Table 3–7, the New York SMSA ranked

TABLE 3-6.  Forcible Rape Rates Among Ten Largest Standard Metropolitan Statistical Areas, 1971-1975

| SMSA | 1975 Total Crimes | Rate | Rank 1975 | 1974 | 1973 | 1972 | 1971 |
|------|-------------------|------|-----------|------|------|------|------|
| Los Angeles | 3,581 | 51.2 | 1 | 1 | 1 | 1 | 1 |
| Detroit | 2,172 | 48.7 | 2 | 2 | 3 | 7 | 5 |
| San Francisco-Oakland | 1,521 | 48.5 | 3 | 4 | 2 | 2 | 3 |
| New York | 4,013 | 41.9 | 4 | 3 | 4 | 5 | 8 |
| Washington, D.C. | 1,255 | 41.4 | 5 | 5 | 5 | 3 | 4 |
| Dallas-Ft. Worth | 935 | 36.9 | 6 | 6 | 7 | 4 | 2 |
| St. Louis | 851 | 35.6 | 7 | 7 | 6 | 6 | 6 |
| Chicago | 2,198 | 31.2 | 8 | 8 | 8 | 8 | 7 |
| Philadelphia | 1,289 | 26.1 | 9 | 9 | 9 | 9 | 9 |
| Boston | 778 | 22.9 | 10 | 10 | 10 | 10 | 10 |

Source: Based on *Uniform Crime Reports, 1971, 1972, 1973, 1974, 1975.*

highest in 1975 with a rate of 889.4 per 100,000 population, more than four times the national rate, and maintained that high ranking from 1971 through 1975. Detroit maintained second highest position throughout the same period.

TABLE 3-7.  Robbery Rates Among the Ten Largest Standard Metropolitan Statistical Areas, 1971-1975

| SMSA | 1975 Total Robberies | Rate | Rank 1975 | 1974 | 1973 | 1972 | 1971 |
|------|----------------------|------|-----------|------|------|------|------|
| New York | 85,088 | 889.4 | 1 | 1 | 1 | 1 | 1 |
| Detroit | 26,974 | 604.2 | 2 | 2 | 2 | 2 | 2 |
| Washington | 14,347 | 473.6 | 3 | 4 | 5 | 4 | 3 |
| Los Angeles | 29,455 | 421.2 | 4 | 5 | 4 | 3 | 6 |
| San Francisco-Oakland | 12,428 | 396.5 | 5 | 7 | 6 | 6 | 4 |
| St. Louis | 9,216 | 385.2 | 6 | 6 | 7 | 7 | 7 |
| Chicago | 26,368 | 374.7 | 7 | 3 | 3 | 5 | 5 |
| Boston | 10,481 | 308.0 | 8 | 8 | 8 | 9 | 10 |
| Philadelphia | 14,047 | 284.7 | 9 | 9 | 9 | 8 | 8 |
| Dallas-Ft. Worth | 5,393 | 212.7 | 10 | 10 | 10 | 10 | 9 |

Source: Based on *Uniform Crime Reports, 1971, 1972, 1973, 1974, 1975.*

When contrasting the robbery rates in the ten largest SMSA's with those of all SMSA's, few differences are apparent although higher rates of robbery generally appear in Miami and Baltimore than in St. Louis, Boston, Dallas-Ft. Worth and Philadelphia. The high rates of robbery in New York, Detroit, and Baltimore have also resulted in high state ranks—New York, Michigan, and Maryland have maintained the highest rates of robbery from 1971 through 1975.

Aggravated assault, like homicide, is a Part I offense that seems to reflect higher rates in the more southerly parts of the nation. During 1975 there were a total of 484,710 aggravated assaults known to the police, reflecting a rate of 227.4 per 100,000 population. The higher rate of 284.0 appeared in metropolitan areas where 82.1 percent of these assaults occurred, but even higher rates were found in the states of Florida (399.6), South Carolina (359.3), and New Mexico (353.8).

Those metropolitan areas with the highest rates of aggravated assault during 1975 were more often in the south:

| | | |
|---|---|---|
| 1. Tyler, Tex. | | 689.6 |
| 2. Lafayette, La. | | 683.2 |
| 3. Fayetteville, N.C. | | 612.3 |
| 4. Lakeland-Winter Haven, Fla. | | 573.2 |
| 5. Saginaw, Mich. | | 550.5 |

TABLE 3–8.  Aggravated Assault Rates Among the Ten Largest Standard Metropolitan Statistical Areas, 1971–1975

| | 1975 | | Rank | | | | |
|---|---|---|---|---|---|---|---|
| SMSA | Total | Rate | 1975 | 1974 | 1973 | 1972 | 1971 |
| New York | 45,342 | 473.9 | 1 | 2 | 1 | 1 | 3 |
| Los Angeles | 30,797 | 440.3 | 2 | 1 | 2 | 2 | 2 |
| Detroit | 14,417 | 323.0 | 3 | 4 | 4 | 4 | 7 |
| San Francisco-Oakland | 9,452 | 301.5 | 4 | 5 | 5 | 6 | 6 |
| St. Louis | 6,767 | 282.8 | 5 | 6 | 7 | 8 | 8 |
| Chicago | 19,267 | 273.8 | 6 | 3 | 3 | 5 | 5 |
| Dallas-Ft. Worth | 5,716 | 225.4 | 7 | 8 | 6 | 3 | 1 |
| Washington, D. C. | 6,733 | 222.2 | 8 | 7 | 8 | 7 | 4 |
| Boston | 7,093 | 208.4 | 9 | 10 | 10 | 10 | 10 |
| Philadelphia | 9,171 | 185.9 | 10 | 9 | 9 | 9 | 9 |

Source:  Based on *Uniform Crime Reports, 1971, 1972, 1973, 1974, 1975.*

During the 1971–1975 period, metropolitan areas in the south reflected eight of the ten highest rates, and those in the states of Florida and the Carolinas accounted for half of the top ten rates. Among the nation's ten largest metropolitan areas a pattern is manifest. New York and Los Angeles almost invariably had the highest rates, Boston and Philadelphia have had the lowest, and Detroit, San Francisco-Oakland, and St. Louis have been moving up on the scale while Dallas-Ft. Worth and Washington, D.C. have been moving lower on the scale.

There were some 3,252,100 burglaries known to law enforcement agencies in the United States during 1975, reflecting a rate of 1,525.9 per 100,000 population. Some 83.9 percent of these burglaries were reported in metropolitan areas where the rate was 1,747.9, but most striking was the geographical distribution of those high-rate burglary areas. As indicated below, the highest burglary rates have been concentrated in the same four states since 1972, and three of these states—Florida, Nevada, and California—have been among the top four states during the past five years. This distribution pattern generally remains firm when bur-

| State | 1975 | 1974 | 1973 | 1972 | 1971 |
|-------|------|------|------|------|------|
| Arizona | 1 | 1 | 3 | 3 | — |
| Nevada | 2 | 2 | 1 | 2 | 4 |
| Florida | 3 | 3 | 4 | 4 | 3 |
| California | 4 | 4 | 2 | 1 | 1 |

glary rates are broken down by metropolitan area. For example, during 1975, the highest rates of this Part I offense appeared in the following Standard Metropolitan Statistical Areas:

| | | |
|---|---|---|
| 1. | Las Vegas | 3,319.2 |
| 2. | Daytona Beach | 3,266.1 |
| 3. | Tucson | 3,051.4 |
| 4. | Fresno | 2,963.1 |
| 5. | Phoenix | 2,856.4 |
| 6. | Miami | 2,855.8 |
| 7. | Orlando | 2,759.9 |
| 8. | Lakeland-Winter Haven | 2,608.9 |

Las Vegas, with a burglary rate more than twice that of the nation as a whole, ranked first among SMSA's from 1973 through 1975, and metropolitan areas in California and Florida accounted for at least half of the top ten during 1971–1975. This pattern is also apparent when viewing the ten largest metropolitan areas in the United States. As presented in Table 3–9, the California areas of Los Angeles and San Francisco-Oakland have been consistently in the upper ranks, followed by Detroit, Dallas-Ft. Worth, and New York.

The distribution of larceny-theft was not unlike that of burglary. There were some 5,977,770 crimes in this category known to the police during 1975, reflecting a rate of 2,804.8 per 100,000 population. Some 83.5 percent of these were reported in metropolitan areas where the larceny-theft rate was 3,195.6. On a statewide basis, Arizona ranked highest with a rate of 4,747.7 in 1975, followed by Nevada, Florida, Oregon, and Delaware. For previous years, Arizona, Nevada, Florida, California, and Oregon consistently ranked among the highest rate states. Given this distribution, the metropolitan areas in those states logically emerged with the highest rates. For example, in 1975:

| | |
|---|---|
| 1. Daytona Beach | 5,603.1 |
| 2. Phoenix | 5,469.3 |
| 3. Gainesville | 5,420.6 |
| 4. Las Vegas | 5,292.9 |
| 5. Modesto (Calif.) | 5,102.2 |
| 6. Tucson | 5,009.3 |
| 7. West Palm Beach-Boca Raton | 5,003.3 |

TABLE 3–9.  Burglary Rates Among the Ten Largest Standard Metropolitan Statistical Areas, 1971–1975

| | 1975 | | Rank | | | | |
|---|---|---|---|---|---|---|---|
| SMSA | Total | Rate | 1975 | 1974 | 1973 | 1972 | 1971 |
| Los Angeles | 163,158 | 2,332.9 | 1 | 1 | 2 | 1 | 2 |
| San Francisco-Oakland | 72,590 | 2,315.7 | 2 | 2 | 1 | 2 | 1 |
| Detroit | 93,526 | 2,095.1 | 3 | 3 | 5 | 3 | 3 |
| Dallas-Ft. Worth | 52,903 | 2,086.5 | 4 | 4 | 6 | 5 | 6 |
| New York | 199,087 | 2,081.0 | 5 | 6 | 4 | 4 | 4 |
| St. Louis | 48,305 | 2,019.0 | 6 | 5 | 3 | 6 | 5 |
| Boston | 57,628 | 1,693.3 | 7 | 7 | 7 | 8 | 8 |
| Washington, D. C. | 43,360 | 1,431.2 | 8 | 8 | 8 | 7 | 7 |
| Chicago | 95,694 | 1,359.9 | 9 | 9 | 9 | 10 | 10 |
| Philadelphia | 61,185 | 1,240.2 | 10 | 10 | 10 | 9 | 9 |

Source:  Based on *Uniform Crime Reports, 1971, 1972, 1973, 1974, 1975.*

During the 1971–1975 period, the distribution was similar. In terms of the ten largest SMSA's, however, where the larceny-theft rates were somewhat lower than these smaller urban areas, the pattern was more mixed. As indicated in Table 3–10, the Dallas-Ft. Worth region recently emerged as highest rated in the larceny-theft category, while San Francisco-Oakland has been consistently high. St. Louis and Chicago have been rising on the scale as New York and Los Angeles have been descending.

The distributional rates of motor vehicle theft, when compared with those of other Part I offenses, were curiously different. Initially, there were some 1,000,500 motor vehicle thefts known to the police during 1975, with a rate of 469.4 per 100,000 population. Of these thefts, 91.5 percent occurred within metropolitan areas where the rate was 586.2 per 100,000 population. Unlike other forms of property crime, which reflected their highest rates in the south, southwest, and west, this variety of predatory behavior was highest rated in the New England (652.8) and Middle Atlantic states (534.1). On a state basis, Massachusetts had the highest rate in 1975 (1,571.1), followed by Rhode Island (1,016.8), and these states occupied the same positions during the entire 1971–1975 period. Boston, Worcester, and Fall River, Massachusetts as well as Providence, Rhode Island have ranked among the top ten of all SMSA's during the five year period, as have New York, Detroit, and Gary. The extremely high rate of motor vehicle theft in Boston is

TABLE 3–10.   Larceny–Theft Rates Among the Ten Largest Standard Metropolitan Statistical Areas, 1971–1975

| SMSA | 1975 | | Rank | | | | |
| | Total | Rate | 1975 | 1974 | 1973 | 1972 | 1971 |
|------|-------|------|------|------|------|------|------|
| Dallas-Ft. Worth | 113,580 | 4,479.6 | 1 | 2 | 3 | 6 | 5 |
| San Francisco-Oakland | 134,285 | 4,283.7 | 2 | 1 | 1 | 1 | 1 |
| Detroit | 166,430 | 3,728.2 | 3 | 3 | 4 | 3 | 2 |
| St. Louis | 86,422 | 3,612.1 | 4 | 6 | 6 | 8 | 8 |
| Washington, D. C. | 109,315 | 3,608.2 | 5 | 4 | 2 | 5 | 6 |
| Chicago | 239,713 | 3,406.5 | 6 | 5 | 7 | 9 | 9 |
| Los Angeles | 215,307 | 3,078.6 | 7 | 7 | 5 | 2 | 3 |
| New York | 240,517 | 2,514.0 | 8 | 8 | 8 | 4 | 4 |
| Boston | 78,813 | 2,315.8 | 9 | 9 | 9 | 7 | 7 |
| Philadelphia | 96,664 | 1,959.4 | 10 | 10 | 10 | 10 | 10 |

Source: Based on *Uniform Crime Reports, 1971, 1972, 1973, 1974, 1975.*

indicated in Table 3–11, where that metropolitan area has ranked first every year during the 1971–1975 period.

In retrospect, although these *UCR* figures suggest specific ideas about the extent and distribution of crime, they must be interpreted with considerable caution. The fact that certain types of offense behavior reflect higher rates in the statistics of one area as opposed to another does not *always* mean that such is the case. The crime rates reflected in the *Uniform Crime Reports* are directly related to the extent to which victims report crimes to the police. As is discussed later in this chapter, the rate of reporting of crimes to local agents of the law is related to police-community relations, community perceptions of the criminal justice process, and community size and characteristics. On the other hand, the concentration of high crime rates in given areas can emerge as a result of a given community's population composition, social and economic make-up, and differential opportunity structures for committing crime.

## THE UNRELIABILITY OF CRIMINAL STATISTICS

The *Uniform Crime Reports* can represent a preliminary knowledge base from which we can draw some insights about the magnitude and trends of crime in the United States, but the *UCR* is not without its

TABLE 3–11.  Motor Vehicle Theft Rates Among the Ten Largest Standard Metropolitan Statistical Areas, 1971–1975

|  | 1975 | | Rank | | | | |
|------|------|------|------|------|------|------|------|
| SMSA | Total | Rate | 1975 | 1974 | 1973 | 1972 | 1971 |
| Boston | 64,718 | 1,901.6 | 1 | 1 | 1 | 1 | 1 |
| Detroit | 49,052 | 1,098.8 | 2 | 2 | 3 | 5 | 5 |
| New York | 90,799 | 949.1 | 3 | 4 | 2 | 3 | 3 |
| Los Angeles | 60,355 | 863.0 | 4 | 3 | 4 | 2 | 2 |
| St. Louis | 17,997 | 752.2 | 5 | 7 | 6 | 6 | 6 |
| San Francisco-Oakland | 21,752 | 693.9 | 6 | 6 | 5 | 4 | 4 |
| Chicago | 48,038 | 682.7 | 7 | 5 | 7 | 7 | 8 |
| Philadelphia | 28,687 | 581.5 | 8 | 8 | 8 | 9 | 9 |
| Washington, D. C. | 14,799 | 488.5 | 9 | 9 | 9 | 8 | 7 |
| Dallas-Ft. Worth | 12,015 | 473.9 | 10 | 10 | 10 | 10 | 10 |

Source:  Based on *Uniform Crime Reports, 1971, 1972, 1973, 1974, 1975.*

problems. The major difficulty with all crime statistics, of course, is their incompleteness, and this, indeed, affects the *UCR* compilations. Yet this is beyond *UCR* control. On the other hand, there are definitional and reporting problems that do impact on the reliability of the FBI data.

As we have noted earlier in this chapter, the FBI has produced standardized definitions of the 29 crime categories used in their statistical reports. These definitions, along with reporting forms, are sent to police agencies across the country as guidelines for compiling local crime data in a standardized format. In the final analysis, however, numerous categories become contaminated since different jurisdictions have alternative definitions of crime which are utilized in their reports to the FBI. Purse snatching, for example, is defined in some jurisdictions as larceny-theft and as robbery in others since it often involves physical contact with the victim. Furthermore, the *UCR* tends to contradict itself in categorical matters as well. In its reports of "crimes known to the police" it includes robbery as a part of "violent crime"; yet in its discussions of "crime cleared by arrest," it designates robbery with the property offenses.

An additional difficulty emerges when not all law enforcement agencies report to the *UCR* system, a phenomenon clearly reflected in the FBI data. This results in incomplete information in some tabulations, and the necessity for estimations in others. Perhaps even more serious are the issues of validity and reliability of the data reported to the *UCR.* Information and record systems at the local level range from excellent to poor; some agencies have sophisticated electronic data processing systems while others have only rudimentary filing mechanisms. In one small police department recently observed, many reports by victims were kept on small pieces of paper filed in a shoe box; on one occasion many of these reports became lost when the shoe box was used for an officer's picnic lunch. An example of problems with filing and tabulation systems that impact on the compilation of criminal statistics was apparent in St. Petersburg, Florida during 1973. The figures on St. Petersburg published by the FBI and the Florida State Department of Law Enforcement were consistent with one another, yet were significantly different from those in St. Petersburg Police files.[16] The extent to which this kind of inconsistency exists is not known, but its presence in one system suggests that it may be apparent in others.

The unreliability of criminal statistics as measures of the magnitude and trends of crime goes far beyond the difficulties found in the *Uniform Crime Reports.* Crime, by its very nature, is not easily measurable. It is subject to both concealment and nonreporting—concealment by victims and offenders and nonreporting by authorities—and, as a result, crimes known to the police generally fall significantly short of the full volume and range of offenses. More specifically, there are wide areas of criminal behavior that rarely find their way into official tabulations. In sex and family relationships there are numerous instances in which the criminal law is in sharp conflict with social norms and human emotions, resulting in the concealment of homosexual relations, seduction, statutory rape, fornication, adultery, sodomy, illegal abortion, desertion, and nonsupport. In the independent professions there are unreported violations by clients and practitioners, primarily in the area of illegal abortions and child adoption practices, fee-splitting, illegal prescription practices by both physicians and pharmacists, falsification of claims, perjury, and conflicts of interest. Among business and corporate professionals there are instances of consumer fraud, fencing of stolen merchandise, short-changing, price fixing, concealment of income, and numerous other white collar offenses. Employees are responsible for an almost uncountable number of cases of embezzlement and pilferage while customers are responsible for numerous instances of shoplifting, tag-switching and petty check forgery. Among public officials, businessmen, and employers there are acts of commission and omission in the form of bribes and other corruption. To these one can add the "victimless crimes" and syndicate rackets involving prostitution and commercialized vice, drugs, gambling, and loan-sharking which result in a further level on nonreporting clientele. Finally, these areas are even further compounded by the millions of victims of the more conventional Part I and Part II offenses who do not report the crimes to the police for fear of publicity or reprisals, a lack of confidence in the police, or a desire not to involve themselves with crime control or criminal justice procedures.[17]

At an alternative level, that of criminal justice authorities, criminal statistics can often be subject to concealment or manipulation for political and public relations purposes. Police agencies wishing to secure more equipment and personnel, for example, typically report all officially known complaints. Yet, if such equipment and/or personnel had been obtained in previous years, the agencies may report fewer crimes to suggest an efficient use of the prior funding.[18] In addition, the complex process that occurs between the commission of a crime and its official recording at the local level can significantly influence the reliability of statistics. Efforts by the National Opinion Research Center during the 1960s suggested that police failed to respond to one-fourth of the complaints received regarding various crimes, a tendency known by professionals in criminology for many years.[19] In 1950, for example, New York City experienced substantial increases in all Part I offense categories listed in the *Uniform Crime Reports.* In an attempt to explain the increases, the New York City Institute of Public Administration examined the situation and found that it resulted from the demands of the new police commissioner that more honest records be compiled. As such, rather than a crime wave, New York had experienced a "crime reporting wave:"

> In most cases arising prior to October 1950, the information furnished by a complaint quickly found its way to a wastebasket. This practice was referred to cynically as "canning" a complaint or referring the matter to "Detective Can."[20]

And finally, other information has suggested that as much as 20 percent of citizen complaints may not be recorded, depending on the presence or absence of a suspect, the victim-offender relationship, and the victim's interaction with the police.[21]

In recognition of the gaps and abuses in our data on crime, the history of criminal statistics in the United States reflects more than six decades of attempts to emphasize the necessity for implementing a comprehensive criminal statistics program. The first appeared with the publication of Robinson's *History and Organization of Criminal Statistics in the United States.*[22] His plan was based on the model designed by the Bureau of Census for collecting mortality statistics, with the responsibility for compilation resting with individual states and cities. In 1931 the U.S. National Commission on Law Observance and Enforcement (the Wickersham Commission) recommended the development of a comprehensive plan for a complete body of statistics covering crime, criminals, criminal justice, and penal treatment at federal, state, and local levels, with the responsibility of the program entrusted to a single federal agency.[23] More than 30 years later, in 1967, the President's Commission on Law Enforcement and Administration of Justice again called for a national criminal statistics program,[24] and as recently as 1973 the same plea has been made by the National Advisory Commission on Criminal Justice Standards and Goals.[25]

## VICTIM SURVEY RESEARCH

Since the greatest source of error in official criminal statistics results from victim concealment of crimes, the President's Commission on Law Enforcement and Administration of Justice initiated the first national study of crime victimization in an effort to determine the parameters of unreported crime.[26] In 1965 the University of Chicago's National Opinion Research Center (NORC) questioned 10,000 households, asking whether any member of the household had been a victim of crime during the previous year and whether the crime had been reported. More detailed surveys of high and medium crime-rate precincts were made in Boston, Washington, and Chicago. The surveys suggested that the amount of crime in the United States was several times that reported in the *Uniform Crime Reports (UCR)*. The NORC survey suggested, for example, that forcible rapes were three-and-a-half times the reported rate, burglaries three times greater, aggravated assaults and larcenies of $50 and over more than double, and robbery 50 percent greater than the reported rate. The overall number of personal injury crimes reported to NORC was almost twice the *UCR* rate and the amount of property crimes more than twice as much. For certain specific offenses, the Washington survey showed from three to ten times as many crimes as the number indicated by police statistics. Even these rates were believed to understate the actual amounts of crime partly because, as Albert D. Biderman pointed out, "most incidents of victimization, even many that are 'serious' legally, are not highly salient experiences in a person's life."[27]

During January 1971, surveys were conducted in a representative sample of homes and businesses in Montgomery County, Ohio (Dayton) and Santa Clara County, California (San Jose).[28] The subject of these surveys was the extent to which citizens and businesses in the two counties had been the victims of crime in the preceding year. These surveys again suggested that the incidence of crime was significantly higher in both cities than had been apparent in official statistics. For example, when comparing these survey findings with 1970 *UCR* data for Dayton, the following selected disparities could be seen:

| Type of Crime | Survey Data | UCR Data |
| --- | --- | --- |
| Robbery | 3,638 | 1,752 |
| Burglary | 34,292 | 6,813 |
| Aggravated assault | 1,440 | 972 |

More recently, the results of the Law Enforcement Assistance Administration's (LEAA) survey of the incidence and characteristics of crime suggested that unreported crime was twice as high as reported crime in 11 of 13 cities studied.[29] The survey was conducted for LEAA by the Bureau of Census from July-October, 1972, and was based on victimization data from the previous 12 months. A portion of the findings, based on victimization rates for rape, robbery, assault, household larceny, burglary, and auto theft, indicated the following:

| City | Ratio of Unreported Crime to Reported Crime |
|------|---------------------------------------------|
| Philadelphia | 5.1 to 1 |
| Denver | 2.9 to 1 |
| Los Angeles | 2.9 to 1 |
| Chicago | 2.8 to 1 |
| Detroit | 2.7 to 1 |
| Dallas | 2.6 to 1 |
| Portland | 2.6 to 1 |
| Cleveland | 2.4 to 1 |
| Atlanta | 2.3 to 1 |
| Baltimore | 2.2 to 1 |
| New York | 2.1 to 1 |

Subsequent efforts by LEAA have even further documented the extent of unreported crime. A survey of 60,000 households and 15,000 business establishments selected to be representative of all households and businesses in the 50 states and the District of Columbia estimated that during the first six months of 1973, crimes of violence and theft accounted for approximately 18 million victimizations of persons aged 12 and above, households, and businesses.[30] These 18 million victimizations involved those specific crimes found within the *UCR* Part I offense category, and again suggested that the gap between reported and unreported crime was considerable. Yet difficulty emerges when attempting to compare the LEAA data with the *UCR*, or when attempting to estimate the actual incidence of crime across the nation. Initially, the *UCR* bases its crime rates on the total population, while the LEAA surveys relate only to those who are aged 12 and above. Secondly, in the victimization surveys, the yardstick for the measurement of crime is the *victimization* rather than the *incident*, and for crimes against persons the number of victimizations is normally greater than the number of incidents since more than one person can be involved in any given incident. Thirdly, several crimes are broken down in terms of victimizations of persons, households, and businesses. As such, during the January-June period, the personal larceny-theft rate was 4,670 per 100,000 population, the household larceny-theft rate was 5,140 per 100,-000 households. Yet larceny-theft from business establishments was not recorded. These data cannot be combined to determine the overall larceny-theft rate, with the result that the LEAA victimization surveys in their present form can tell us little more than we already inadequately know about the extent of crime. What they do offer, however, is significant information on the characteristics of victims and offenders, victim-offender relationships, and the circumstances under which offenses occurred. Furthermore, since much of the LEAA research was undertaken on an in-depth basis, data were obtained on citizen attitudes and perceptions relative to the fear of crime, personal safety, police effectiveness, and the quality and functions of the criminal justice system.

Apart from the LEAA victimization surveys, one study during 1974 did suggest a method for utilizing victim survey research for estimating the actual incidence of crime.[31] The site was Pueblo, Colorado, and a total of 1,800 households (17.2 percent of those in the city) were selected for study in a manner that would insure the statistical reliability of the findings when estimates were projected to the total population of the city. All persons who had been victims of crime during the preceding twelve months (May 1973–April 1974) were personally interviewed, and the following were projected as to the incidence of crime in Pueblo:

| Crime | Total Offenses |
|---|---|
| Burglary (inc. attempts) | 1,715 |
| Robbery | 360 |
| Auto theft | 720 |
| Theft from vehicles | 2,847 |
| Other larcenies | 3,928 |
| Malicious mischief | 2,933 |
| Forgery/counterfeiting | 51 |
| Fraud | 429 |
| Consumer fraud | 669 |
| Assault | 960 |
| Sex offenses (excluding forcible rape, vice) | 806 |

In an effort to determine the reliability of these projections, Pueblo Department of Police statistics on reported crimes were examined for the corresponding period of time (May 1973–April 1974). An interpretation of the victimization data and the official statistics suggested that the projections reflected a high degree of accuracy. There were, for example, 1,715 burglaries (residential) projected to have occurred in Pueblo during the May 1973–April 1974 study period. The survey data also projected that only 58 percent (995) of these 1,715 burglaries were reported to the police, suggesting, therefore, that some 995 residential burglary reports should have appeared in police files. An analysis of the police files yielded 1,043 residential burglary cases reported during the survey period—a variation of less than 5 percent from the projected number of reports. In the case of robbery (which included purse snatching by study definition), 360 of these offenses were projected to have occurred in Pueblo during the May 1973–April 1974 study period. The survey also projected that some 58 percent of these robberies were reported to the police, suggesting that approximately 209 robberies ought to have been in the Pueblo police files. An examination of the files yielded 212 cases—a variation of only three cases. And in most other offense categories where comparable data were available, the difference between the projected reports and actual reports was only minimal. This would suggest, then, the victimization survey technique can indeed be utilized for more appropriately estimating the incidence of crime.

Perhaps a major application of the victimization survey is its use for law enforcement and criminal justice planning. Proper planning for the development and effective utilization of law enforcement resources necessarily begins with the collection and analysis of data that reflect a community's needs for police services as well as the type of activities to be performed by the police. These data include crimes committed, arrests, and calls for services. As such, the nature and extent of crime in any given community, combined with the activities of its local law enforcement agencies, give direction to the total criminal justice process. Victim survey research has served to discover the victim of crime as a source of data, and the information derived from the surveys can indeed be used for examining the distribution of crime in a community, for evaluating the effectiveness of innovative programs, for developing police-sponsored public education programs, for describing the characteristics of victims and high crime areas, for sensitizing police to the needs of the victim, and for developing police training programs that include methods for interacting with the victim.[32]

Police agencies have traditionally required information on the extent and distribution of crime in order to more effectively deploy manpower to high crime areas, yet this need is not typically met by existing data systems. Many police agencies are complex organizations with sophisticated detection equipment, highly trained personnel, and intricate computer systems for analyzing data on crime. Yet the most sophisticated equipment, the most highly trained officer, or the most complex computer is unable to analyze trends of crime, draw profiles of victims and offenders, or even examine distributions of crime if the data provided are based on incomplete or biased information. The Pueblo study demonstrated that victim surveys can measure the extent of crime by collecting information from a primary source—*the victim*—unfiltered by the victim's indecisions about reporting, or police decisions about responding, officially recording, or reporting to the FBI.

This type of victim research can also play an important role in evaluating police effectiveness. First, if crime is reduced by specialized police or community programs, such a reduction would be reflected in the victim survey data. Secondly, the NORC study sponsored by the President's Commission in the mid-1960s implied that the discrepancy between official statistics and victim reports might be used as an indicator of community perceptions of police effectiveness,[33] and the majority of the victimization surveys to date have found that the major reason victims did not report crimes to the police was their lack of confidence in their local law enforcement agency. In the Pueblo study, for example, 58 percent of the respondents reported lack of confidence as the major reason for the non-reporting.[34]

Currently, police agencies in many metropolitan areas have established community relations endeavors for providing information to citizens about police activities and procedures, for reducing tensions between the police and the community, and for structuring crime prevention programs. Victim survey research data can be directly applied to these goals. Most surveys have focused, for example, on why individuals do not report crimes to the police. Many responses indicated a lack of knowledge about police procedures. The victims found in several studies reported that they did not feel it was worth the trouble and inconvenience to involve themselves with the procedures that police used for collecting information and investigating a case. In Pueblo, for example, 17 percent of the victims failed to report because they did not care to be involved with the police or were afraid of the publicity that police involvement would entail.[35] This suggested the need for a public education program that would inform the citizenry as to the nature of police investigation and its dependence on community cooperation.

Target hardening, the process of making citizens conscious of mechanisms for preventing and reducing their risk of criminal victimization, has become a major emphasis in the media, community crime prevention efforts, and police-community relations programs. The victimization survey has direct application here since it can provide both the police and the community with profiles of crime-specific victims, places, and contexts in which given crimes are more likely to occur. In the NORC study, for example, it was learned that the victims of violent personal crimes and small scale property crimes were more likely to be of lower socioeconomic status and residing in areas characterized by poverty and substandard housing; members of the middle and upper status levels who were more likely victimized were found to be residing in neighborhoods adjacent to these areas.[36] Within this context, information relative to the nature and extent of forcible rape has been employed to establish centers for educating women about those sections of the community where this crime is most likely to occur. By making forcible rape a public issue and supplying peer group and emotional support, these centers have encouraged the official reporting of forcible rape. Increased information on the victims of this crime can be used by police for further identifying those areas and populations which have the highest risk of victimization, and the greatest need for information, educational programs, and services.

As a final issue, studies of the victim have broad implications for changes in police and court practices. Victimization surveys have documented, for example, that many individuals fail to report crimes to the police due to embarrassment over the personal nature of some crimes. This is especially apparent in the case of forcible rape, and increased sensitivity by the police and prosecutors to a victim's emotional trauma and sense of loss might well increase victim willingness to report. In a major study of forcible rape in San Francisco during 1973 and 1974, it was found that even when victims were willing to report a sexual assault, some were expected to make their own way to the police station and subject themselves to an intensive personal interview in a highly unsupportive environment; and several were exposed to callous and unrelenting interrogation by police and prosecutors. Furthermore, even though a forcible rape may have indeed occurred, the charges were often dropped or the case dismissed if the offender in the case had been an acquaintance of the victim.[37] In a similar perspective, with robberies, burglaries, or other crimes involving theft, police are usually dependent on the victim for providing information about the time and place of the crime, the circumstances under which it occurred, a description of the stolen goods, and a profile of the suspects. Without this kind of information police procedures would be difficult, yet traditionally, the police have done little to increase victim willingness to cooperate. Victim survey research has indicated why such willingness has not been extended by victims, and suggests the procedures that require altering as well as the particular victim populations that are most sensitive to police indifference.

## SELF-REPORTED CRIMINAL BEHAVIOR

Since the 1930s, research in crime has been producing studies confirming the limitations of official criminal statistics. The early efforts included rudimentary victim surveys,[38] but were primarily involved with the collection and analysis of self-reported offense behavior. The numerous investigations documented that criminal and delinquent behavior was far more widespread than official records indicated. In the 1940s, for example, a mail questionnaire was sent to some 1,800 persons requesting that they indicate which of 49 selected criminal offenses they may have committed.[39] The data documented, for example, that 89 percent of the men and 83 percent of the women were guilty of some crime, and that, in many categories of crime, the extent of involvement was considerably more widespread than police files would even begin to suggest.

Studies of self-reported crime have been generated not only as a check on the limitations of standard recording mechanisms, but in addition, to determine:

—how extensive crime commission may be among the "normal" population;
—what kinds of crime are committed that typically remain unknown;
—how the official system of control selects its cases;
—whether certain categories of offenders are over- and under-selected by official control mechanisms; and,
—whether explanations and theories of crime developed for officially known offenders are applicable for nonregistered offenders.[40]

Self-reported studies have provided numerous insights regarding these issues, but research of this nature has not been without its limitations and problems. First, there are the methodological questions of validity and reliability. When the respondents admit to criminal behavior, are their answers true? Was what they did really a crime? Do they underreport or exaggerate their offense behaviors? How accurate are the respondents' estimates as to the frequency of their behavior?[41] Secondly, how representative is the data that are collected? Typically, self-reported studies have focused on specialized populations, generally with small samples, and their findings cannot be projected to any base population. Lastly, the majority of self-reported studies have focused on groups of juveniles, stressing on the incidence of unrecorded delinquency, and few efforts have been targeted on populations of adults, or adult offenders.

Among the more recent efforts to examine the extent of unrecorded crime among an adult population involved the collection of extensive self-reported data from two populations of arrested narcotic addicts.[42] During 1970, 38 male and 52 female narcotic addicts were extensively interviewed, and it was found that the intensity of their criminal involvement was even greater than anticipated. As suggested by Table 3–12, the sample of 38 males had been responsible for almost 7,000 personal and property crimes during a median period of four years. Furthermore, less than 1 percent of these crimes were cleared by arrest,

TABLE 3–12.   Unreported Criminal Involvement Among a Sample of 38 Male Narcotic Addicts, New York, 1970

| Nature of Criminal Offense | Total Offenses During Median Period of 4 yrs. | Total Offenses Committed | Percent of Sampling Committee Offense |
|---|---|---|---|
| Burglary | 2,341 | 35% | 74% |
| Shoplifting | 1,272 | 19% | 39% |
| Theft from vehicle | 1,053 | 16% | 21% |
| Other larcenies | 570 | 8% | 16% |
| Sneak theft | 500 | 7% | 3% |
| Vehicle theft | 411 | 6% | 13% |
| Assault & robbery | 292 | 4% | 29% |
| Armed robbery | 184 | 3% | 32% |
| Purse snatching | 85 | 1% | 32% |
| Picking pockets | 58 | <1% | 16% |
| Total | 6,766 | 100% | 100% |

Source:  James A. Inciardi and Carl D. Chambers, "Unreported Criminal Involvement of Narcotic Addicts," *Journal of Drug Issues*, (Spring 1972), pp. 57–64.

or more specifically, one arrest resulted for every 120 crimes committed. A similar distribution also emerged for the sample of women. The study suggested that although not all drug-dependent persons are necessarily criminally involved, those who are officially known as criminal addicts may reflect a level of criminal behavior even higher than previously estimated.

In general, despite sample biases and other methodological limitations, the body of self-reported studies that have accumulated over the past four decades have offered several significant conclusions and contributions to criminological research. First, it is clear that the extent of crime is far greater than previously believed. The work of Sir Leon Radzinowicz, for example, concluded that based on self-reported estimates, 85 percent of all crimes in Great Britain are not known to the police.[43] Second, the studies documented that, while crime may not be a way of life among average citizens, it is also not uncommon for them, and many of their crimes were serious enough to warrant imprisonment had they become known. Finally, the majority of studies suggested that crime was as common among the upper and middle classes as in the lower and working classes.[44]

## EPILOGUE

It is likely that we will never fully know the extent of crime in the United States. Official statistics include only those crimes known to the police and cannot account for those unreported by victims or the innumerable offenses evolving from sex, family, and business relationships. Victim survey research can more closely approximate the extent of Part I offenses, but the technique is expensive and could not be undertaken in every community on a regular basis. Self-reports can more appropriately focus on all categories of offense behavior, but as already noted there are methodological limitations which would preclude their reliable application on a more widespread basis. Furthermore, the self-report study is an expensive tool, perhaps even more so than the victimization study. On the other hand, the three mechanisms might be combined for a closer examination of specific issues in crime. It has been suggested, for example, that official statistics, victimization data, and self-reports could generate a reasonable estimate of the nature of drug-related crime in a given community.[45] Victimization data could be collected for estimating the extent of reported and unreported crime, official statistics could be used for verifying victimization estimates, as was done in the Pueblo study, and self-reported data from drug-using and non-drug-using populations could be used for estimating the proportion of crimes that are drug-related. Similar efforts could be undertaken for other kinds of populations and crimes, resulting in a better understanding of the prevalence of crime in the streets, in business, the corporate sector, government, and the "normal" population.

## SUGGESTED READINGS

CRESSEY, DONALD R., "The State of Criminal Statistics," *National Probation and Parole Association Journal*, 3 (July 1957), pp. 230–41.

DOLESCHAL, EUGENE, "Hidden Crime," *Crime and Delinquency Literature*, 2 (October 1970), pp. 546–72.

ENNIS, PHILIP H., *Criminal Victimization in the United States: A Report of a National Survey* (Washington, D. C.: U. S. Government Printing Office, 1967).

FERDINAND, THEODORE N., "The Criminal Patterns of Boston Since 1849," *American Journal of Sociology*, 73 (July 1967), pp. 84–99.

HOOD, ROGER, and SPARKS, RICHARD, *Key Issues in Criminology* (New York: McGraw-Hill, 1970).

McCLINTOCK, F. H., "Facts and Myths About the State of Crime," in Roger Hood (ed.), *Crime, Criminology and Public Policy* (New York: Free Press, 1974), pp. 33–46.

ROBINSON, LOUIS NEWTON, *History and Organization of Criminal Statistics in the United States* (New York: Hart, Schaffner & Marx, 1911), reprinted in 1969, Patterson Smith Publishing Corp., Montclair, New Jersey.

SHULMAN, HARRY MANUEL, "The Measurement of Crime in the United States," *Journal of Criminal Law, Criminology and Police Science* 57 (1966), pp. 483–92.

VIANO, EMILIO C., (ed.), *Victims and Society* (Washington, D. C.: Visage Press, 1976).

WHEELER, STANTON, "Criminal Statistics: A Reformulation of the Problem," *Journal of Criminal Law, Criminology and Police Science* 58 (1967), pp. 317–24.

WOLFGANG, MARVIN E., "International Criminal Statistics: A Proposal," *Journal of Criminal Law, Criminology and Police Science*, 58 (1967), pp. 65–69.

# 4

# The Search for Causes: A Lost Cause in Criminology

The Rosetta stone, now in the British Museum, was found in the Nile River delta by an engineer among Napoleon's troops in 1799. It was a basalt slab erected in 195 B.C. to honor Ptolemy Epiphanes and was inscribed in three languages—Greek, demotic Egyptian, and hieroglyphic. The significance of the stone was that it furnished Egyptologists with the key through which they could decipher the meaning of Egyptian hieroglyphics, and since that time the Rosetta stone has served as a symbol for that which might unravel the more elusive mysteries of nature and human behavior. In a like manner, it has been suggested that the fervent efforts of researchers in crime down through the ages have often reflected the belief in a *criminologists' stone*—that one monolithic approach or theory that would ultimately account for the entire range of behaviors interpreted as crime.[1]

A belief in the criminologists' stone was evident as early as a century ago in the work of Italian criminologist Cesare Lombroso, who once reflected:

Suddenly, one morning, on a gloomy day in December, I found in the skull of a brigand a very long series of atavistic abnormalities ... analogous to those that are found in inferior vertebrates. At the sight of these strange abnormalities—as an extensive plain is lit up by a glowing horizon—I realized that the problem of the nature and generation of criminals was resolved for me.

With this "revelation," Lombroso gave substance to the *anthropological* study of crime and criminals, suggesting that the criminal was an *atavism*—a throwback to an earlier stage in the evolution of man.

Yet time dictated that Lombroso had encountered a parallax view of crime causation, and so like Coronado's quest for the seven cities of Cibola, Sir Walter Raleigh's pursuit of El Dorado, and Juan Ponce de Léon's search for the fountain of youth, the criminologist's search for his elusive "stone" has continued. A *medical* approach has sought to study the influence of physical disease on crime; a *biological* approach has attempted to relate crime to heredity; *physiological* and *biochemical* approaches have correlated crime with both normal and abnormal physiological functions and types; a *psychological* approach has analyzed motivation and diagnosed personality deviations; an *IQ* approach has characterized low intelligence as the morphology of evil; a *psychiatric* approach has designated mental disease as the root of crime; a *psychoanalytic* approach has traced behavior deviations to the repression of basic drives; a *geographical* approach has tried to demonstrate the influences of climate, topography, natural resources, and geographical location on crime; an *ecological* approach has investigated the impact of the spatial distribution of persons and institutions upon behavior patterns; an *economic* approach has looked for relationships between various economic conditions and crime; a *social* approach has considered educational, religious, recreational, occupational, and status factors as they may relate to crime; a *cultural* approach has examined the influence of various institutions, social values, and patterns that characterize groups, and the conflicts between the cultures of different groups, on crime; a *sociological* approach has been concerned with the nature and effects of social values, attitudes, and relationships on behavior; and a *multi-factor* approach has sought to embrace the combination of all of these variables that may result in crime.[2]

Still, the criminologists' stone has not been found. Many megaliths have risen and fallen, and understandably so, for as sociologist Robert K. Merton has commented:

> ... the assumption that a single theory will account for the entire range of behavior placed in this category [crime and delinquency] ... is not too remote, in logical structure, from the assumption of a Benjamin Rush ... that there must be *a* theory of disease, rather than distinct theories of disease ... just as classifying enormously varied conditions and processes under the one heading of disease led some zealous medical systematists to

believe that it was their task to evolve a single overarching theory of disease, so, it seems, the established idiom, both vernacular and scientific, of referring to "juvenile delinquency" [or crime] as though it were a single entity, leads some to believe that there must be *a* basic theory of "its" causation. . . .[3]

The following commentary offers an overview of the history of ideas in criminology's persistent search for the elusive causes of crime. It can be seen in this review that explanations for the root of crime followed the paths of both intellectual and scientific fad and fashion, and that many of the more recent explanatory positions have been linked in many ways to those ideas that had been rejected in years past. Furthermore, it is of interest that, while many perspectives on crime causation were only theoretical or hypothetical in nature, they, nevertheless, had a significant impact on the treatment of criminals during the period they were in vogue.

## EARLY THEORIES OF CRIME

Prior to the beginnings of scientific criminology no real search for the causes of crime was undertaken. Persons whose behavior was viewed as criminal were interpreted as being possessed by some evil spirit or devil, or they were understood to have simply made the conscious choice to be "bad." The *demonological* explanation of crime has been perhaps the most enduring. Primitive and preliterate anamism held that spirits infused every object or being, operating in ways that controlled the behavior of the persons and objects that served as temples or vessels. Hence, magic emerged as a practical procedure to change the conduct of those possessed, especially when the spirits were considered evil and disruptive.

This notion of *demonology* became more formalized during the Middle Ages; crime or criminal behavior was a curse of some deity or possession by the devil; ritual and procedure became instruments for determining guilt or innocence; and prayer, punishment, torture, or death became tools for chasing or destroying the evil demons. Witchcraft was among the alleged behaviors associated with demonic intervention, and the history of civilization suggests that those believed to be witches were ruthlessly pursued, often conceived of as capital offenders.

The most celebrated hysteria over witchcraft in America occurred in the Puritan colony of Massachusetts Bay during the latter part of the seventeenth century.[4] History has not fully suggested how the phenomenon actually began in this small settlement, but with a legacy dating back to prehistory and a consciousness of witches and witch-priests in Britain from the fourth century, a belief in witchcraft was logically possible among the Puritans. Their rigid religious orientation included creeds which assured the fires of hell and the reality of the devil as an adversary who had the ability to possess souls for sinister purposes. The "outbreak" of witchcraft began in the home of a local minister, Reverend Samuel Parris, when several young girls were reported to have been seized by fits and convulsions. When questioned, they accused three village women who were then induced to confess to all manner of dealings in evil, and to indict friends and neighbors for similar practices. During 1692, trials, torture, and executions for witchcraft were common throughout the colony, and the most damning piece of evidence that could be introduced was the *devil's mark* or *witch's mark* which a prosecutor would reveal on the accused's body.[5] The devil's mark took the form of a scar or strip of oddly shaped dark skin, while the witch's mark was a piece of protruding flesh, or what appeared to be a secondary pair of nipples on which the witches' imps and familiars were supposed to feed. Both witch's and devil's marks were alleged to have been awarded to the witch when initiated into the devil's evil cult, and sealed with sexual intercourse between him and his neophyte. While these marks are accepted today as birthmarks, moles, warts, or other common imperfections, their appearance on an accused witch meant certain conviction, followed by torture and/ or death.

At the center of the Massachusetts witch frenzy was Cotton Mather, a zealous local clergyman, whose *Wonders of the Invisible World* reflected the epitome of Puritan fanaticism.[6] His zeal was similar to that of Matthew Hopkins, the infamous seventeenth-century British witch finder who was dedicated to the discovery of witchcraft and was responsible for the conviction and execution of some 200 alleged witches.[7] Mather's efforts included experiments with those "possessed" and the collection of evidence for trial. During his reign of terror, spirited also by his father, Increase Mather, who often presided over the court cases, dozens of innocent citizens were put to death, while an even greater number were either punished, tortured, or otherwise degraded.

The *classical* school of criminological thought, emergent in Europe during the second half of the eighteenth century, represented an abandoning of the supernatural as an explanation for the causes of crime and a guide to criminal procedure. It was grounded in the idea that man was a self-determining being, acting on the basis of reason and intelligence, and therefore responsible for his behavior. And its orientation included the notions that:

—the human "will" was a psychological reality, a faculty of the individual which regulated and controlled behavior;
—the will was "free," and hence, there were no limitations to the choices an individual could make;
—"God," the devil, and nature could influence the will, yet in specific actions of the individual the will was "free."

Within this frame of thinking, crime was simply the result of an individual's conscious and rational decision to break the law. Yet the influence of the classical school was not in its explanations of a cause of crime, but in its efforts to reform the then contemporary system of punishments.[8]

Prominent among the classical writers was Cesare Bonesana, Marchese di Beccaria, an Italian mathematician and economist whose interest in criminal procedure and penal practice had resulted from frequent visits to his intimate acquaintance Alessandro Verri, a prison official in Milan.[9] Beccaria objected to many of the policies of criminal justice procedure, especially to both the capricious and purely personal justice that judges were applying as well as to the severe and barbaric punishments of his time. Penalties were almost totally discretionary, and judges exercised the power to add to the punishments nebulously prescribed by law, in terms of their personal views of the circumstances involved. Under this scheme, the practice of power was both arbitrary and tyrannical, and punishments included having offenders branded, mutilated, torn limb from limb, fed to animals, slowly starved, scalded, burned, hanged, enslaved, crucified, and stoned or pressed to death.

Beccaria's *Dei delitti et delle pene (Of Crimes and Punishments)*, published in 1764, outlined a more liberal doctrine of criminal law, and included the following essential points:

1. Since the criminal law placed restrictions on individual freedom, the law should be limited in scope. The function of the law was to serve the needs of a given society, not to enforce moral virtue, and as such, to prohibit an action necessarily increases rather than decreases crime.

2. In the administration of justice, the presumption of innocence should be the guiding factor, and at all stages in the criminal justice process the rights of the suspected, the accused, the convicted, and the sentenced should be protected.

3. The criminal law should define in advance both the offenses and their punishments. Thus, there should be a complete written code of criminal law.

4. Punishment should be retributive: " ... everyone must suffer punishment so far to invade the province of his own rights as the crime he has committed has penetrated into that of another."

5. The severity of punishment must be limited; it should be proportionate to the crime; it should not go beyond the point that already prevents the offender from further injuring others or beyond the point that already deters others.

6. The nature of the punishment should correspond with the nature of the offense; a fine, thus, would be appropriate for simple thefts while corporal punishment and labor would satisfy crimes of violence.

7. There must be certainty of punishment; penalites must be applied with speed and certainty.

8. Punishment should not be used to make an example of the offender for society, nor should the punishment include reformatory measures, since enforced reformation by its very nature is of little use. Furthermore, the punishment should be based on the objective criterion of the crime, and not varied to suit the personality of the offender.

9. "It is better to prevent crimes than to punish them ... " and prevention consists in a clear and limited code of laws, supplemented by the rewording of virtue.[10]

As for the causation of crime, Beccaria and other classicists such as Jeremy Bentham, William Blackstone, and Samuel Romilly viewed the potential offender as an independent and reasoning individual who weighted the consequences of crime and decided the balance of advantage. All individuals were assumed to have the same powers of resistance, and, hence, to deserve the same punishment for the same crime and to react similarly to identical punishments.

The classical school clearly ignored the notion of individual differences and the significance of particular situations. It attempted to approach first offenders and repeaters on the same basis of the criminal act committed, and it sought to treat the insane, the incompetent, and minors in the same fashion as the competent. A *neo-classical* school of thought responded with a more softened approach which suggested that free will indeed determined the nature of human conduct, but acknowledged that free will could also be affected by pathology, incompetence, insanity, or other conditions that made it impossible for an individual to exercise free will.[11] Furthermore, this school of thought also accepted the validity of mitigating circumstances which might influence an individual's ability to choose between right and wrong.

Within the realm of criminal jurisprudence, the perspectives of the classical and neo-classical schools continue to stand at the foundation of many contemporary criminal justice processes. And while they also endured in the area of crime causation for more than a century, a *positive* school of criminology was developing which rejected the notion that behavior was self-determining. The basis of positivism was a conception that crime causation was related to factors natural to man and his world. It was grounded in a doctrine of *determinism,* one which held that the individual was not an independent creature who might act in any manner of choice, but rather, behavior was "determined" by one's ancestors, or by biology, or by some other physical, natural, social, or cultural factor.

The early deterministic theories of crime causation were initially influenced by the emerging concepts of physiognomy and phrenology. *Physiognomy* was the belief that character could be read by observation and measurement of the face.[12] Although this judgment of moral and ethical structure from facial features was primarily the work of J. K. Lavater (1741-1801), the principles behind his ideas were apparent in the writings of Socrates,[13] and they ultimately led to the development of *phrenology*—the search for relations between the skull, the brain, and social behavior.[14]

Franz Joseph Gall, a European anatomist, has been credited with the initial doctrine of phrenology, which contended that irregularities in the shape of the skull and unusual protuberances in the cranium resulted from abnormalities in the structure of the brain. These in turn were related to the personal characteristics of individuals. Gall's work was elaborated by the American physician Charles Caldwell, who maintained that human conduct was the consequence of organs and faculties of the mind incorporated in the physiological cells and tissues of the brain. These, in turn, followed the physiological laws of heredity, and of growth and decay.[15]

Phrenology was discounted for its hypothetical nature, but it was also rejected during the nineteenth century on the grounds of its fatalism, for it denied that man was the "master of his fate." Nevertheless, it did provide the setting within which later deterministic theories of crime could impact the intellectual posture of western civilization.

## THE EMERGENCE OF SCIENTIFIC CRIMINOLOGY

The emergence of scientific or modern criminology has been traditionally dated with the work of the Italian physician Cesare Lombroso.[16] Richard Quinney has argued, however, that this is a myth in criminology:

> ... Such judgments on the founding of modern criminology are based on the assumption that there were no efforts before the Italian criminologists to take the discussion of crime out of the realm of theology and metaphysics and into the objective description and analysis of crime as a natural phenomenon.[17]

He notes that a scientific orientation in criminology grounded in a sociological frame of reference appeared long before Lombroso even began his work. In 1839, for example, R. W. Rawson and Joseph Fletcher reported on rates of crime in England and Wales, refuting theories which attempted to associate crime with poverty or race or population density, and suggesting that crime was a profession for which persons received training in prisons, jails, and specific kinds of neighborhoods.[18] Other studies of this period focused extensively on the relationship of social and economic conditions to crime,[19] and the interaction of crime with the changing criminal law.[20] Within this context, however, Lombroso turned attention away from the study of crime as a social phenomenon, and he has been consequently accused of being an anomaly to criminology.[21]

Lombroso and his immediate followers—Enrico Ferri and Raffaele Garofalo—have also been regarded among the founders of the "positive" school of criminology. Their approach to the study of crime was positivistic in that they applied the logic and method of the natural sciences, in contrast to the speculative approach of the classical school. And as noted earlier, the positive school placed emphasis on the determinism of conduct, an orientation that continues to dominate much of modern criminology.

The initial conceptualization of the positive school was one of *biological determinism,* a notion which suggested that the causes of crime were the result of some biological or physical element.[22] It was spirited by the work of Lombroso, who had been heavily influenced by the efforts of both Franz Joseph Gall and Charles Darwin. In 1876 Lombroso's *L'uomo delinquente (The Criminal Man)* marked the synthesis of a line of thought that had been developing in Europe for some time. According to his thesis, there was a born criminal type; the criminal was an *atavism,* a throwback to an earlier stage in the evolution of humankind, a more ape-like evolutionary ancestor. The criminal could be identified by certain "stigmata of degeneration," including a slanting forehead, excessive dimensions of the jaw and cheek bones, ears of unusual size, peculiarities of the eyes, abnormal dentition, excessive length of arms, or other constitutional defects.[23] And these designations applied to both male and female criminals alike, except in the case of prostitutes, Lombroso suggested, the typical criminal characteristics might not be immediately evident:

> ... the art of making up, imposed by their trade on all of these unfortunates, disguises or hides many characteristic features which criminals exhibit openly ... if external anomalies be rare in prostitutes, internal ones, such as overlapping teeth, a divided palate ... are more common among them....[24]

Lombroso ultimately modified his thoughts to include a discussion of environmental factors that might be causally related to criminal behavior, concluding that biological atavism did not necessarily apply to all criminals.[25] Yet even in modified form his views regarded most offenders as defective or degenerate in some way, and his positivism and biological base exerted a significant influence on both European and American criminology.


## TWENTIETH-CENTURY BIOLOGICAL DETERMINISM

Despite severe attacks on his work, the Lombrosian perspective initiated an orientation towards the study of crime that has received support for almost a century. Charles Goring, for example, a medical officer at Britain's Parkhurst Prison, made careful measurements of some 3,000 English convicts as well as large groups of noncriminals. Goring anticipated that in order to substantiate Lombroso's contentions, the criminals, all of whom were recedivists, as compared to the general population, should reflect significant differences in head width and height, degree of receding forehead, and in cranial circumference and symmetry. Yet his findings reflected no such differences.[26]

Biological theories of crime also suggested that the propensity to commit crime might be inherited, and among the better known efforts in this respect was Richard Dugdale's study of the Juke family in 1874. The family came from the Finger Lake region of New York State, and Dugdale traced its 709 members back to the year 1740. His findings indicated that 20 percent of the Juke family had been either habitual thieves, prostitutes, or had been prosecuted for bastardy, and from this he concluded the crime was caused by "bad" heredity; that although environment played a role in the development of criminality, the biological transmission of feeblemindedness resulted in degeneracy.[27] This inspired the study of other families which allegedly transmitted negative behavioral traits, resulting in Goddard's investigation of the Kallikak family, Estabrook and Davenport's examination of the Nam family, and Estabrook's follow-up of the Jukes in 1915.[28] These concluded that heredity or "poor germ plasm" could facilitate a transmission of crime, alcoholism, feeblemindedness, harlotry, illigitimacy, and pauperism.[29]

Other attempts to demonstrate a relationship between crime and heredity examined the relative criminality of identical and fraternal twins. The theory was based on the notion that *identical* twins were the product of a single egg and would therefore have identical heredity; *fraternal* twins, on the other hand, were the product of two eggs fertilized simultaneously, thus having heredity only in the manner of ordinary siblings. From this it was decided that the similar behavior of identical twins emerged from their identical heredity. During the late 1920s and early '30s numerous studies found that in following up pairs of identical and fraternal twins, there were a greater number of instances in which both members of the identical pairs were criminal than was the case with the fraternal pairs. And from this it was concluded that the criminality was inherited.[30]

Biological determinism was not limited to investigations of evolutionary throwbacks and heredity. In 1928 neuropathologist Max G. Schlapp combined with popular mystery writer Edward H. Smith with the purpose of demonstrating that most forms of criminality were the result of endocrine imbalances, that the criminal was the victim of disturbances in his body chemistry.[31] In 1938 biochemist Louis Berman contended that criminality was a consequence of glandular and metabolic dysfunctioning.[32] In 1939 Ernest A. Hooton, within the Lombrosian ethos, maintained that crime was a consequence of offenders' physical inferiority, and that such "criminal stock" should be eliminated by sterilization and segregation.[33] In 1947 Joseph Wilder indicated that criminal behavior resulted from *hypoglycemia,* a condition characterized by a low level of sugar in the blood.[34] In 1949 William H. Sheldon's theory of crime and delinquency offered a relationship between body structure and behavior.[35] And in 1955 Edward Podolsky suggested that *hypocalcemia,* a lack of calcium in the blood stream, exhibited a deviant influence on behavior.[36]

More recently, advances in the fields of molecular biology and micropathology have hypothesized a link between chromosome abnormalities and crime. It is postulated on the theory that the male cytogenetic makeup includes one X chromosome and one Y chromosome, with the latter mediating the development of primary and secondary sexual characteristics. Research has speculated that one in every 700 males possesses an XYY chromosomal makeup, with the extra Y chromosome possibly causing such behavioral traits as social isolation, sexual deviation, and criminality. Those prominent in chromosome research have tended to be conservative in their statements about the relationship between crime and chromosomes,[37] but some European courts have already accepted the XYY theory as a defense to criminal behavior. In 1968, for example, the French case of Daniel Hugon who was accused of murdering a prostitute, offered the XYY defense. Hugon was judged to be sane at the time of the homicide, but his XYY defense was permitted in mitigating the sentence.[38]

In retrospect, while the recent interest in the XYY syndrome might suggest a revival of the "biological criminal," biologically-based explanations of crime causation currently receive little support in American criminology. And justifiably so. From the "atavistic man" to the "XYY man," the logical base of each theoretical posture has been structurally weak. The influences of environmental, cultural, social, and legalistic factors were continually ignored. The samples secured for research investigation were typically biased. They included convicted criminals, prison inmates, or adjudicated delinquents, and rarely were non-criminal control populations introduced. And in addition, many of the samples were so small that any conclusions drawn from them had little meaning. Finally, interpretations were often based on unsound reasoning, contorted logic, or blatant prejudice; obvious confounding factors were often ignored in an effort to support the overall theoretical drive. Yet in spite of these difficulties, the biological school continues to persist in contemporary European criminology. Perhaps this is due, as

Quinney has suggested, to the prestige of the natural sciences in Europe, to the enduring European tradition of accepting physical features as indicators of behavior, or to nationalistic political structures which have emphasized the importance of physical superiority vs. inferiority.[39]

## FROM ECLECTIC THEORY TO SOCIOLOGICAL THEORY

Biological theories of crime causation were essentially *eclectic* in approach; they were marked by explanations based on specific tangible factors, and later on a configuration of factors which typically focused on the characteristics of the offenders—their ancestry, heredity, or physical and biological or genetic structure. The perspective of the *psychogenic* approach to crime rested on a parallel base, for this approach looked for the roots of crime within the offenders—their innate impulses, emotional instabilities, mental conflicts, repressions, and drives.[40] Yet they were more hypotheses than they were theories, and they were never subject to verification. Psychopathy, for example, was often suggested as a cause of criminal behavior, while the latter was often targeted as an indicator of psychopathy.[41]

In reaction to these and many other particularistic explanations which sought the roots of crime in terms of but a single, and perhaps narrow, class of phenomena, a multiple-factor approach emerged which stressed the notion that the criminal act was the consequence of any number of diverse sets of factors. William Healy's *The Individual Delinquent* reflected this posture.[42] In his formulation of the causes of delinquency, he examined the medical, psychological, psychiatric, and social characteristics of 823 chronic offenders. On each case, Healy diagnosed the reasons for their deviation, finding an average of 3.5 factors per individual. Nathaniel Hirsch postulated a similar view, suggesting that some 60 percent of the influences which contributed to crime came from within the individual, 39 percent emerged from the environment, and 1 percent was the result of accident.[43]

In general, the framework of these and other multiple-factor studies offered little to causation theory, for the enumeration of "factors" designated to be pertinent added to several hundred operating in an unstable number of indefinite combinations. And as to the relative importance of given factors on crime causation as designated by Hirsch and others, George B. Vold has commented:

Such application of multiple factor thinking, which determines the importance of a factor from its frequency of occurrence ... as logic it is about on
the par with that which would be involved if the assumption were made
that the element hydrogen is twice as important as the element oxygen in
the compound water....[44]

The more sociological view of crime, criminality, and crime causation began to emerge in the United States when the *relative* causes of
crime became more fully understood:

> ... Only in freeing himself from an absolute conception of the world could
> the student of crime perceive crime as being a violation of one of a number
> of possible codes, with the behavior of the offender seen as a consequence
> of participation in one of several social worlds.[45]

The sociological study of crime moved slowly during the first two
decades of the twentieth century, hampered somewhat by the influences of Lombroso's criminal anthropology and evolutionary theory.
Yet during the 1920s and 1930s a sociological theory of criminology was
ultimately achieved at the University of Chicago. Criminal behavior
was perceived to be similar to other social behaviors, and it was interpreted as being circumscribed by conflicting cultural values, memberships in social groups having deviant value systems, social roles in
deviant groups, the varying nature of conduct norms, attitudes toward
law and society, and the nature, frequency, and duration of criminal
associations.

The commitment to this sociological perspective was influenced by
the Chicago sociologist Robert E. Park, an ex-newspaperman whose
main scholarly interests were in the areas of human ecology, collective
behavior, and race relations. With respect to the urban community,
Park theorized that land-use patterns emerged apart from deliberate
planning, but through processes of competition, segregation, invasion,
and succession, and that these processes produced "natural areas"
within a human community.[46] Park sent his students out to study the
natural areas of Chicago—the ghetto, the ganglands, hotel life, skid row,
the marginal man, the "gold coast," and the slum—and the impact of
ecological structure on suicide rates, divorce rates, and crime rates.
Among Park's students was Clifford R. Shaw, who found that delinquency was concentrated in the deteriorated areas of the city, and that
these areas maintained their high rates of delinquency in spite of constant population changes.[47] Through a number of case studies Shaw and

his collaborators found that slum youth were participants in a culture where delinquency was a prescribed behavior,[48] that crime was acquired in a social and cultural setting through a process of interaction.

From a broader stance, criminologist Donald R. Taft later commented on certain conditions in the society as a whole that served as a stimulus to criminality.[49] American society, he suggested, was characterized by materialism, a growing impersonality, individualism, political democracy, group loyalties, insistence on the importance of status, survivals of frontier traditions, race discrimination, a lack of scientific orientation in the social field, tolerance of political corruption, general faith in the law but disrespect for some law, and an acceptance of quasi-criminal exploitation. The values which ensue from these conditions are accepted by both "criminals" and "noncriminals," and as such, the general nature of the social order was the cause of crime. More specifically:

> It has been contended that a society characterized by such values must expect considerable crime.... The general structure and culture of our society have made for crime in several ways: (1) They have provided a differential and underprivileged experience for millions of people. Thus slums, gangs, broken homes, demands for escape through the use of alcohol or drugs—such abnormal experiences of the underprivileged are implicit in such values as individualism, materialism, the necessity to gain status in some group.... In a society cherishing such values some individuals *must* be underpriviliged—some *must* fail.... (2) Our society involves the relative tolerance, acceptance, and even the approval of exploitive behavior either of the white-collar crime type or that of the noncriminal exploiter. The values in the general culture explain these two types of unsocial behavior more *directly* than they explain "no-collar crime," the crime of the underprivileged. But the prevalence and acceptance of white-collar crime and noncriminal exploitation also help explain "no-collar" crime. The prestiged classes hand on to the underprivileged the value basis of their crimes.[50]

Taft's view was indeed a sociological one, for it suggested that criminal behavior, like all behavior, was part and product of social relationships. Persons react to a social structure and a system of values and institutions, and they participate in relationships as active agents of social and cultural conditions. According to Taft, there are "criminogenic" aspects to our sociocultural order. In such a materialistic culture not all can be successful and the potential failures will strive for their share of material success. Other social values, those that place little importance on the mechanisms of equalization, create a situation where social and material goals become primary regardless of the means utilized to attain them.

Columbia University sociologist Robert K. Merton also noted the "criminogenic" aspects of American culture.[51] In his discussion of "social structure and anomie," Merton stressed that the competitive struggle for wealth and materialistic goals is deemed valuable to all, yet the ultimate products of status, power, and wealth were available to few through legitimate means. Thus, there emerges a gap between aspirations and achievable goals, resulting among many a normless struggle for material reward.

The somewhat culturally deterministic views of Taft, Merton, and others,[52] offer a case for the analysis of crime in terms of culture conflict. As noted in Chapter 1, Jerome Michael and Mortimer J. Adler have argued that crimes are merely instances of behavior which are prohibited by the criminal law, that "... the criminal law is the formal cause of crime."[53] This comment of more than four decades ago gives direction to an explanation of crime as it may emerge from conflicting sets of norms, and in this behalf, Richard Quinney has unearthed for us one of the earlier perspectives on the issue. He offers a comment by Edwin H. Sutherland, who had examined law, criminal behavior, and punishment as all part of a conflict process:

> This process begins in the community before the law is enacted, and continues in the community and in the behavior of particular offenders after punishment is inflicted. This process seems to go on somewhat as follows: A certain group of people feel that one of their values—life, property, beauty of landscape, theological doctrine—is endangered by the behavior of others. If the group is politically influential, the value important, and the danger serious, they secure the enactment of a law and thus win the cooperation of the State in the effort to protect their value.[54]

Thorsten Sellin's *Culture Conflict and Crime* similarly regarded the criminal law as a body of rules which prohibited specific forms of conduct and has prescribed certain punishments for violations of these rules. He further observed that the types of conduct the rules prohibited and the nature of the sanctions attached to their violation depended directly on the interests of those in the population who influenced legislation:

> ... In some states, these groups may comprise the majority, in others a minority, but the social values which receive the protection of the criminal law are ultimately those which are treasured by dominant interest groups.[55]

Crime, in this orientation, can emerge from, or be the result of, a conflict between the norms and values and goal orientations of a social or culture group and the legal codes that have been imposed by an alternative group that has the greater power to shape public policy. Yet within this framework, the crime that emerges from group conflict can occur when the purposes and interests and valued goals of groups become competitive with one another in other ways. Albert K. Cohen's concept of the "delinquent subculture" offers an illustration. He suggested that working-class boys are handicapped in attaining social and economic status. Some do, but most do not. Thus, they band together into gangs, providing them with an arena for striking back at the middle-class values which they oppose and with status as a subcultural group. These subcultures are "nonutilitarian," "malicious," and "negativistic." They are nonutilitarian in that gang members defy legal codes often simply for the approval given by their peers; they are malicious in that they enjoy the discomfort of their victims since such discomfort is the result of their defiance of norms; and they are negativistic since they repudiate the standards of the middle-class culture.[56]

An alternative view of delinquency that might be interpreted within the conflict mode was offered by Walter B. Miller who contended that there were certain "focal concerns" within lower-class cultures that could often lead to antisocial conduct. He defined "focal concerns" as ". . . areas or issues which command widespread and persistent attention and a high degree of emotional involvement."[57] These areas or issues could be found in the middle class, but carried higher priorities within the lower class. They included a preoccupation with "toughness," the sensitivity to "smartness," excitement, autonomy, a belief in fate, and a chronic awareness of "trouble." The illegal activity often found in lower-class areas represented an adolescent adaptation to the lower class cultural concerns which were often in conflict with those of the wider society.

Much of what appears in *conflict theory* often seems to reflect on economic concerns. The conflict approach focuses on the political power base occupied by those who have the influence to shape public policy, and how this base and ensuing power and influence serve to extend a criminal status to those of conflicting norms or interests. And a political power base often rests on a strong economic base, or at the very least the two are intricately woven. As such, it is the "underprivileged," the "working class," or the "marginal" that so many theorists are referencing when they discuss crime in terms of group conflict. Furthermore, much of what remains unspoken in the theoretical terrain, but which is often nevertheless apparent, is in many ways reminiscent of the early theories of economic determinism. As early as 1516 Thomas More's *Utopia* commented on the issue of crime and its relation to the poor economic status of certain groups. Similar observations were made in 1798 by Thomas Malthus in his *An Essay on the Principle of Population as it Affects the Future Improvement of Society,* and by Karl Marx in his *A Contribution to the Critique of Political Economy* in 1859. More recently, many public pronouncements about the causes of crime have targeted an economic base, suggesting, for example, that "poverty" is the cause of crime. But a direct cause and effect relationship between poverty and crime is an oversimplification that criminology has never taken seriously. Much of our statistical data on crime does suggest that high rates of certain kinds of crime appear more concentrated in areas of low income, and that the majority of our known offenders are of low socioeconomic status. But concomitants other than low income are indeed operating in these "high-crime" areas. There are, as we have seen, cultural explanations, and there is the issue of differential law enforcement in certain territories, as well as differential justice for those who have the economic means for better representation in the halls of justice. And finally, there are differential opportunity structures for committing crime. The studies of self-reported criminal behavior noted in the previous chapter indicated that crimes were committed by persons at all status levels. Persons of middle and high social and economic status have the opportunity to commit the less visible and rarely prosecuted white-collar offenses. Such opportunities are not typically available to the slum-dweller, whose only opportunities for crime are the more visible offenses of burglary, robbery, and other thefts. This would necessarily return us to the issue of conflict in its widest sense, escorting us to a conception of crime causation that emerges from one group's ability to remain unmolested by the criminal justice process through the maintaining and influencing of norms and codes that support its valued goals. This would also suggest that within alternative social, cultural, and economic groups, the selection of crimes and the methods of committing crimes may be *learned* behaviors.

A conception of crime as learned behavior was discussed almost a century ago by the French magistrate and sociologist Gabriel Tarde. In his *Les Lois de l'imitation (Laws of Imitation)* in 1890, Tarde contended that patterns of crime and delinquency were learned and adopted by a process of conscious imitation, or by the unconscious suggestion of presented behavioral movements, in much the same manner that fads and fashions might be adopted. Patterns of criminality were thereby learned and could be passed from person to person and from generation to generation.[58] In a later publication, Tarde reiterated the elements of "imitation-suggestion" as a process of learning to commit crime, maintaining that it was similar to a trade apprenticeship, the only difference being that "the true seminary of crime" was to be found in "each public square or each crossroad of our towns."[59]

A more developed theory of crime as learned behavior appeared in Edwin H. Sutherland's conception of "differential association." It grew from his study of professional thieves, which suggested to Sutherland that many criminals learned the knowledge and motivations as well as all the skills necessary for engaging in criminal behavior.[60] In its more complete form, Sutherland's theory of differential association included a series of nine propositions:

1. Criminal behavior is learned.
2. Criminal behavior is learned in interaction with other persons in a process of communication.
3. The principal part of the learning of criminal behavior occurs within intimate personal groups.
4. When criminal behavior is learned, the learning includes (a) techniques of committing the crime, which are sometimes very complicated, sometimes very simple; (b) the specific direction of motives, drives, rationalizations, and attitudes.
5. The specific direction of motives and drives is learned from definitions of the legal codes as favorable or unfavorable.
6. A person becomes delinquent because of an excess of definitions favorable to violation of law over definitions unfavorable to violation of law.
7. Differential associations may vary in frequency, duration, priority, and intensity.
8. The process of learning criminal behavior by association with criminal and anticriminal patterns involves all of the mechanisms that are involved in any other learning.
9. While criminal behavior is an expression of general needs and values, it is not explained by those general needs and values since noncriminal behavior is an expression of the same needs and values.[61]

Sutherland's theory of differential association represented a major breakthrough in criminology, for it was a theoretical conception that attempted to "normalize" criminal behavior—"normal" in the sense that it was "learned" through the same processes that other, noncriminal, behaviors were learned. Sutherland's ideas were not peculiarly unique or new, but in the form presented they represented an integrated theory. They suggested a chain of interrelationships and correlates in a person's associations and learning experiences that made crime reasonable and understandable as normal, logical behavior; and they suggested a framework within which we might better understand many of the subculture and conflict theories of crime, while also realizing the simple-minded nature of the efforts which sought to explain crime in terms of broken homes, poverty, physical abnormalities, or weather conditions.

On the other hand, differential association theory has been subject to some criticism. Quinney has indicated that it was formulated at such a high level of abstraction that it has not been possible to fully test it with empirical data.[62] Yet he also pointed to a series of studies which have partially substantiated the variables of association (frequency, duration, priority, and intensity),[63] and analyses of some life histories of offenders have also given substance to the differential association process.[64] An alternative criticism notes that the theory fails to explain the totality of crime, or as Hartjen questions: "Differential association may very well account for professional theft and similar kinds of conduct, but what about statutory rape and other compulsive types of crime that involve little if any training?"[65] Indeed, it does fail to explain impulsive and irrational acts that result in crime, or perhaps other types of criminal conduct, but as presented by Sutherland the differential association theory seemed to focus only on those kinds of criminality that were more systematic in nature, such as theft, gang delinquency, forms of white-collar crime, and perhaps others such as syndicate racketeering. More appropriately, it is a theoretical perspective that does have its outer limits, yet at the same time no plausible alternative of comparable scope has been advanced;[66] it is a theory that has not suffered the fate of other theories of crime—those that misguidedly announce the finding of the "criminologists' stone."[67]

Since the initial formulation of the differential association theory, it has been the subject of continuing analysis, examination, and sometimes further extension or modification. In 1956, for example, Daniel Glaser suggested that in addition to the face-to-face association process of learning noted by Sutherland, indirect pattern imitation was also a mechanism for learning criminal behavior. Referred to as "differential identification," it holds that ". . . a person pursues criminal behavior to the extent that he identifies himself with real or imaginary persons from whose perspective his criminal behavior seems acceptable."[68]

This comment emerges as a logical extension to the original theory, and its mechanism is clearly evident in the reflections of a professional pickpocket and burglar who had patterned his early behavior after that of his criminal reference group:

> They were known as the Old Border Gang, and among them were several well-known and successful crooks. . . . When I saw one of these great men pass, my imagination was fired with ambition to be as he was! . . . I grew to think the career of the grafter was the only one worth trying for . . . so I began to pilfer left and right.[69]

An interesting application of the differential association theory was offered by criminologist Donald R. Cressey. Based on the idea that criminal behavior was "learned," he listed a series of principles for the unlearning of criminal behavior and how they might be applied to the rehabilitation of offenders.[70] The cornerstone of the concept suggests the development of anticriminal norms in the individual and represents one of the crucial elements in the rehabilitation process currently manifest at *Synanon* and other therapeutic communities for the treatment of drug users:

> The most effective mechanism for exerting group pressure on members will be found in groups so organized that criminals are induced to join with noncriminals for the purpose of changing other criminals. A group in which criminal A joins with some noncriminals to change criminal B is probably the most effective in changing criminal A, not B; in order to change criminal B, criminal A must necessarily share the values of the noncriminal members.[71]

In sum the differential association theory has provided an exciting episode in criminological thinking, and it continues to do so. Current research documents how many individuals become involved in criminality through a chain of circumstances and associations analogous to that of any other normal vocational life adjustment. Furthermore, as a criminological theory, it has outrun the capacity of both psychology and social psychology to provide adequate, scientific answers to the question of why there are selective differences in human association.[72]

## CHANGING PERSPECTIVES ON CRIME CAUSATION

During recent decades, numerous students of crime and criminal justice have looked to the criminal law for an explanation of the causes of crime. In Chapter 1, it was suggested that crime was a social construction, for it "came into being" through the codification of law. With this as a point of departure, some have begun to look at causation in terms of the highly relative manner in which criminal definitions are applied to different segments of society. Howard S. Becker's initial discussion of the genesis and definition of deviance contended that ". . . one who cannot be trusted to live by the rules agreed on by the group . . . is regarded as an *outsider.*"[73] In linking this to "causation," Quinney suggested that the probability that the deviant or criminal label will be applied tends to vary according to the extent to which the behaviors of the powerless conflict with the interests of the powerful.[74] As such, the application of criminal definitions would appear to be some type of *political enterprise,* and crime itself would be *political behavior.*

An early elucidation of the notion of the *politicality of crime* appeared in the writings of Frank Tannenbaum some four decades ago. In his discussion of societal reaction to deviant (or criminal) behavior —what he referred to as the "dramatization of evil"—he suggested that one's reputation is a type of public definition, and that the process of making a criminal is one of "tagging, defining, identifying, segregating, describing, emphasizing [and], making conscious and self-conscious. . . ."[75] Edwin M. Lemert, a decade later, introduced the idea of politicality when he viewed societal reaction in terms of the rivalry of groups struggling to maintain their position in a hegemony of power relations. Innovation in behavior, he maintained, represented a departure from recognized patterns of social action and tended to be viewed as unfavorable since it upset a system of reciprocity between groups; the reaction of society to these innovative behaviors involved the triad of awareness, policy determination, and reform.[76] Stated differently, George B. Vold offered that crime may indeed be ". . . political behavior, and the criminal becomes in fact a member of a 'minority group' without sufficient public support to dominate the control of the police power of the state."[77]

These conceptions of Quinney, Tannenbaum, Lemert, and Vold have their foundations in the writings of the economic determinists, as well as in the later criminological discussions of conflict and "criminogenesis." In *A Contribution to the Critique of Political Economy,* Karl Marx discussed the power-conflict view of society, and argued that the mode of production determined the character of social, political, and spiritual existence:

In the social production which men carry on they enter into definite relations that are indispensable and independent of their will; these relations of production correspond to a definite stage of development of their material powers of production. The sum total of these relations of production constitutes the economic structure of society—the real foundation, on which rise legal and political superstructures and to which correspond definite forms of social consciousness. The mode of production in material life determines the general character of the social, political, and spiritual processes of life.[78]

Society, in Marx's view, was organized around the pursuit of human needs, and the essential character of social interaction was the facilitation of such need-acquisitions through a division of labor. During the course of history, classes emerged which seized the primary modes of production and exploited the subordinate classes for their own acquisitive purposes. These classes not only dominated the social structure, but through their possession of economic strength they also controlled the primary determinants of political power. Power, in turn, was used as the vehicle for the maintenance of both the class structure and the prevailing economic order. Thus, capitalist and working-class interests were polar and tended to conflict for dominance. Marx further claimed that within this framework, law was a tool employed by the capitalists for the maintenance of their position through the exploitation of workers, and as such, law represented a means for the institutionalization of conflict.[79]

"Criminogenesis," as noted earlier in the work of Donald R. Taft, also reflects on a highly stratified society whose materialistic orientation places a high value on the acquisition of wealth and power.[80] In his view, as well as to some extent in that of other conflict theorists, the ensuing competitive struggle for favorable goals or for fostering group interests can result in criminal behavior, or the definition of opposing behaviors as criminal.[81] Ultimately, those groups who have the greater ability to translate their interests into public policy are hence more capable of shaping the nature and direction of legislation and of law enforcement and administration. Quinney has carried this interpretation even further in his contention that groups whose interests are in conflict with those represented in prevailing law are highly vulnerable to having their behavior defined as criminal; that the probability of criminal labeling taking place depends heavily on prevailing criminal conceptions, community expectations of law enforcement, and the ideological structure of the criminal justice system.[82] Crime control becomes a concrete means through which the dominant classes protect their interests; it acts as a coercive means of checking threats to economic relations, and the legal system serves to legitimize or illegitimize behavior systems:

1. American society is based on an advanced capitalist economy.
2. The state is organized to serve the interests of the dominant economic class, the capitalist ruling class.
3. Criminal law is an instrument that the state and dominant ruling class use to maintain and perpetuate the social and economic order.
4. Crime control in capitalist society is accomplished by institutions and agencies established and administered by a governmental elite, representing dominant ruling class interest, to establish domestic order.
5. The contradictions of advanced capitalism—the disjunction between existence and essence—requires that the subordinate classes remain oppressed by whatever means necessary, especially by the legal system's coercion and violence.
6. Only with the collapse of capitalist society, based on socialist principles, will there be a solution to the crime problem.[83]

Perspectives of this order provide us with an Aristotelian view of crime causation, claiming that the law is the "formal" cause of crime and the capitalist structure is its "material" or prior cause. The collapse of the capitalist structure would indeed eliminate the property relations from which much predatory crime originates, but it would not necessarily eliminate behaviors which would be deemed threatening to the new socialist order. Hence, laws of an alternative content would necessarily be written, and new bureaucracies for their enforcement and administration would be structured. New sets of "interests" would logically emerge, as would innovative types of criminalization.

More pragmatically, we are confronted in American society with a political and capitalist democracy in which crimes not only occur, but do so with rather high frequency. And too, much of this "crime" results from a legal structure that has, in many ways, been built to preserve the interests of an elite ruling class. But then, too, there are many other types of crime. There are the impulsive, irrational, and even logically premeditated acts of violence which result from differences of opinion in social relations. There are the purely political crimes that emerge from protests against an already established order. There are the infringements of the law that would not occur if they were not infringements—some persons break laws as a protest against the real or imagined irrationality of the prohibition or against the legitimacy of the prohibiting authority. In sum, we are confronted with the fact that there are likely as many *causes* of crime as there are *types* of crime, and this, as we already understand, is a phenomenon that is constantly in a state of change.

## POSTSCRIPT—LOMBROSO RIDES AGAIN

The hereditarian thesis of crime has experienced a long and persistent career. The notion of a "born criminal type" marked by physical and mental stigmata emerged in Europe many centuries before Cesare Lombroso cast him in a Darwinian role, and since that time, the theory has sought to explain criminality in terms of feeblemindedness (low IQ), constitutional inferiority, strange electroencephalograms, and aberrant chromosomes. More recently, this collective body of thought has been referred to as "degeneration theory"—an analytic scheme which suggested that both personal and social afflictions were the result of a core malady of "degeneration," and that degeneration itself was heritable:

> According to the Degeneration Theorists, degeneration might take any number of forms—criminality, poverty, insanity, drunkenness, feeblemindedness, cancer—so that insane parents might have a feebleminded daughter and a criminal son and drunken grandchildren. What was inherited was not a specific affliction but degeneration per se, a pervasive kind of rot which could manifest itself in any one of a number of forms. Thus criminal behavior was a sign that the culprit also bore, within him or her, the seeds of mental deficiency, insanity, and a willingness to live off welfare. By the same token, the lame, the unemployed, and those who appeared mentally unsound were suspected of criminality.[84]

Despite the logic and impact of modern criminological thought, the Lombrosian ethos continues to plague the social sciences. In a recent issue of *Atlantic Monthly,* Richard Herrnstein of Howard University commented on a "low capacity residue" of humanity that will emerge in modern society who will be unable to master the common occupations, who will be unable to compete for success and achievement, and who are "... most likely to be born to parents who have similarly failed...."[85] Or more currently, David Rosenthal of the National Institute of Mental Health has stated in the March 1975 issue of *Criminal Justice and Behavior:*

Findings from family studies, twin studies, and adoption studies indicate that hereditary factors are ... implicated in criminality. It is not a single genotype crime gene that provides the thrust toward crime, but a variety of phenotypical characteristics that are heritable in more or less degree.[86]

It seems that among many of us, it is still not fully realized that crime is only a *social* construction, that crime is only *subjectively* defined, that crime is only what we want to perceive it to be, and that crime is simply what the political power base feels it ought to be. It seems that there are those who still suspect that low IQ, or perhaps even physical anomalies as well, are somehow the cause of crime, that there are lines "... connecting low intelligence, low social class, and low behavior."[87]

## SUGGESTED READINGS

COHEN, ALBERT K., *Delinquent Boys: The Culture of the Gang* (Glencoe, Ill.: Free Press, 1955).

FINK, ARTHUR E., *The Causes of Crime: Biological Theories in the United States, 1800–1915* (Philadelphia: University of Pennsylvania Press, 1938).

HARTJEN, CLAYTON A., *Crime and Criminalization* (New York: Praeger, 1974).

HOOD, ROGER, (ed.), *Crime, Criminology and Public Policy* (New York: Free Press, 1974).

MICHAEL, JEROME, and ADLER, MORTIMER J., *Crime, Law and Social Science* (New York: Harcourt, Brace, 1933; Montclair, N.J.: Patterson Smith, 1971).

QUINNEY, RICHARD, *The Social Reality of Crime* (Boston: Little, Brown, 1970).

RADZINOWICZ, LEON, *Ideology and Crime* (New York: Columbia University Press, 1966).

SCHAFER, STEPHEN, *Theories in Criminology* (New York: Random House, 1969).

SCHUESSLER, KARL, (ed.), *Edwin H. Sutherland: On Analyzing Crime* (Chicago: University of Chicago Press, 1973).

SELLIN, THORSTEN, *Culture Conflict and Crime* (New York: Social Science Research Council, 1938).

SHAW, CLIFFORD, R., *The Jack Roller* (Chicago: University of Chicago Press, 1930).

VOLD, GEORGE B., *Theoretical Criminology* (New York: Oxford University Press, 1958).

WEST, J. D. (ed.), *Criminological Implications of Chromosome Abnormalities* (Cambridge: University of Cambridge, Institute of Criminology, 1969).

# 5

# From Bonnie and Clyde
# To Watergate: An Observation
# of Behavior Systems in Crime

The search for causal explanations of crime has endured since the founding of the discipline of criminology, and it will likely persist. Both researchers and students of crime, deviance, and criminal justice, however, have long since become either dissatisfied or frustrated with the traditional approaches to causation theory. It has been believed that if we could determine *the* cause or causes of crime, we could then logically develop approaches and strategies for the prevention of crime, the control of crime, and the rehabilitation of criminals. These have not come to pass. "Theories" and "solutions" continue to emerge, and crime continues to increase.

The alternative approach to the study of crime has involved a focus on specific modes of criminal behavior. In its broadest sense, this strategy has sought to examine the wide range of behavioral styles in crime, with the purpose of establishing a knowledge base about the phenomena of given crimes and criminals, while also generating a fuller understanding of trends, patterns, and behavior systems in crime. And from this, it has been anticipated that more meaningful theoretical formulations might develop and more appropriate treatment and control mechanisms might emerge. Yet the types of crime, the circumstances within which they occur, and the characteristics of offenders are exceedingly numerous, and those concerned with their systematic study have been confronted with the almost endless dilemma that whatever they may observe are unique events. The Platonic and Nietzschean problem, that social phenomena are unique and will never be repeated again in spite of their resemblance to other recurrent events, has forced the debate over the scientific applicability and usefulness of the "particular" vis-a-vis the "general." Social and criminal phenomena are indeed unique and never occur at the same time and place and under the same circumstances on more than one occasion. The observed characteristics of syndicate racketeering in Chicago during the 1920s, for example, cannot necessarily be used to predict patterns of organized crime in other urban areas. Similarly, the manifest nature of one "delinquent subculture" may not, with any strong degree of certainty, help to understand the behavior of other delinquent groups within similar social circumstances.

Yet one of the goals of social science is the observation and analysis of discrete events with the purpose of uncovering some degree of natural and historical order which can be useful in the explanation and perhaps even the prediction of other occurrences. This is the very essence of scientific pursuit, whether it be criminology, sociology, economics, or the study of the physical world. Science deals with systematic statements of the probability that actual or even hypothetical recurrences of phenomena can, for whatever purpose, be regarded as identical.[1] It must face the issue that events, situations, and circumstances are indeed relative and variable, and that they are continually changing and altering in both the physical and social worlds.

The physical sciences face less of a problem in this respect due to the more concrete nature of their subject matter. Light, for example, will travel at a speed of 30 billion centimeters per second in this galaxy as well as in the next; or similarly, the nucleus of the Lithium atom will always contain three protons and four neutrons regardless of its relative position in the vast spectrum of space and time. Criminology, on the other hand, is less of an exact science. Its subject matter—crime and criminals—is continually subject to the changing influences of its operating milieu and greater environment, to the dynamic structures and processes of the social worlds in which it is manifest. The only recourse left to criminologists and other social scientists has been the construction of *types,* conceptual and theoretical models of social conduct and organization that can serve to organize a variety of phenomena.

European sociologist and historian Max Weber offered a strategy in this direction for the social sciences with the conceptualization of an "ideal type":

An ideal type is formed by the one-sided accentuation of one or more points of view and by the synthesis of a great many diffuse, discrete, more or less present and occasionally absent concrete individual phenomena, which are arranged according to those one-sidedly emphasized viewpoints into a unified analytical construct.[2]

To Weber there was no knowledge that was not hypothetical. Reality was infinite and no concept could ever wholly reconstruct the endless diversity of particular phenomena. In his conception of the "Protestant ethic" and "spirit of capitalism," Weber rejected the metaphysical notions that science could penetrate the essence of all things and provide a reflection of "true" reality. *Capitalism* as an "ideal type" represented a reflection of a particular kind of economic activity. As an analytical construct, it never existed in reality in its pure form, yet it symbolized the embodiment of those characteristics manifested by a particular economic doctrine. As such, it provided a base for the intellectual and scientific understanding of a reality.

Weber's ideal types were essentially *classifications*—sets of variables linked into logically possible combinations—and have suggested the construction of *typologies.*[3] The typology is a multidimensional classification whose attributes and variables have been linked by a special set of explanatory criteria. Classifications and typologies have become useful methodological tools for the study of social and criminal behavior. It has already been realized, for example, that a considerably relative and diverse range of activities and personages fall within the concepts of "crime" and "criminals." Thus, any attempt to develop a framework within which these phenomena might be better understood necessarily requires their organization into some orderly grouping, a situation well recognized by both criminology and criminal justice.

## CRIMINAL TYPES AND TYPOLOGIES

Ever since Cesare Lombroso first announced his "discovery" of a "born criminal" type, students and observers of criminal behavior have attempted to classify the various forms of crime and criminality into logical and meaningful categories. Many of the earlier efforts focused on particular offenders, viewing their behaviors as homogeneous entities merely segmentalized by differences in mental and/or physical characteristics. This was especially evident in the pioneer works of Italian criminologists Enrico Ferri, Raffaele Garofalo, and C. Bernaldo de Quirós.[4] Of interest in this respect was the later work of German psychiatrist Ernst Kretchmer, who identified three major constitutional types—the *asthenic,* the *athletic,* and the *pyknic.*[5] Kretchmer applied his constitutional forms to a system of mental disorders identified decades before by Emil Kraeplin, the nineteenth-century European psychiatrist on whose work modern conceptions of paranoia are based,[6] and constructed one of the earliest classifications of constitutional groups with their corresponding mental disorders. Kretchmer made no correlations between criminality and his physical types, but numerous theorists of crime have drawn heavily upon his work.[7]

The observation that the totality of criminal activity constitutes fundamentally different types of behavior in alternative social situations is of relatively recent origin, and the pursuit of typological thinking within this framework has yielded some interesting contributions during recent decades. These, furthermore, have followed several divergent lines of investigation. One method of typological enterprise has been directed towards the study of variations in different kinds of lawbreaking. The resulting classifications have designated such groupings as "violent offenders," "property offenders," "white-collar crime," or "organized crime" and have primarily been used as a means for organizing the content of textbooks.[8] Those analyzing criminal behavior within the context of these broad types have discussed a need for the direct investigation of specific forms of deviant conduct. The ensuing research has provided focused views of such behavior systems as check forgery,[9] white-collar crime,[10] and embezzlement.[11] Other approaches have provided some insight on criminality and criminal offenders through the abstraction of given factors from the characteristics of specific offender populations. Criminologist Ruth Cavan, for example, attempted to classify offenders as conformers to subcultural groups, law-abiding violators, segmental criminals, professional criminals, or maladjusted law violators, all based on the extent to which each had withdrawn from the control of the prevailing social organization.[12] Or similarly, Clarence C. Schrag focused on role patterns exhibited within a prison community which were identifiable through inmate argot (slang). The classifications developed from his perspective reflected differences in terms of background characteristics, offense behavior, and institutional conduct.[13] Essentially, classifications and typologies framed in these terms have not satisfactorily differentiated types of crime or criminal behavior, nor have they accounted for the full spectrum of criminality.

The oldest form of classifying crimes and criminals is based on the legal categories of offenses. Thus, criminals can be referred to as "murderers," "robbers," "rapists," or any other labels that might appear in criminal codes. Yet as Clinard and Quinney have pointed out, the method has a variety of disadvantages:

> ... (1) It tells nothing about the person and the circumstances associated with the offense, nor does it consider the social context of the criminal act ...; (2) it creates a false impression of specialization by implying that criminals confine themselves to the kind of crime for which they happen to be caught or convicted; (3) it is a common practice in order to secure easy convictions to allow offenders to receive a reduced sentence by "plea copping" or pleading guilty to a lesser charge that may only slightly resemble the original charge or offense; (4) because the legal definition of a criminal act varies according to time and place, the legal classification of crime presents problems for comparative analysis; and (5) most important of all, the use of legal categories in a classification assumes that offenders with a certain legal label, such as burglars, robbers, auto thieves, and rapists, are all of the same type or are the product of a similar process.[14]

In an attempt to mitigate the disadvantages of the legal classifications and at the same time make use of their empirical base, criminologist Julian B. Roebuck constructed an arrest history typology which was based upon legal offense categories studied within the framework of criminal careers.[15] Rather than categorizing offenders according to their most recent offense, he developed *arrest patterns* as longitudinal measures of behavior. Roebuck established specific criteria for "patterning" an offender's total arrest history, and assumed that particular patterns made manifest particular behavior systems in crime. The method was able to isolate a variety of integrated criminal types, but it did have its limitations. First, the number of possible arrest patterns that could be developed was almost infinite; second, a significant portion of the sample to which the method was applied emerged as "jack-of-all-trades" offenders having no discernible pattern around any particular type or types of crime; and most importantly, the unreliability of "arrests" as an indicator of behavior was always present.

More recently, Marshall B. Clinard and Richard Quinney have developed a multidimensional typology of criminal behavior systems that represents a comprehensive framework within which we can begin to more fully understand and analyze many varieties of offense behavior. Their model included eight behavior systems in crime constructed in terms of four classification characteristics.[16]

1. Violent personal crime
2. Occasional property crime
3. Occupational crime
4. Political crime
5. Public order crime
6. Conventional crime
7. Organized crime
8. Professional crime

The typological construction is based upon four characteristics: (1) the criminal career of the offender, (2) the extent to which the behavior has group support, (3) correspondence between criminal behavior and legitimate behavior patterns, and (4) societal reaction.

1. *Criminal Career of the Offender.* The extent to which criminal behavior is a part of the offender's career. Includes conception of self, identification with crime, progression in crime, and the degree to which criminal behavior has become a part of the life organization of the offender.

2. *Group Support of Criminal Behavior.* The extent to which the offender's criminal behavior is supported by the norms of the group or groups to which he belongs. Includes the differential association of the offender with criminal and noncriminal norms, the social roles of the offender, and the integration of the offender into social groups.

3. *Correspondence between Criminal Behavior and Legitimate Behavior Patterns.* The extent to which the type of criminal behavior is consistent with legitimate patterns of behavior in the society. Includes the degree to which the criminal behavior corresponds to the valued goals and means that are regarded as legitimate by the dominant power segments of society. Includes the extent of conflict between value systems.

4. *Societal Reaction.* The extent to which society reacts to the criminal behavior. Includes the various forms of informal reaction, such as disapproval and censure, and the forms of official reaction, such as enforcement of law, prosecution, conviction, and sentencing.

The types of criminal behavior systems in the typology are shown in the following table. Eight distinct patterns of crime are delineated in relation to the four characteristics. The career continuum is used to order the criminal behavior systems. The ranking of the criminal behavior systems on each continuum is based on available research evidence.

There are undoubtedly other ways of dividing crime into types along the career continuum in reference to group support of criminal behavior, correspondence between criminal behavior and legitimate behavior patterns, and societal reaction. The behaviors and associated phenomena that run along the continua have been, for our purposes, abstracted and segmented into eight distinct types. The typology serves the purpose of allowing us to present existing research on various forms of crime.

The eight types of criminal behavior systems which we have constructed may be summarized as follows:

1. *Violent Personal Crime.* Includes such forms of criminal activity as murder, assault, and forcible rape. The offenders do not conceive of themselves as criminals. They are often persons without previous records, but because of certain circumstances commit a personal offense. The offenses are not directly supported by any group, though there may be subcultural definitions which are favorable to the general use of violence. The behaviors are in sharp contrast to the middle class values of the society. There is a strong reaction to the offenses.

2. *Occasional Property Crime.* Includes some auto theft, shoplifting, check forgery, and vandalism. The offenders do not usually conceive of themselves as criminals and are able to rationalize their criminal behavior. They are usually committed to the general goals of society and find little support for their behavior in group norms. The offenses are in violation of the values of private property. Societal reaction often involves arrest, especially for the offender who already has a criminal record.

3. *Occupational Crime.* Includes embezzlement, fraudulent sales, false advertising, price fixing, fee-splitting, black market activity, prescription violation, and antitrust violation. Violators do not conceive of themselves as criminals and rationalize their behavior as being merely a part of their daily work. Their behavior may be tolerated by their peers. They accept conventional values and attempt to seek a greater share of the rewards in the conventional world. The illegal behavior corresponds to the social and economic philosophy of the achievement of ends in the society. Because such crime is committed by persons in high status positions and the violation of law is often complex and not highly visible, there is little reaction from the public when these violations occur.

4. *Political Crime.* Includes treason, sedition, espionage, sabotage, military draft violations, war collaboration, radicalism and the various other forms of protest which may be defined as criminal. The offenders occasionally violate the law when they feel that illegal activity is essential in achieving necessary changes in society. The offenders are committed to the larger society or to an order which they are trying to bring about. Their behavior is prescribed and supported by their own groups. Democratic societies are based on the right to petition, yet societal reaction is strong when such behavior is regarded as a threat to the society.

5. *Public Order Crime.* Includes drunkenness, vagrancy, disorderly conduct, prostitution, homosexuality, traffic violation, and drug addiction. The violators may conceive of themselves as criminals when they are repeatedly defined as criminals by others. They may vacillate between criminal values and the values of a larger social order. They may associate with other offenders. There is some correspondence between the illegal behavior of public order offenders and legitimate patterns. Some of the forms of public order crime (for example, prostitution) are desired by parts of the legitimate society. Other forms (for example, drunkenness and vagrancy) are regarded as merely representative of "failure" in the existing economic system. There may be informal punitive reaction as well as arrest and limited incarceration.

6. *Conventional Crime.* Includes robbery, larceny, burglary, and gang theft. The offenders pursue crime as a part-time career, usually supplementing a legitimate income through crimes of gain. Many juvenile gang members may be beginning a career in illegal activity. While there may be some identification with the larger society, there is likely to be greater commitment to a criminal subculture. There is usually association with other offenders. The behavior corresponds to the goals of economic success; but there is public reaction to the behavior because the value on the sanctity of private property is violated.

7. *Organized Crime.* Includes racketeering, organized prostitution, organized gambling, and control of narcotics. The offenders pursue crime as a livelihood. In the lower echelons they conceive of themselves as criminals, associate primarily with other criminals, and are isolated from a larger social order. In the top levels the individuals associate as well with persons of legitimate society and often reside in the better residential areas. There is considerable correspondence between the illegal activities of organized crime and legitimate society. The principles of large-scale enterprise are shared by legitimate society. Illegal services desired by legitimate society are provided by organized crime. The public tolerates organized crime, partly because of the desired services it provides and partly because of the difficulty in dealing with its operation.

8. *Professional Crime.* Includes confidence games, shoplifting, pickpocketing, forgery, and counterfeiting. Professional criminals pursue crime as a livelihood and as a way of life. They conceive of themselves as criminals, associate with other criminals, and have high status in the world of crime. They are usually isolated from the larger society and are committed to a career of crime. There is some correspondence between professional crime and dominant behavior patterns in that professional criminals are, after all, engaged in full-time employment. Also, law-abiding persons are some times involved as accomplices in an attempt to obtain money in a quick and easy manner. Societal reaction is not usually strong. Many cases of professional crime are "fixed" in the course of legal processing.[17]

This conceptual presentation of behavior systems in crime, like others preceding it, is not without its limitations. Initially, several of the classification characteristics such as "group support" and "correspondence between criminal and legitimate behavior patterns" are at a level of abstraction that lends difficulty to measurement.[18] Secondly, some of the behavioral categories are entirely too broad; they include diverse classes of crime which, in themselves, reflect a wide spectrum of behavior systems. "Public Order Crime," for example, emerges as one "system" that attempts to consider drunkenness, prostitution, gambling, and other infringements of the public morality. Yet each of these reflects one or more behavior systems that the typology cannot necessarily account for. Finally, and equally as important, this schema does

## Typology of Criminal Behavior Systems

| Classification Characteristics | 1<br>Violent Personal Crime | 2<br>Occasional Property Crime | 3<br>Occupational Crime | 4<br>Political Crime |
|---|---|---|---|---|
| | *Low* | *Low* | *Low* | *Low* |
| Criminal Career of the Offender | Crime not part of offender's career; usually does not conceive of self as criminal | Little or no criminal self-concept; does not identify with crime | No criminal self-concept; occasionally violates the law; part of one's legitimate work; accepts conventional values of society | Usually no criminal self-concept; violates the law out of conscience; attempts to change society or correct perceived injustices; desire for a better society |
| | *Low* | *Low* | *Medium* | *High* |
| Group Support of Criminal Behavior | Little or no group support, offenses committed for personal reasons; some support in subcultural norms | Little group support; individual offenses | Some groups may tolerate offenses; offender integrated in groups | Group support; association with persons of same values; behavior reinforced by group |
| | *Low* | *Low* | *High* | *Medium* |
| Correspondence between Criminal Behavior and Legitimate Behavior Patterns | Violation of values on life and personal safety | Violation of value on private property | Behavior corresponds to pursual of business activity; "sharp" practices respected; "buyer beware" philosophy; hands off policy | Some toleration of protest and dissent, short of revolution; dissent periodically regarded as a threat (in times of national unrest) |
| | *High* | *Medium* | *Low* | *High* |
| Societal Reaction | Capital punishment; long imprisonment | Arrest; jail; short imprisonment, probation | Indifference; monetary penalties, revocation of license to practice, seizure of product or injunction | Strong disapproval; regarded as threat to society; prison |
| Legal Categories of Crime | Murder, assault, forcible rape, child molesting | Some auto theft, shoplifting, check forgery, vandalism | Embezzlement, fraudulent sales, false advertising, fee-splitting, violation of labor practice laws, antitrust violations, blackmarket activity, prescription violation | Treason, sedition, espionage, sabotage, radicalism, military draft violations, war collaboration, various protests defined as criminal |

| 5 Public Order Crime | 6 Conventional Crime | 7 Organized Crime | 8 Professional Crime |
|---|---|---|---|
| *Medium* | *Medium* | *High* | *High* |
| Confused self-concept; vacillation in identification with crime | Income supplemented through crimes of gain; often a youthful activity; vacillation in self-concept; partial commitment to a criminal subculture | Crime pursued as a livelihood; criminal self-concept; progression in crime; isolation from larger society | Crime pursued as a livelihood; criminal self-concept; status in the world of crime; commitment to world of professional criminals |
| *Medium* | *High* | *High* | *High* |
| Partial support for behavior from some groups; considerable association with other offenders | Behavior supported by group norms; status achieved in groups; principal association with other offenders | Business associations in crime; behavior prescribed by the groups; integration of the person into the group | Associations primarily with other offenders; status gained in criminal offenses; behavior prescribed by group norms |
| *Medium* | *Medium* | *Medium* | *Medium* |
| Some forms required by legitimate society; some are economic activities | Consistent with goals on economic success; inconsistent with sanctity of private property; behavior not consistent with expectations of adolescence and young adulthood | Illegal services received by legitimate society; economic risk values; large-scale control also employed in legitimate society | Engaged in an occupation; skill respected; survival because of cooperation from legitimate society; law-abiding persons often accomplices |
| *Medium* | *High* | *Medium* | *Medium* |
| Arrest; jail; prison; probation | Arrest; jail; probation; institutionalization; parole; rehabilitation | Considerable public toleration; arrest and sentence when detected; often not visible to society; immunity through politicians and law officers | Rarely strong societal reaction, most cases "fixed" |
| Drunkenness, vagrancy, disorderly conduct, prostitution, homosexuality, gambling, traffic violation, drug addiction | Robbery, larceny, burglary, gang theft | Racketeering, organized prostitution and commercialized vice, control of drug traffic, organized gambling | Confidence games, shoplifting, pickpocketing, forgery, counterfeiting |

not include all of the behavior systems that circumscribe violations of criminal codes.[19]

In a revision of their work, Clinard and Quinney expanded their typology to include *corporate criminal behavior*—a system involving violations of criminal laws created to regulate such activities as restraint of trade, false advertising, fraudulent sales, misuse of trademarks, and the manufacture of unsafe foods and drugs.[20] To this, one might also wish to add such behavior systems as *governmental crime,* or even *environmental crime.*

## BEHAVIOR SYSTEMS IN CRIME

As noted earlier, the construction of types in criminology serves to reduce the phenomena of crime to more systematic observation. Furthermore, typologies can emerge as guides for research, they can assist in the formulation of hypotheses, and they can represent the basis of theory construction. Yet the typological endeavor is a difficult one, for the only characteristic that criminal behaviors have in common is their designation as "criminal" by some recognized authority. This can result in the emergence of perhaps as many behavior systems in crime as there are unique types of crime, according to the perspective of the observer. The more common difficulty, however, is that there are many instances where one type of crime, depending on supporting conditions and variables, can fall into any number of "behavior systems." The crime of homicide offers an interesting example. Homicide resulting from some difference of opinion in personal relationships may fall into the category of violent personal crime. Should a homicide occur as a by-product of an armed robbery, it may be a case of what Clinard and Quinney termed "conventional crime." On the other hand, if the homicide was actually an assassination, perhaps it might be termed "political crime." Homicide through a gangland contract would appear to be associated with the behavior system of "organized crime." The death of a patient during the performance of an illegal abortion is legally termed a homicide, and this could fall within the context of "occupational crime." At the outset, this might suggest that the role of assassin or "hit man," for example, emerges as a component of a larger order of behavior—political crime or organized crime—and hence, the wider spectrum of criminal behavior should be focused on for the purpose of constructing types. But this is an oversimplification. The point is that no matter how detailed and specific a typology might be, each behavior system may have a whole series of subsytems. The "enforcer" in an organized crime syndicate, for example, reflects an essentially different behavior system in crime than that of a syndicate attorney who may be employed to "fix" court cases. Furthermore, more than one level of criminal behavior can occur concurrently. Many of the activities of lower echelon syndicate racketeers could easily be construed as "conventional" criminal behavior.

Conversely, there are criminal activities that in themselves appear to be a behavior system, but after close scrutiny they emerge as many different orders of behavior. Arson, for example, is a typical case. Much of the literature on the subject is within a psychological or psychiatric orientation, and the phenomenon is discussed under the term of *pyromania*. The offender is typically viewed as a compulsive neurotic whose behavior is triggered by some "irresistible impulse."[21] An alternative view includes the issue of pyromania, but suggests that the majority of arson cases are actually property crimes where the offender has materialistic ambitions.[22] Yet a recent analysis of arsonists demonstrated that arson would fall within the context of six different behavior systems, and perhaps even more.[23] There were "revenge firesetters," for example, whose crimes resulted from anger, hatred, or jealousy in personal relationships. They sought revenge by fire, by burning the victims' residence or personal property, or by burning the victims themselves. There were "excitement firesetters" who enjoyed watching fires or the operations of fire equipment, and who often received the label of "pyromaniac" after clinical observation. There were "criminal-vindication firesetters" where arson was used for hiding the evidence of other crimes, such as burglary or homicide. There were "insurance-claim firesetters" who would incinerate business property in order to collect insurance money. There were "vandalism firesetters" who destroyed property by fire as part of their adolescent peer group activities. And there were "institutionalized firesetters," a special group of individuals designated as "mental defectives" who had been socialized in institutions since birth and who recognized arson as a mechanism for engineering a transfer from a "defective" institution to a "criminal" institution. Each of the six types of firesetters had alternative motivations and mechanisms for lighting fires, and further, each type generally lighted their fires under differing sets of circumstances. And to these six types one might add the "professional torches" in the ranks of organized crime, the "firebombers" of activist and political liberation organizations, and the large number of skid row vagrants who, for some reason, have been overrepresented among arson arrestees.

The case of arson has some interesting implications for typological research. On the one hand, it suggests the importance of the overall behavior system rather than the particular criminal code that has been violated. Revenge by arson, for example, is likely "violent personal crime" and fire can be construed as merely a type of weapon. Vandalism firesetting is an instance of "occasional property crime," and insurance-claim firesetting may indeed be another example of "occupational crime." The issue, however, is that while the *behavior system* may be the most appropriate unit of analysis, criminal behavior must be closely examined before it can be placed into a typology. Furthermore, some account must be taken of the various subsystems of activity before any multidimensional typology can begin to generate meaning-ful explanations of behavior systems in crime. In the balance of this chapter, a variety of crimes and criminal behavior systems are dis-cussed. Each will be viewed in terms of its possible relevance for typological construction, or according to the problems it may pose for typological analysis.

## Homicide

Traditionally, homicide is the willful killing of one human being by another, and includes murder, manslaughter, justifiable homicide, and excusable homicide.[24]

*Murder,* in most jurisdictions, consists of at least two degrees. First-degree murder typically includes the notions of *premeditation* and *malice aforethought.* Premeditation refers to the prior formation of the intent to kill—the conscious decision prior to the act of killing to take a human life, even if such a decision occurs only moments before the act. Malice aforethought refers to the deliberate intention to take the life of another—the desire to kill. Second-degree murder includes mal-ice aforethought, but not premeditation. Yet murder is to be distin-guished from *manslaughter,* which involves premeditation but not malice aforethought. Therefore, manslaughter would likely be charged in a case where one individual was killed during a spontaneous or sudden fistfight, or in the instance of a pedestrian killed due to the negligence of a driver under the severe influence of alcohol. By con-trast, *excusable homicide* includes deaths from accidents or misfor-tunes that may occur during some lawful act, as in the case of a hunter who mistakes another for an animal in the limited visibility of a swamp. *Justifiable homicide* includes those instances of death which result from legal demands—the execution of a prisoner, the killing of a fleeing prisoner by a prison guard, or the shooting of an armed robber by a police officer. Acts of self-defense may be deemed justifiable or excusable depending on the circumstances surrounding the case. And finally, *criminal homicide* includes murder and manslaughter, while attempted murder is usually classified as an assault.

Criminal homicide, as noted in earlier chapters, is relatively infrequent when compared with the extent to which other violations of the criminal law occur. During 1975 there were some 20,510 homicides in the United States, representing less than one-half of one percent of all known Part I offenses.[25] Furthermore, as suggested by Table 5–1, the vast majority of criminal homicides fall into what Clinard and Quinney have referred to as "violent personal crime." During 1975, for example, two-thirds or 67.6 percent of all homicides were the outgrowth of arguments or differences in personal relations, and of these, almost half occurred within families or among lovers. Their proportions, furthermore, varied little over the period 1970–1975. Felony murder, defined in the *Uniform Crime Reports* as those killings resulting from robbery, burglary, sex motives, gangland and institutional slayings, and other felonious activities, accounted for 32.4 percent of the criminal homicides in 1975. The actual felony–murder doctrine, however, varies somewhat from the conceptualization used by the *Uniform Crime Reports.* Under its provisions, if a death occurs during the commission of a felony, the person committing the initial offense can also be charged with first-degree murder.[26] As such, should an individual commit the felonious crime of arson by setting fire to a house, and if a fireman were killed fighting that fire, the arsonist would be charged with first-degree

TABLE 5–1.  Percent Distribution of Murder Circumstances, 1970–1975

| Year | Total Number | Total Percent | Spouse killing spouse | Parent killing child | Other relative killings | Romantic triangle and lovers' quarrels | Other arguments | Known felony type | Suspected felony type |
|------|--------|---------|--------|--------|----------|----------|--------|--------|--------|
| 1970 | 16,000 | 100.0 | 12.1 | 3.1 | 8.1 | 7.1 | 40.8 | 20.4 | 8.4 |
| 1971 | 17,780 | 100.0 | 12.8 | 3.5 | 8.4 | 6.3 | 41.5 | 20.4 | 7.1 |
| 1972 | 18,670 | 100.0 | 12.5 | 2.9 | 8.9 | 7.1 | 41.2 | 22.1 | 5.3 |
| 1973 | 19,640 | 100.0 | 12.3 | 3.2 | 7.7 | 7.5 | 40.3 | 21.6 | 7.4 |
| 1974 | 20,710 | 100.0 | 12.1 | 2.7 | 8.0 | 6.2 | 43.2 | 22.2 | 5.6 |
| 1975 | 20,510 | 100.0 | 11.5 | 3.0 | 7.9 | 7.3 | 37.9 | 23.0 | 9.4 |

Source: *Uniform Crime Reports,* 1970–1975.

murder. Thus, the felony–murder provision can be applied even though premeditation and malice aforethought were lacking. In addition, the felony–murder doctrine has even been applied to cover a charge of first-degree murder against one of a pair of robbers when it was a police officer who killed the second robber.[27] And in Dade County, Florida, a 1972 statute extends the felony–murder issue to charge dealers and distributors of heroin with first-degree murder if the drug causes the death of another person.[28]

Firearms predominate as the weapon most often used in criminal homicide. Table 5–2 indicates that some two-thirds of all murder weapons during recent years were some type of firearm; although the use of firearms in homicides has increased, the predominance of guns as major weapons has been a persistent pattern. Furthermore, as suggested by Figure I, the majority of firearms used in murders are handguns. During 1975, for example, 66 percent of the weapons used in criminal homicides were firearms, and of these, 78 percent (or 51 percent of all weapons) were handguns. The "personal" weapons used in homicides include hands, fists, and feet, while "other" weapons typically include blunt instruments, poison, explosives, arson, and drowning.

Perhaps the most persistent characteristic of criminal homicide is the victim-offender relationship. In the majority of cases, according to FBI data, approximately two-thirds of the participants are either members of the same family, business acquaintances, drinking partners, or social

TABLE 5–2.  Percent Distribution of Murders by Type of Weapon Used, 1966–1975

| Year | Total | | Firearms | Knives, cutting instruments | Other weapons | Personal weapons |
|------|--------|---------|----------|------------------------------|---------------|------------------|
|      | Number | Percent |          |                              |               |                  |
| 1975 | 20,510 | 100.0   | 65.8     | 17.7                         | 7.5           | 9.0              |
| 1974 | 20,710 | 100.0   | 67.9     | 17.6                         | 6.8           | 7.7              |
| 1973 | 19,640 | 100.0   | 67.0     | 17.8                         | 6.6           | 8.6              |
| 1972 | 18,670 | 100.0   | 66.2     | 19.0                         | 6.6           | 8.2              |
| 1971 | 17,780 | 100.0   | 65.1     | 19.8                         | 6.5           | 8.6              |
| 1970 | 16,000 | 100.0   | 65.4     | 18.9                         | 7.6           | 8.1              |
| 1969 | 14,640 | 100.0   | 64.5     | 19.9                         | 7.4           | 8.2              |
| 1968 | 13,690 | 100.0   | 65.4     | 18.7                         | 8.3           | 7.6              |
| 1967 | 12,130 | 100.0   | 63.6     | 20.0                         | 7.7           | 8.7              |
| 1966 | 10,950 | 100.0   | 60.0     | 23.0                         | 8.0           | 9.0              |

Source: *Uniform Crime Reports,* 1966–1975.

Figure 1
## MURDER BY TYPE OF WEAPON USED, 1975

DUE TO ROUNDING, DOES NOT ADD TO 100%

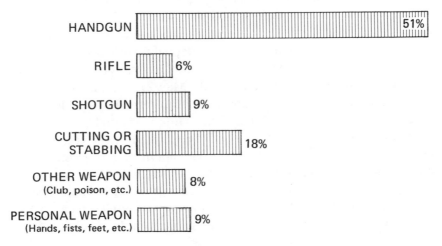

SOURCE: Federal Bureau of Investigation, *Crime in the United States: 1975* (Washington, D.C.: U.S. Government Printing Office, 1976), p. 17.

companions who may vacation, party, or travel together. The most intensive study of homicide patterns ever conducted also found the same phenomenon. For the period 1949 through 1952, criminologist Marvin E. Wolfgang of the University of Pennsylvania analyzed a total of 588 criminal homicides in Philadelphia. In 65 percent of the cases, the victim was a close friend of the offender, a family member, paramour, or homosexual partner. Furthermore, some 41 percent of the women victims were killed by their husbands.[29] These findings, combined with those of the *Uniform Crime Reports,* have implications for criminal justice in the United States, for they suggest that criminal homicide is largely a societal problem whose complete prevention is almost totally beyond police or any other form of criminal justice intervention.

Of the remaining criminal homicides in the United States, almost all are related to some other offense, or at least suspected to be so. During 1975, as noted in Table 1, 32.4 percent were known or suspected felony types. The majority of these killings occurred in connection with robbery offenses, while prostitution and commercialized vice, rape and other sex offenses, and drug law violations accounted for most of the remainder. Again, a portion of these can result from differences of opinion in personal relations—between prostitute and john, drug user and dealer—or as an unforeseen consequence in a forcible rape situation. And finally, there are those instances of homicide which seemingly have no explanation in rational goal-oriented terms, as in the instance of convicted murderers, Nathan F. Leopold, Jr. and Richard A. Loeb. Leopold was a graduate of the University of Chicago in 1924 and the son of a multimillionaire shipping magnate; Loeb was a 1924 University of Michigan graduate, and the son of Sears, Roebuck and Company vice-president Albert A. Loeb. On May 21, 1924, after weeks of intricate planning, the two kidnapped and murdered 14-year-old Robert Franks, a distant relative of Loeb. The crime was quickly discovered and the killers apprehended, and both Leopold and Loeb received life sentences for murder plus 99 years for kidnapping. Some accounts suggest that the crime was an outgrowth of Loeb's fanatic dream to commit an important crime in a perfect manner,[30] although Nathan Leopold himself commented in 1958 that the murder was undertaken for reasons which still remained incomprehensible to him.[31]

## Assault

The majority of the violent personal crimes that do not result in death occur from some type of assault—either aggravated or simple. *Assault,* in legal terms, is simply an intentional "attempt" or "threat" to physically injure another person, and does not refer to the actual infliction of injury.[32] *Battery* is the nonlethal culmination of an assault, while *assault and battery* is an assault carried into effect by doing some violence to the victim.[33] *Aggravated assault* refers to an assault with the intent to commit murder, rape, robbery, or to inflict serious bodily harm,[34] and *simple assault* is one in which the intended bodily harm fails, or where no serious harm was ever intended.[35]

Few systematic studies of assault have been undertaken, but evidence has suggested that most assaults, along with homicide, might be examined within the broader perspective of personal violence:

> The ostensible motives in homicide and assault are often relatively trivial, usually involving spontaneous altercations, family quarrels, jealous rages, and the like. The two crimes are similar; there is often no reason to believe that the person guilty of homicide sets out with any more intention to harm than the one who commits an aggravated assault. Except for the seriousness of the final outcomes, the major distinction is that homicides most often involve handguns while knives are most common in assault.[36]

Official statistics on aggravated assaults, however incomplete they may be, tend to support these notions. Although Americans concerned with "crime in the streets" reflect a fear of assault by strangers, this conception is seemingly based more on myth than fact. Street muggings do indeed occur, yet according to the President's Commission on Law Enforcement and Administration of Justice, nearly two-thirds of all known aggravated assaults result from domestic quarrels, altercations, jealousies, and arguments over money or property; victim-offender relationships have been intimate, close, and frequent, primarily involving family members and close friends.[37] The risk of serious personal assault in 1975 was approximately 1 in 440,[38] and based on our knowledge of victim-offender relationships, this risk was twice as great from family members or acquaintances than from strangers.

## Forcible Rape

Sexual assault, more commonly known as *forcible rape,* is legally defined as having "carnal knowledge" (sexual intercourse) of a female, against her will through the use or threat of force.[39] This is to be distinguished from *statutory rape* which is the carnal knowledge of a female under a stated age (usually 16 or 18), with or without her consent.[40]

Forcible rape is an offense that has been difficult to fully analyze, for it is significantly underreported to police, it has been subject to numerous misconceptions, myths, and prejudices, and it has been confounded by many paradoxes.

One of the more complete analyses of forcible rape patterns involved an examination of 646 instances of rape occurring in Philadelphia during the years 1958 and 1960.[41] In this study, the findings suggested the following to be *misconceptions* about rape:

—that blacks are more likely to attack white women than black women;
—that rape is primarily a hot-season crime;
—that rape usually occurs between total strangers;
—that rape usually is associated with drinking;
—that rape usually is an explosive act;
—that rape usually is mainly a dead-end street or dark alley event;
—that rape usually is a violent crime in which brutality is inflicted upon the victim;
—that victims usually are responsible for their own victimization, either consciously or by default.

These, for the most part, are indeed myths and misconceptions. Available data suggest that rape is an interracial act, apparent among all racial and ethnic groups; it occurs in all seasons, and alcohol is a factor in perhaps only one-third of all rape situations. Rape is not predominately an explosive act; it is a planned event in the vast majority of cases. Brutality is the exception rather than the rule, and verbal coercion or threat are used to initially subdue the victim; furthermore, the number of rapes actually precipitated by the victim are comparatively small. Finally, the majority of rapes do not occur in dead-end streets and dark alleys; a high percentage of these offenses are committed by family members and others previously known to the victims, and hence, occur in places where the victim and offender initially met each other.[42]

This latter issue, the victim-offender relationship, is one that has evoked much prejudice about forcible rape. There are indeed many findings which suggest that there are personal relationships between the victim and offender in instances of rape. In Amir's study, the victim and offender were known to one another in 48 percent of the cases.[43] More recently, a survey of forcible rape cases by the District of Columbia Crime Commission demonstrated an even higher proportion of previous personal relationships between victim and offender:

> Almost two-thirds of the 151 victims surveyed were attacked by persons with whom they were at least casually acquainted. Only 36 percent of the 224 assailants about whom some identifying information was obtained were complete strangers to their victims; 16 (7 percent) of the attackers were known to the victim by sight, although there had been no previous contact. Thirty-one (14 percent) of the 224 assailants were relatives, family friends or boyfriends of the victims, and 88 (39 percent) were either acquaintances or neighbors.[44]

Data as these may indeed be reliable, but they have often been construed to mean that most rapes are "victim-precipitated"—a situation ending in forced intercourse when a woman first agreed to sexual relations, or clearly invited them verbally and through gestures, but then retracted before the act.[45] The idea of victim precipitation can be carried even further to suggest that the victim of rape is often a willing partner, and therefore no "rape" actually takes place, or as one person stated on a Los Angeles television show:

> ... in the majority of women who are raped, I think that probably 75 percent of them are actually enjoying it or asking for it.[46]

Attitudes and interpretations such as these have served to make rape the only crime in which the victims can become the accused—victims must prove their good reputation, mental soundness, and impeccable propriety; past encounters with the accused, or sometimes evidence of any prior crime or sexual activity, leads to the suggestion that the victim may have fabricated her story, or may have tried to "trap" the defendant. This has resulted in a lack of sympathy on the part of many male jurors during the prosecution of rape cases, especially when it becomes evident that the complainant and defendant were known to one another prior to the crime. And it has led to the support of legislation which states that before an act can be legally accepted as rape, every material element of rape—penetration, force, and the identity of the rapist—must be corroborated by evidence other than the victim's testimony.[47] Yet the real issue surrounding forcible rape is not the victim's acquaintance with the offender, her chastity, criminal record, prior sexual experience, or even the notion of victim precipitation. Rather, merely because a woman may have consented to intercourse on some prior occasion does not mean that she must forever forfeit her right to choose sexual partners. Under the law, each of us has the right of sexual self-determination, and the criminal justice process becomes biased should it examine rape within the context of a woman's prior sexual encounters.

There is, too, the instance of falsely accused rape, of which the case of the Scottsboro boys provides an excellent example. In April 1931 nine boys ranging in age from 13 to 21, all black, had a fight with four white youths while they were all hitching a ride on a freight train. The white boys, and two girls accompanying them, were thrown from the train, with one reporting the incident to the authorities. When the train arrived at the next station, Scottsboro, Alabama, where the sheriff was waiting with a posse, the nine boys were arrested and charged with raping the white girls, Victoria Price and Ruby Bates. Physicians examined the two women, but there was no medical evidence of rape. All were convicted, eight were sentenced to death, and the appeal process began. During a later trial, Ruby Bates reversed her testimony, indicating that neither she nor Victoria Price had ever been raped, but had concocted the charge in an attempt to avoid being arrested for vagrancy. But the convictions remained, and the Scottsboro boys continued to serve time in prison. As the years passed, eight of the nine were released on parole, some having spent two decades in prison.[48]

Equally peculiar in our perception of rape is the denial of men as victims and of women as offenders. The law, initially, defines *victims as women* and *offenders as men.* Mass media, secondly, reports only those rapes of *women* by *men.* Yet studies have indicated that other types of rape do indeed occur, especially in correctional institutions. A report on the Philadelphia prison system documented 156 cases of sexual assault during a 26-month period in that system alone;[49] in many American prisons and jails, young male prisoners are raped within a day or two after their arrival;[50] and rape through forced oral-genital contact and body contacts which attempt to simulate heterosexual intercourse are well known in women's institutions.[51]

## Property Offenses

Property crimes are among the more widespread of offenses, and can appear in any variety of forms:

1. theft (secret taking and removing of another's property, as in burglary or sneak theft);
2. larceny (open taking and removing of another's property, but without violence);
3. robbery and brigandage (taking and removing property through the use of compulsion, violence, and coercion);
4. unlawful appropriation of something found;
5. unlawful appropriation of entrusted property;
6. removal of landmarks;
7. property damage (simple, not creating a general danger);
8. dangerous property damage (through arson, explosion, or flooding);
9. swindling (taking property or removing it through fraud or deceit);
10. extortion (as blackmail, but by violence or threat of violence);
11. blackmail (coercion through threat of disclosure);
12. misuse of trust (misuse of the rights entrusted in regard to another's property, or misuse of another's weakness, inexperience, or need);
13. usury (misuse in the field of credit transaction);
14. criminal bankruptcy;
15. buying, receiving, or possessing stolen goods;
16. plagiarism;
17. forgery;
18. counterfeiting; and,
19. pickpocketing.[52]

This discursive listing suggests a wide variety of behaviors, many of which have little or no relation to one another. Many of these can be included in the activities of white-collar, professional, organized, and "heavy" criminals, discussed later in this chapter, each of which reflects alternative behavior systems in crime. By far, however, the crimes of larceny, theft, burglary, vandalism, and forgery account for the majority of known property crimes, and studies suggest that these are committed primarily on an occasional basis.

In their discussion of the "occasional property offender," Clinard and Quinney have pointed out, as noted earlier, that property crime as such is typically the activity of an amateur offender:

> Many property offenders commit only an occasional theft of some kind. Such criminal behavior is incidental to their way of life. The offenses are so rare that such offenders in no way make a living out of crime, and they do not play criminal roles. Occasional property offenders do not identify with crime or conceive of themselves as criminals. Their offenses show little sophistication in the techniques of crime. Most of them have little real knowledge about criminal activities or of the criminal argot or vocabulary of crime.[53]

To these can be added the amateur offenders who steal on a more regular basis, but who nevertheless show little sophistication in crime or identification with criminal roles—the nonprofessional shoplifters who steal merchandise for their own use; the employees of department stores and other business establishments who pilfer money and goods to supplement their wages; the adolescent delinquents who burglarize and vandalize property as part of peer group activity; the central city drug users who engage in various predatory behaviors for the purpose of obtaining funds for drug supplies. Combined, these offenders account for the majority of known property crimes, which involve substantial dollar losses to their victims. During 1975, for example, there were 10,230,282 major property offenses (burglary, larceny–theft, motor vehicle theft) known to the police in the United States, representing a dollar loss of $3.8 billion. As suggested by Table 5–3, the average loss per

TABLE 5–3.  Property Crime by Number of Offenses and Economic Loss, 1975

| Type of Offense | Total Offenses | Average Loss (in dollars) | Total Losses (in billions) |
|---|---|---|---|
| Burglary | 3,252,129 | $ 422 | $1.4 |
| Larceny–theft | 5,977,698 | $ 166 | $ .9 |
| Vehicle theft | 1,000,455 | $1,457 | $1.5 |
| Total | 10,230,282 | $ 371 | $3.8 |

Source: *Uniform Crime Reports, 1975.*

victim was $371, ranging from $166 for larceny–thefts to $1,457 in cases
of motor vehicle theft.

Of all varieties of property crime, larceny reflects ostensibly the most
divergent number of behaviors, from sneak thefts such as shoplifting,
thefts from buildings, and "snatch-and-run" thefts from vehicles to the
more interpersonal acts of purse-snatching and pocket-picking. As apparent in Table 5–4, the proportional distribution of each type of larceny
has remained relatively constant over time, although some minor fluc-
tuations are evident. These data would suggest that pickpocketing,
purse-snatching, and thefts from buildings and coin-operated machines
have maintained a steady level in the overall larceny picture, while an
increasing proportion of thefts of bicycles, thefts from vehicles, and
shoplifting have become apparent. Also, the dollar value of each larceny has increased from $74 in 1960 to $156 in 1970 and $166 in 1975.
These official data, as indicated below, also suggest that during 1975, the
largest dollar loss per larceny occurred with miscellaneous thefts from
buildings:[54]

| | |
|---|---|
| from buildings | $258 |
| from vehicles | $207 |
| pocket-picking | $135 |
| purse-snatching | $ 83 |
| shoplifting | $ 33 |

There is an implication in these data, however, that perhaps only
those larcenies with the higher dollar losses become known to the

TABLE 5–4.   Percentage Distribution of Larcenies by Type, 1970–1975

| Year | 1970 | 1971 | 1972 | 1973 | 1974 | 1975 |
|---|---|---|---|---|---|---|
| Pocket-picking | 1.1 | 1.0 | .9 | 1.0 | 1.1 | 1.0 |
| Purse-snatching | 2.2 | 2.5 | 1.9 | 1.9 | 2.2 | 1.9 |
| Shoplifting | 7.1 | 8.0 | 8.7 | 8.4 | 10.9 | 11.1 |
| From vehicles (except accessories) | 16.8 | 16.7 | 16.6 | 16.9 | 17.6 | 18.5 |
| Vehicle accessories | 20.4 | 18.8 | 17.3 | 15.8 | 15.9 | 18.7 |
| Bicycles | 10.9 | 13.2 | 12.8 | 12.8 | 16.9 | 13.2 |
| From buildings | 16.1 | 16.4 | 16.8 | 16.2 | 17.4 | 16.8 |
| From coin machines | 1.6 | 1.4 | 1.3 | 1.3 | 1.4 | 1.3 |
| All others | 23.9 | 22.0 | 23.7 | 25.9 | 16.8 | 17.6 |

Note: Percentages do not total to 100.0 due to rounding.
Source: *Uniform Crime Reports, 1970–1975.*

police. A recent study of active professional pickpockets indicated, for example, that even among these highly skilled thieves the average "score" was only $10 to $25.[55]

Causation factors in property are not fully defined, although Edwin M. Lemert's study of 1,023 cases of "naïve" check forgery offers some suggestions relative to a variety of occasional offenders.[56] He found check forgery to be characteristic of those with substantial educational and occupational backgrounds, who rarely had delinquent or criminal backgrounds. The majority of those investigated were immersed in a progressive condition of social isolation—increasing alienation from conventional social bonds through divorce or separation from their families—aggravated further by other isolating conditions such as loss of job or physical mobility. In addition, many of the subjects had experienced financial imbalances through gambling losses, alcoholic sprees, or business failures. Given these conditions, combined with a set of circumstances or course of action to which the offender felt committed, check forgery was seen as an immediate solution to the situational tensions of the moment. Out of funds at a time when they might be needed to maintain an activity or relationship, the offender used forgery to stabilize the situation. Check forgery was selected over other forms of crime since it required no special skills, it was of an impersonal nature, and because no other alternatives were available.

Studies have suggested that the vast majority of shoplifters may not be altogether unlike the naive check forger. In Mary Owen Cameron's investigation of department store shoplifters, most were amateur thieves and reflected little or no experience in crime or with criminal processing.[57] Most had no knowledge about arrest procedures, readily admitted their guilt, confessed prior thefts to store detectives, and consistently offered to pay for the stolen merchandise, failing to understand that they had been arrested and faced criminal processing.

## Vocational Crime

It has been suggested that violent personal crime—homicide, assault, and forcible rape—are often situational offenses, that they emerge from differences of opinion in personal relations, and that generally, crime is not a part of the offender's social role. Similarly, the property offender is for the most part an occasional criminal, and crime is not pursued within a career context. These offenses are to be contrasted with *career* or *vocational crime,* which might be defined as *offense behavior that is pursued as an occupational career for the purpose of obtaining a*

*steady flow of income; the development of the criminal vocation begins*
*with an initiation and socialization into the world of crime, attended*
*by a maturation process involving the acquisition of skills, knowledge,*
*and associations appropriate for maintaining the desired occupation.*[58]
The types of vocational crime are threefold: (1) professional crime; (2)
professional "heavy" crime; and (3) organized crime.

*Professional crime* refers to the nonviolent forms of criminal occupation pursued with a high degree of skill to maximize financial gain and
minimize the risks of apprehension. The more typical forms of professional crime include picking pockets, shoplifting, confidence games,
burglary, sneak-thieving, extortion, and forgery and counterfeiting.
Many of these varieties of crime are also undertaken by other types of
criminals, but with the professional criminal or thief, they occur
within a unique social organization and occupational structure.[59] Or
more specifically, professional criminals make a regular business of
stealing. It is their means of livelihood, and as such, they devote their
entire working time and energy to stealing. Professional criminals
operate with proficiency; they have a body of skills and knowledge that
is utilized in the planning and execution of their work, and they are
contemptuous of amateur thieves. They are graduates of a developmental process that includes the acquisition of specialized attitudes, knowledge, skills, and experience. Furthermore, professional criminals make
crime their way of life; they organize their lives around criminal pur-
suits and develop a philosophy regarding their activities and profession; they identify themselves with the world of crime where they are
members of an exclusive fraternity that extends friendship, understanding, sympathy, congeniality, security, recognition, and respect.
And finally, professional criminals are able to steal for long periods of
time without going to prison; they commit crimes in a manner that
reduces the risks of apprehension, and they are able to effectively cope
with confrontations with the criminal justice system through the
"fixing" of cases.

Professional crime is centuries old, having emerged as an outgrowth
of the disintegration of the feudal order in Europe during 1350–1550,
and its evolution was hastened by the mobility and economic changes
that resulted from that disintegration. It first appeared among English-
speaking peoples during the years of Shakespeare's youth—the Eliza-
bethan period of British history. Professional crime emerged in the
United States during the urbanization of America, and since that time
it has remained relatively unchanged. The types of crime, techniques

and skills, attitudes and philosophies, interactional setting, patterns of recruitment and training, style of life, and to some extent the argot of twentieth-century professional criminals are characteristically similar to those of centuries ago. Professional crime has decreased in recent years, however, and this has occurred primarily from the lowered profitability of the profession due to the greater difficulty in "fixing" the contemporary criminal justice process.[60]

*Professional "heavy" crime* involves highly skilled offenses for monetary gain, but employing elements of coercion and the use or threat of force, violence, or property damage. The specific crimes include armed robbery, hijacking, and sometimes burglary, arson, and kidnapping—much of which Clinard and Quinney referred to as "conventional crime." The crimes are committed with surprise and speed to diminish the risks of apprehension.[61]

A view of the history of crime suggests that central to a conceptualization of professional "heavy" crime is the notion of *banditry*. In its purest form, banditry is the practice of marauding by organized or semi-organized groups. It emerges on the frontiers of society and is characteristic of segments of the outcast or oppressed. Methods are highly visible and pitiless, while goal orientations are occupational and economic. Banditry endures until such time as its effective arena is encroached upon by civilization and is suppressed or dispersed when the advancing society can no longer contain it. The specific action patterns of banditry vary as does the essence of frontier or civilization; implicit in the closing of old frontiers is the emergence or expansion of newer ones.

The phenomena of banditry or professional "heavy" crime are manifest in piracy, in the grand manner of *Blackbeard* and *Henry Morgan.* Piracy was banditry on a maritime frontier. Spirited initially by the Spanish discovery of America in 1492, the West Indies became the frontier of Europe and remained so for some three hundred years. The buccaneers and pirates of the Caribbean were the counterparts of the notorious highwaymen of seventeenth- and eighteenth-century England, the desperadoes of the American West, the public enemies of the depression-ridden 1930s, and the billion-dollar cargo hijackers of the contemporary postindustrial era. Each had its own unique frontier, miscreant populations, and intruding civilization, yet common to all were corresponding patterns of social change which defined the context of their genesis, rise, and decline.

Predominant in the history of "heavy" crime were the outlaws of the

American West, the organized groups of cattle thieves and rustlers, the bank bandits, and robbers of train and stage—Jesse and Frank James, the Younger brothers, the Daltons, and "Butch" Cassidy. The more modern bandits of the "heavy" type have been associated with the social change and public apathy of the 1930s. Armed with machine guns, these newer outlaws re-created the frontier pattern of swift and rapid assault followed by an immediate and elusive retreat. Fast cars and intricate systems replaced the bridled desert and canyon escape routes of the American West, but their crimes and methods of committing them were essentially the same. Characteristic of this era were such principals as John Dillinger, Bonnie Parker and Clyde Barrow, Ma Barker, Alvin Karpis, Charles "Pretty Boy" Floyd and "Machine Gun" Kelly.

Contemporary "heavy" crime most often appears as armed robbery, which has been discussed by Werner J. Einstadter as having three tactical levels:

1. *The Ambush*—little planning; participants attack an establishment in guerrilla fashion; randomness in selection of victim; high incidence of violence.
2. *The Selective Raid*—some planning; limited analysis of site conditions; tentative plan of approach.
3. *The Planned Operation*—well-planned and well-structured in every aspect; risks are held to a minimum.[62]

*Organized crime, syndicated crime, or racketeering* generally refers to any business operations structured for the purpose of economic gain through illegal activities. As such, it concentrates on the distribution of illegal goods and services—gambling, prostitution, *loan-sharking* (usury), distribution of illicit drugs—and is characterized by:

—a hierarchical structure involving systems of rigidly defined relationships with mutual obligations and privileges;
—monopolistic control of established and defined spheres of influence within specific geographical areas;
—dependence upon the threat of and/or use of force and violence to maintain discipline, restrain competition, and secure cooperation;
—maintenance of immunity from intervention by and interference from agencies of the criminal justice system; and,
—large financial gains secured through specialization in one or more enterprises.[63]

As discussed already in Chapter 2, organized crime in America was spirited by national prohibition during the 1920s, and today it exists as a series of loosely connected complex business organizations. It is maintained by a division of labor that includes financiers, purchasing agents, transportation specialists, attorneys, accountants, training personnel, and enforcers. In describing the structural arrangement of organized crime in the United States, current testimony has indicated that:

1. there is a nationwide alliance of tightly knit "families" of criminals;
2. the "members" of these "families" are Italians and Sicilians by birth or national origin;
3. each "family" has a boss who directs the activities of its "members" (see Chart II);
4. the "families" are linked together as members of *La Cosa Nostra;*
5. the leaders of the more powerful "families" combine as a "Commission" to direct the motions of *La Cosa Nostra;* and
6. "families" are linked to non-*Cosa Nostra* syndicates by an elaborate series of "treaties" and "understandings."[64]

This popular conception of organized crime suggests that syndicate racketeering is primarily an Italian and Sicilian phenomenon with all-embracing national and international connections.[65] Yet this is a disputed issue. Others have suggested that the "syndicate" is not a syndicate at all; that organized crime is simply a loosely connected confederation of both Italian and non-Italian gangsters; and that the infamous *Mafia* is no more than a decentralized and unregimented collection of semi-aligned bands of western Sicilian farmers and businessmen having no bearing on and little in common with the operations of organized crime in the United States.[66]

*Professional crime, professional "heavy" crime,* and *organized crime* can be considered as "vocational" in nature since the participants in each behavior system view their respective offense patterns as their "calling." It is this degree of commitment that differentiates the vocational aspect from non-career-oriented varieties of criminality:

> The *professional thief* has the most highly developed of criminal careers. His skill at engaging successfully in specialized crimes has accorded him great prestige among other criminals. His longevity in crime results not just from ability, but also from his motivations, by a set of justifications which make his activities and way of life seem reasonable to him. The ensuing philosophy of life reflects a criminal self-image, one which confers

# Figure 2
## AN ORGANIZED CRIME FAMILY

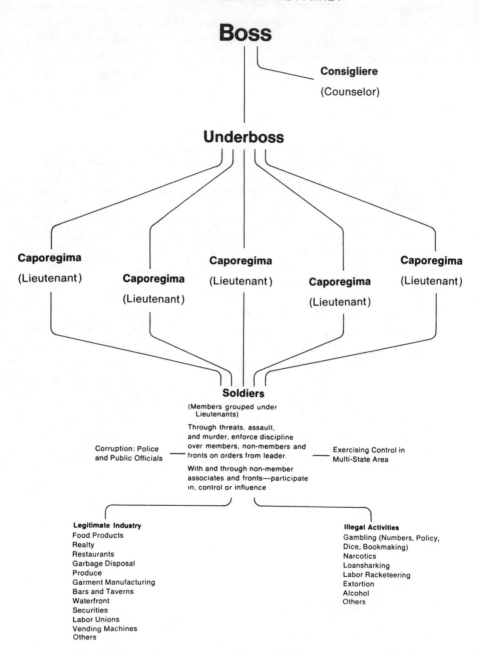

SOURCE: President's Commission on Law Enforcement and Administration of Justice, *The Challenge of Crime in a Free Society* (Washington, D.C.: U.S. Government Printing Office, 1967), p. 194.

a degree of worth upon any illegal movements and functions pursued. The *professional "heavy" criminal* also has a career and self-concept of a criminal nature. His vocation in crime typically begins with involvement in a culture that is either neutral or opposed to the law of the wider society. A career, identified with crime, and criminal self-conception emerge as a result of repeated offenses and of arrests and convictions which create a stigma that prevents entry into more law-abiding social outlets. Finally, while members of the *organized underworld* also have a criminal self-conception and commitment like that of other career offenders, in contrast to the *professional* offenders, they often live a segmented life, seeking the seclusion of respectability within the prestige system initialed by the larger society.[67]

The three varieties of vocational or career crime, although sharing conceptions and commitments to life-styles essentially isolated and different from the wider society, differ significantly in their approaches to criminal behavior. The professional thief is a *passive* property offender, the "heavy" criminal is a more *violent* predator, and those in organized crime are concerned with illegal goods and services. Yet these differences actually reflect only "ideal types" of behavior, for in many circumstances the actors in one particular career behavior system may pursue the activities of the others. This is especially apparent in the organized underworld. As a hierarchical complex, the leaders at the foundation of a criminal syndicate rule over a middle echelon of management personnel who, in turn, control a tertiary level of workers. Authority, responsibility, and activity vary from one rank to another. Those in minor positions, for example, often manifest careers similar to those of the professional "heavy" offenders or even professional thieves. The situation becomes even more complex when it is realized that organized crime groups vary in size, with even the powerful leaders in the small organizations engaging in the activities found at all levels of a large crime cartel. As such, while professional crime, professional "heavy" crime, and organized crime may represent three distinct behavior systems in crime, each also contains a series of subsystems of roles, activities, and behaviors.

## Crime in Business and Government

Our scholarly interest in crime in business and government dates back to Edwin H. Sutherland's original formulation of the concept of "white-collar crime."[68] In his presidential address to the American Sociological Society in 1939, Sutherland used the term to refer to those persons of "respectable" and "high social status" who violated any variety of legal codes during the normal course of their occupational activity. As such, *white-collar crime can be defined as those offenses committed by persons acting in their occupational roles. The offenders are businessmen and members of the professions who, in the course of their everyday occupational activities, violate the basic trust placed in them or act in unethical ways.* The offenders are typically "ideal" members of the community—physicians, attorneys, business owners, bank tellers, office workers.

The white-collar crime concept originally referred to members of the upper classes, but more recently, the concept has been expanded to include persons at all occupational levels. Donald J. Newman suggested that farmers, repairmen, and others in essentially non-white-collar occupations could be classified among business criminals through such activities as watering milk for public consumption or making unnecessary repairs on television sets.[69] Marshall B. Clinard, in his research on wartime black market operations included all of those violators, regardless of their social status.[70] Consequently, the concept was expanded by Richard Quinney to include all violations that occur during the course of any legitimate occupational activity, and he termed the expanded concept "occupational crime."[71] More recently, Clinard and Quinney have taken those white-collar offenses committed within the corporate sector and retitled them "corporate crime."[72]

Within this context, the expanded concept of white-collar crime would include any variety of illegal activities:

—*in the business sector*—financial manipulations, unfair labor practices, rebates, misrepresentation of goods and consumer deception by false labeling, *fencing* of stolen goods, short-changing, over-charging, black-marketeering;
—*in the labor sector*—misuse of union funds, failing to enforce laws affecting unions, entering into collusion with employers to the disadvantage of union members, illegal mechanisms for controlling members;
—*in the corporate sector*—restraint of trade, infringement of patents, monopolistic practices, environmental contamination, misuse of trademarks, manufacture of unsafe goods, false advertising;
—*in the financial sector*—embezzlement, violation of currency control measures, stock manipulation;
—*in the medical sector*—illegal prescription practices, fee-splitting, illegal abortions, fraudulent reports to insurance companies;
—*in the legal sector*—misappropriation of funds in trusts and receiverships, securing prejudiced testimony, bribery, instituting fraudulent damage claims;

—*in the criminal justice sector*—accepting bribes, illegal arrest and detention practices, illegal correctional practices;
—*in the civil sector*—illegal commissions, issuance of fraudulent licenses and certificates, illegal tax evaluations, misuse of campaign funds, illegal campaign practices.

At all levels of white-collar criminality, the offenders generally have no criminal self-concept. The violations tend to be part of one's work, and they are rationalized in one manner or another. Businessmen may look at their illegality as "sharp" business practices, while other offenders may rationalize that the laws are "unfair" or that whatever they gained "was coming to them."

The notion of white-collar crime might be expanded even further to include *governmental crime*—the *bribery and corruption among high governmental officials, and activities of government agencies which serve to truncate the rights and humanity of the population as a whole.* Governmental crime has surfaced recently with the many disclosures of FBI and CIA covert activities on American and foreign soil which have been outright violations of the law and constitutional rights.[73] Perhaps most interesting in this respect was the Watergate affair.

When the offices of the Democratic National Committee, located in the Watergate buildings in Washington, D.C., were broken into in June 1972, our knowledge of the vast spectrum of crimes being committed by the state began to take form. We learned that acts of spying and sabotage were connected to the highest level of the United States government, the presidency itself. And the Watergate discovery served to sharpen our perspective. It uncovered a "second government," one which had been previously unsuspected, but nevertheless had been operating for perhaps decades:

> Beneath Watergate is a government with "a combination of vast and complicated interlocking forces, pulling in the CIA here and organized crime there, using politicians one time and émigré thugs the next, which seems to regard government as a tool for financial enrichment." These operations are usually beyond the reach of citizens.[74]

## CRIMINAL BEHAVIOR SYSTEMS AND SOCIAL CONTROL

In the preceding section a variety of behavior systems in crime have been briefly discussed—violent crime, property crime, career crime, and white-collar crime. Each of these, as has been illustrated, can have a number of independent subsystems of behavior, and to these can be added other forms of activity—*crimes against the public order or morality,* as in prostitution, drunkenness, gambling, and illicit drug use, and *political crime,* as in espionage, treason, and revolution. Again, each of these can interpreted as being independent behavior systems. Before concluding this discussion of criminal behavior, however, it is important to note the differential levels of societal reaction to particular types of crime, and to ponder these alternative reactions.[75]

Edwin M. Lemert's definition of the generation of the definition of deviance and crime asserted that:

> The deviant person is one whose role, status, function and self-definition are importantly shaped by how much deviation he engages in, by the degree of its social visibility, by the particular exposure he has to the societal reaction, and by the nature and strength of the societal reaction.[76]

Lemert uses such terms as "how much deviation," "degree of social visibility," and "nature and strength" in his proposition. Yet of these, *it is suggested that "degree of visibility" stands as the primary determinant of societal reaction; it is the degree of visibility that most often determines social definitions, penalties, and rejection.* Social visibility can be observed in three dimensions: as seen by the victim, as seen by the societal control system, and as seen by the society at large.

Victim-offender relationships contribute significantly to the conferring of visibility on the deviant act. In violent personal crime, there is physical contact between the victim and the offender. Such contacts are violations of the moral precepts of the "sanctity of the human body" and "thou shalt not kill." Violations of these precepts are direct assaults upon middle-class morality and are looked upon as "heinous." The offender is then defined as something different or sick, a killer, a fiend, something cruel and diabolically wicked. The visibility of violent personal crime is enhanced by the fact that offenses are readily detected. Even where the assaulted victim is hidden, the mere absence of the victim enhances visibility.

In crimes against property, the victim-offender relationship is less personal. The victim may be an individual, a group, or a business organization. Yet offenses of this type are inconsistent with the sanctity of private property, violations of the canons of ethics of the middle-class value system.

The importance of wealth and material goods has been increasingly stressed in the growth of industrialized society. The American aggregate, as an embodiment of materialism and conspicuous consumption, reacts in a particularly hostile manner to those who encroach upon the rewards of economic success. Societal outcry in the form of calls for compensation and justice for victims has long since called attention to such offenders. Repeated transgressions have resulted in repeated castigations, thus enhancing their social visibility.

The victim of political crime, public order crime, and organized crime is society as a whole. Political criminals are visible according to the very nature of their acts. In an attempt to bring about change, their doctrines are advertised as disruptions of the status quo. The political criminal (the radical left-wing insurgent, the traitor) is deviant in that his ideas and acts are visibly in contrast with the traditional doctrines of the polity.

Public order criminals generate a complex of overt situations which offend the public morality. Most of the offenders are visible to the victim—the individual in society—who views such behavior as immoral and undignified. Vagrants, disorderly persons, hoboes and tramps, drunkards, and some prostitutes and homosexuals display their nonconformity before the public eye. Because they are visible, they become defined as different, and their deviant status is also ascribed to their presumed cohorts who are not as visible. Organized crime represents a threat to free enterprise. Although it provides goods and services to many of those who define it as deviant, it tends to be labeled deviant nevertheless. The criminals themselves are not visible, but the results of their efforts are often visible in the form of public order crimes: gambling, drug sales, prostitution and commercialized vice. Syndicated crime is an elusive entity which when detected, is made highly visible by the moral crusaders and rule enforcers. When made visible by the reactions of such individuals, the society as a whole has been awarded a better picture of the deviant enterprise and can react accordingly.

White-collar crime is the least visible of all forms of criminality. Such crime is pursued during the normal events of business activity. Business activity then acts as a shield, and the deviance is not seen.

Professional crime occupies a unique position in the complex of victim-offender relationships, a position which inhibits the victim in calling attention to the deviant act. This situation was described by Sutherland:

The shakedown (extortion from homosexuals and certain other violators
of law) is safe because the victims, being themselves violators of the law,
cannot complain to the police. The confidence game is safe for the same
reason, for the victims have entered into collusion with the thieves to
defraud someone else and were themselves defrauded in the attempt.
Stealing from stores is relatively safe because the stores are reluctant to
make accusations of theft against persons who appear to be legitimate customers.[77]

Furthermore, when the victim is not himself a deviant, the thief's
ability to manipulate people permits him to arrange restitution rather
than face complaint and prosecution. In either case, the overt act is
neither intrinsically visible nor made visible by the victim.

Social visibility is not only observed or ascribed by the victim, but
also by the social control system. The social control system is dominated by the *moral entrepreneurs*—the moral crusaders, the rule makers, and the rule enforcers.[78] Visibility is built into some deviant acts,
but as seen earlier, when the victim is the society as a whole, the
individual often views such acts as no more than immoral behavior.
Some offenders themselves are visible—hoboes, tramps, drunkards,
streetwalking prostitutes—but their activities are not directed against
the person or property of the citizen. Again, they are visible, but the
citizen is often apathetic since this type of deviance falls into the category of "crimes without victims." But as Becker has indicated, the
existing rules do not satisfy the moral crusader, "because there is some
evil which profoundly disturbs him."[79] Evil is socially visible to him,
and he, being fervent and righteous, feels justified to do away with it.
Crusaders of this type point out such acts to the society, making them
more visible. Having now seen what the crusader called deviant, the
society urges the lawmakers to *label* the acts officially as deviant. This
process is instigated by the reaction of the crusader to visible behavior
toward which the citizen was only apathetic; ". . . social groups create
deviance by making the rules whose infraction contitutes deviance,
and by applying those rules to particular people and labeling them as
outsiders."[80]

Many examples can be cited for this process and generation of the
definition of deviance. Intoxication was a quality visible only to those
who (1) had the opportunity to observe the condition, (2) had the knowledge to recognize such a condition, (3) defined such a condition to be
a nuisance, and (4) did not derive pleasure from such a condition. The

prohibitionists emerged from this group and pointed out this "evil" to all others, making intoxication visible to greater numbers in the society. Reformers of this type were common in the last century and the early part of this century as we have noted in earlier chapters. In cases where the offense is highly visible to the victim, the processes of definition and labeling of deviance bypass the efforts of the crusaders and are enacted directly by the rule makers. Those acts which have been traditionally accepted as deviant maintain that label because they are highly visible as disruptions of what had been defined as the status quo. Violent personal and property crime fall into this category.

It has been observed that many forms of professional crime are visible to the victim, yet due to the victim's involvement in an act which he himself labels as deviant, such visibility is not transmitted to the moral crusaders, rule makers, and rule enforcers. Under these circumstances, social visibility remains low, and, consequently, societal reaction remains low. But what of the instances where the professional criminal commits deviant acts which are classifiable as predatory crime—burglary, larceny, and the like? The crime is highly visible to the victim, and such economic assaults are communicated to the power holders in the criminal justice system. However, the professional criminal possesses a complex of skills and techniques which enable him to commit his acts of theft without being detected. When the theft is observed, it is usually attributed to those groups which are more visible than the professional—the amateur or "heavy" property offender. The professional, thus, is able to steal for long periods without being caught, affording him the opportunity to accumulate substantial sums of money. When he is caught committing a deviant act, being a good actor and able to manipulate people, he puts his wealth and linguistic dexterity to work for him and employs the *fix*:

> In order to send a thief to the penitentiary, it is necessary to have the cooperation of the victim, witnesses, police, bailiffs, clerks, grand jury, jury, prosecutor, judge, and perhaps others. A weak link in this chain can always be found, and any of the links can be broken if you have pressure enough.[81]

Thus, when the commission of a deviant act is made visible by the victim and is transmitted to the rulers of the criminal justice system, or when the act is observed directly by agents of the law, the *fix* shields such visibility from other lawmakers and enforcers and members of the total society. Since the deviant acts of the professionals are not defined as highly visible by the law enforcers, as are those of the members of subcultures of violence, little opposition is found when *fall-dough* (bribe money) is offered.

In discussing the third dimension of social visibility, as it is observed by the society as a whole, a comment on the general theory of labeling is necessary. Becker has stated that "deviance is not a quality of the act the person commits, but rather a consequence of the application by others of rules and sanctions to an 'offender' ... deviant behavior is behavior that people so label."[82] The labeling orientation, as such, is plausible when viewing all societies over a period of time. But after the label has been successfully applied and an act has been defined as deviant, such deviance has been reified to be a quality of the act until a new set of definitions is applied. In this society activities embodied in the types of criminal behavior discussed have been successfully defined as deviant. In all cases visibility brought about the processes of social and legal definition regardless of the effectiveness of the enforcement of the rules. It is, however, the degree of visibility of the deviant act in the eyes of the total society that determines the vigor with which rules will be enforced.

We have seen that professional crime lacks a high degree of social visibility in the eyes of the victim and the forces of social control. The deviance ascribed to the professional thief is such, not because of any quality intrinsic to the professional deviant, but as a result of the labeling of acts which were perpetrated by more visible deviants—the amateur and habitual property offender. It is for this reason that the legal categories of deviance retain their labels, but the professional criminal continues to lack visibility. Victims and rule enforcers continue to shield the visibility of the professionals from the total society. Professional criminals, maintaining this shield, remain immune to the forces of social control. Immunity in turn perpetrates contact among members of the profession. The lack of molestation permits the development of a subculture and social organization aimed at maintaining that status quo—the lack of visibility. An intricate network of relationships and linguistic constructions is developed for the purpose of keeping out "outsiders"—amateur criminals. Codes of ethics are implemented for the purpose of maintaining the status quo from within. A dissemination of information regarding the fix, *fences* (receivers of stolen goods), and untrustworthy members of the profession emerges in order to maintain a defense system against the infiltration of outsiders. Codes of ethics, argot, self-segregation, isolation, and the dissemination of information represent the functional aspects of professional theft. It is essential to the group members that low visibility be maintained, and deviants from the "way of life" are looked upon as a threat. Since deviance is "the other side" of conformity, the professional who violates group norms is no longer accepted and protected, and he, too, becomes an outsider or "deviant" deviant.

Essential to the continuance of low visibility are self-segregation and isolation. The size and complexity of the city offer such advantages to the professional criminal. The city offers not only a highly mobile wealth upon which the thief may prey, but also anonymity and areas into which he may creep and remain unseen. The natural areas of the professional criminals are the "bad lands," submerged regions of disorganization and their underworlds of crime and vice. It is within the crime and vice areas that the professionals segregate themselves. In these sections of the city the social network of the thieves and fences maintains itself and remains isolated from the rest of society. The hangouts, meeting places, residential hotels, and rooming houses provide an arena in which the thief can maintain his social contacts. When arriving in a new and unfamiliar city, he naturally gravitates to that neighborhood.

Not only does the vice area represent a place of social contact, but it stands as a defined cultural territory for the total social system of *grifting* (professional thieving). The geographical location, the set of traditions, the occupational specialties and the common language represent boundaries, and as such they define "the contours of the niche they occupy in social space."[83] Furthermore, the vice area represents a location in which the thief is safe from outsiders—the forces of social coercion and control. Criminal districts, more often than not, are immune from such forces due to political corruption and patronage by nondeviant groups who view their taverns, brothels, and gambling houses as places of occasional gratification. The vice area is a highly visible entity, and its visibility is created by the prostitutes, homosexuals, and hoodlums who also gravitate to its confines. Visibility exists because of the subcultures of violence and pleasure houses which stand within its bounds. When the crusaders descend upon such an area, it is not the professional he tries to exterminate, but the hordes of property, organized, and public order criminals.

## SUGGESTED READINGS

ADLER, FREDA, *Sisters in Crime: The Rise of the New Female Criminal* (New York: McGraw-Hill, 1975).

AMIR, MENACHEM, *Patterns in Forcible Rape* (Chicago: University of Chicago Press, 1971).

BERNSTEIN, CARL, and WOODWARD, BOB, *All the President's Men* (New York: Warner, 1974).

CLINARD, MARSHALL B., and QUINNEY, RICHARD, *Criminal Behavior Systems: A Typology* (New York: Holt, Rinehart and Winston, 1973).

CRESSEY, DONALD R., *Theft of the Nation* (New York: Harper & Row, 1969).

CURTIS, LYNN A., *Criminal Violence: National Patterns and Behavior* (Lexington, Mass.: D. C. Heath, 1974).

INCIARDI, JAMES A., *Careers in Crime* (Chicago: Rand McNally, 1975).

MCKINNEY, JOHN C., *Constructive Typology and Social Theory* (New York: Appleton-Century-Crofts, 1966).

MORELAND, ROY, *The Law of Homicide* (Indianapolis: Bobbs-Merrill, 1952).

MORRIS, NORVAL, and HAWKINS, GORDON, *The Honest Politician's Guide to Crime Control* (Chicago: University of Chicago Press, 1970).

PETERSEN, DAVID M., and TRUZZI, MARCELLO, (eds.), *Criminal Life: Views from the Inside* (Englewood Cliffs, N.J.: Prentice-Hall, 1972).

SUTHERLAND, EDWIN H., *White Collar Crime* (New York: Dryden, 1949).

WOLFGANG, MARVIN E., *Patterns in Criminal Homicide* (Philadelphia: University of Pennsylvania Press, 1958).

# 6

# The Discovery of
# Criminal Justice in America

The term "criminal justice" does not refer to some metaphysical explanation of "right" and "wrong," but rather, it is a concept that incorporates the mechanisms through which violations of criminal statutes arc officially handled. More broadly, criminal justice in America exists for the control and prevention of crime, and as a "process" it involves those agencies and procedures structured for the management of both crime and the persons accused of violating the criminal law. As an organizational complex, criminal justice includes the agencies of law enforcement charged with the prevention of crime and the apprehension of criminal offenders and with the cross-purposes of maintaining "order" under the rule of law; it includes the court bureaucracies charged with determining the innocence or guilt of accused offenders and with the sentencing of convicted offenders; and it includes the network of "corrections" charged with the control, custody, supervision, and treatment of those convicted of crime.

The components of criminal justice—police, courts, and corrections —have a long and enduring history. The development of police systems can be traced to the latter part of ninth-century England when Alfred the Great organized the defense of his kingdom against a Danish invasion. Part of Alfred's strategy depended on internal stability. He instituted a system of *mutual pledge* through which ten families (*tithings*) assumed responsibility for the acts of their members, followed by a *hundred,* which was composed of ten tithings or one hundred families. The hundred was under the charge of a *constable,* and "hundreds" within a given geographical area were combined to form *shires*—administrative districts (now called counties) under royal authority governed by a *scirgerefa, shire-reeve,* or *sheriff.*[1] In urban areas, the *night watch* or *watch* system emerged for the protection of city streets during the nighttime hours. Instituted in England in 1233, this system represented the earliest metropolitan police force.[2] The night watch, although an ineffective measure for protection, persisted until the nineteenth century when the first modern police force was founded by Sir Robert Peel in London in 1829.[3] American police systems followed the pattern established by the British, and the first formally organized metropolitan police force in the United States appeared in New York City in 1845.[4]

Court systems are as old as perhaps civilization itself, but for many millennia they were of an inquisitorial nature and intricately tied to punishment and death. Under the *inquisitorial* system, the accused was considered guilty until he could prove himself innocent, and the assumption of guilt was the guiding factor. Inquisitional "justice" became manifest when the accused readily admitted his guilt, usually elicited through torture or other forms of corporal punishment. The system also relied on trials by battle or ordeal, which were based on the theory that if the accused were innocent some form of divine intervention would spare them from pain, suffering, and death.[5] By contrast, the *adversary* system presumed the innocence of the accused with the burden of proof placed on the court. It emerged as a contest between the accused and the state before an impartial judge.[6] The *adversary* system is grounded in the notion of "due process" guaranteed by the United States Supreme Court. *Due process of law* is a phrase impossible to define precisely, but one which asserts a fundamental principle of justice rather than a specific rule of law. It implies and comprehends the administration of laws which do not violate fundamental principles of private rights; it requires in each case an evaluation based on a disinterested inquiry, on a balanced order of facts exactly and fairly stated, on the detached consideration of conflicting claims, and on a judgment mindful of reconciling the needs of continuity and change in complex society. Or as Daniel Webster maintained, due process meant "... the law which hears before it condemns; which proceeds upon inquiry, and renders judgment only after trial."[7]

The history of "corrections" is tied to that of punishment. The various doctrines which circumscribed the desirability and object of punishment have been closely related to prevailing theories of crime and criminal responsibility. When the idea of diabolical possession dominated, conventional notions of punishment included exorcism, execution, or exile, for the purposes of placating a deity and protecting the community from further outrage. When crime was viewed as the willful act of a free moral agent, stress was placed on the idea of social revenge; crime was identified with sin and included acts of voluntary perversity which called for retaliation by group vengeance. With the development of the deterministic theories of crime causation, those deemed degenerate were incarcerated or segregated, and those considered capable of reformation were subjected to "correctional" treatment.

Enforcement, court process, and corrections, as such, have endured in the United States since its founding more than two centuries ago, yet the concept of *criminal justice* is of relatively recent origin. For almost two hundred years, ideas of crime control, reduction, prevention, and overall management were seemingly viewed as independent activities guided by alternative philosophical and pragmatic approaches. "Law enforcement" was an entity structured for "keeping the peace" and maintaining "order." The "administration of justice" was a mechanism for determining the culpability of those accused of violating the law, and punishment and reformation served to further protect society while extending to the offender an opportunity to pay retribution for his wrongdoing. The concept of "criminal justice" was offered in 1933 by Jerome Michael and Mortimer J. Adler in their discussion of the problems and methods of the administration of criminal law:

> We shall use the phrase "criminal justice" as an abbreviation for the phrase "the administration of criminal law." The elements of criminal justice are the criminal law and its enforcement.[8]

Or more specifically:

> It is obvious that the criminal law neither makes nor applies itself; it is made and enforced by men whom we call officials and who in one way or another have become society's representatives for those purposes. By criminal justice we shall mean nothing more pretentious than the administration of the criminal law as it exists at a given time. Viewed most broadly, the administration of the criminal law consists in the application of its treatment content to those who violate its behavior content. The processes of criminal justice therefore include all official activities in the detection of crime, the pursuit, apprehension and prosecution of criminals, and their treatment. . . .[9]

Michael and Adler were concerned with the purposes and goals of what they conceived of as "criminal justice." They were clearly not the inventors of the term, but they were among the first to recognize the need for an integration of the various components involved in the administration of the criminal law. In addition they viewed research as a possible mechanism for defining the gaps and requirements for structuring a unified criminal justice machinery. Yet little of what Michael and Adler had suggested was heard, for their comments were made at a time when kidnappings and bank robberies competed for the national spotlight. Prohibition had been repealed, and many of those from the illegal liquor trades were stepping into other forms of predatory behavior. It was also a time of depression, when in addition to the economic hardships on the nation as a whole, there were many committed to terrorizing both the wealthy and the banking industry. In March 1932, for example, the son of aviation pioneer Charles A. Lindbergh was kidnapped, a case which received worldwide attention. The following year, oilman Charles F. Urschel was kidnapped from his home in Oklahoma City by Alfred L. Bates and George "Machine Gun" Kelly, the man who is credited with nicknaming FBI agents G-men.[10] There was the 14-month period in 1933 and 1934 when John Dillinger robbed more than a dozen banks, led raids on midwestern police stations and city halls, and engineered the escapes of many of his friends from various correctional institutions. And in addition to the more infamous activities of Bonnie Parker and Clyde Barrow, there were the exploits of the Barker-Karpis gang which operated virtually unchallenged in robbing banks, exterminating police officers, and kidnapping business executives.[11]

The crime wave of the 1930s was followed by World War II, and interest was focused on espionage and internal security. And in the 1950s the issue was organized crime and the perceived menace of communist infiltration into American government and politics. But the concept of "criminal justice" was to be revived, primarily as an outgrowth of the nation's "war on crime" initiated during the mid-1960s.

## THE EMERGENCE OF "CRIMINAL JUSTICE"

The notion of "criminal justice" was preceded by "law and order," a highly explosive political slogan which had emerged during the early part of the decade. "Law and order" became a shorthand term for a generalized fear of the violence and demonstrations surrounding the civil rights and antiwar movements and for the concern over street crime and sexual freedom. "Law and order" was the theme of Barry Goldwater's presidential campaign in 1964, and although he lost the election, it became ingrained in the public's perception of crime.

Always quick to sense certain types of public uneasiness, Congress and President Lyndon Johnson responded on July 25, 1965, with the establishment of the *President's Commission on Law Enforcement and the Administration of Justice.* And even before the findings of the Commission were announced two years later, Johnson offered a glimpse of a strategy for his "war on crime":

> The problems of crime bring us together. Even as we join in action, we know that there can be no instant victory. Ancient evils do not yield to easy victory. We cannot limit our efforts to enemies we can see. We must, with equal resolve, seek out new knowledge, new techniques, and new understanding.[12]

The general report of the President's Commission, *The Challenge of Crime in a Free Society,* after hundreds of meetings, tens of thousands of interviews, and numerous national surveys, offered more than 200 specific proposals.[13] Yet much of what the Commission recommended was disappointing—in part a restatement of what had been offered by the Wickersham Commission almost four decades before. More formally known as the National Commission on Law Observance and Enforcement and chaired by the former United States Attorney General George W. Wickersham, this earlier Commission had been established by an act of Congress in 1929 and represented the fulfillment of President Herbert Hoover's campaign promise to conduct a thorough inquiry into the enforcement of the prohibition laws. In fifteen volumes and more than four thousand pages, the findings of the Commission extended beyond the prohibition issue to the causes of crime, criminal statistics, the administration of justice, and corrections.[14] In the areas of statistics, the administration of justice, and corrections, specifically, the recommendations of the Wickersham Commission in 1931 and those of the President's Commission in 1967 were in many ways similar.

The President's Commission did, however, recognize that procedures in the enforcement and administration of law could be even more relative and problematic than the very concept of crime. It has been demonstrated, for example, that the nature of crime can be exceedingly

variable, and that the content of criminal codes and criminal definitions reflect change and diversity from one jurisdiction to another. Yet
from the perspective of a given jurisdiction, official definitions of what
constitutes crime are generally static—acts in violation of specific criminal laws. When "crime," as such, falls within the spectrum of administrative management and control, however, its statically defined
character becomes subject to individual interpretation. Law enforcement agents interpret the definition of a situation to determine if a law
has been indeed violated. Prosecutors and defense attorneys interpret
the law and social situation of the alleged offense to determine which
laws were violated and to assess the culpability of the accused. Juries
interpret the information provided by the police and courts to determine the innocence or the extent of guilt of the defendant. Judges
interpret the evidence presented and the character of the offender to
determine the nature and type of sentence and to insure that "due
process" has been achieved. And finally, correctional personnel interpret their knowledge of law, social science, correctional administration,
and human behavior to determine the appropriate custodial, correctional, rehabilitative, and punitive treatment for each convicted criminal. Within this context, the Commission recognized that "justice" was
a nebulous superstructure of codes, directives, functions, agencies, and
institutions which persisted under the leadership of the individual
interpretations of each actor in its every phase. And further, it was clear
that the various components in the administration of justice were acting independently of one another—police were concerned only with
the apprehension of criminals and utilized the court system simply as
a dumping ground; the courts, in turn, were concerned only with the
processing of cases and utilized corrections as their terminal point. In
this behalf, the President's Commission "discovered" the concept of
"criminal justice." It was described in terms of a "system"—an orderly
flow of managerial decision-making that would begin with the investigation of a criminal offense and end with a correctional placement. As
such, the criminal justice system was conceived of as:

> . . . an apparatus society uses to enforce the standards of conduct necessary
> to protect individuals and the community. It operates by apprehending,
> prosecuting, convicting, and sentencing those members of the community
> who violate the basic rules of group existence. The action taken against
> lawbreakers is designed to serve three purposes beyond the immediately
> punitive one. It removes dangerous people from the community; it deters
> others from criminal behavior; and it gives society an opportunity to at-
> tempt to transform lawbreakers into law-abiding citizens.[15]

## CRIMINAL JUSTICE AS A "SYSTEM"

Realizing that criminal justice in America was composed of a series of bureaucracies operating along alternative and often conflicting paths, the President's Commission also stressed the need for some orderly integration:

> The criminal justice system has three separately organized parts—the police, the courts, and corrections—and each has distinct tasks. However, these parts are by no means independent of each other. What each one does and how it does it has a direct effect on the work of the others. The courts must deal, and can only deal, with those whom the police arrest; the business of corrections is with those delivered to it by the courts. How successfully corrections reforms convicts determines whether they will once again become police business and influences the sentences the judges pass; police activities are subject to court scrutiny and are often determined by court decisions. And so reforming or reorganizing any part or procedure of the system changes other parts or procedures. Furthermore, the criminal process, the method by which the system deals with individual cases, is not a hodgepodge of random actions. It is rather a continuum—an orderly progression of events—some of which, like arrest and trial, are highly visible and some of which, though of great importance, occur out of public view. A study of the system must begin by examining it as a whole.[16]

This, of course, was an idealized concept on the part of the Commission, for the notion of criminal justice operating as a "system" was, and still is, a myth. The unity of purpose and organized interrelationships among police, courts, and corrections are beset with inefficiency, fallout, and failure. In fact this lack of coordination and failure of purpose has been so apparent that the American Bar Association has referred to criminal justice as a "nonsystem."[17] Yet the Commission did offer a simplified view of the flow of criminal justice processing, demonstrating the stages throughout the system and the points at which the accused could be diverted, dismissed, acquitted, discharged, or loop back to an earlier part of the system. In what has become perhaps the most popular representation of the criminal justice flow, Figure I illustrates the various points in the process, indicating, from entry to exit, the nature and direction of client movement. Felonies, misdemeanors, petty offenses, and juvenile cases follow somewhat different paths, and are shown separately in the diagram, but in the descriptions of the major points in the process offered below, these are taken collectively.

*Investigation.* The investigation phase of the criminal justice process begins when a crime becomes known to the police—known through

# A GENERAL VIEW OF

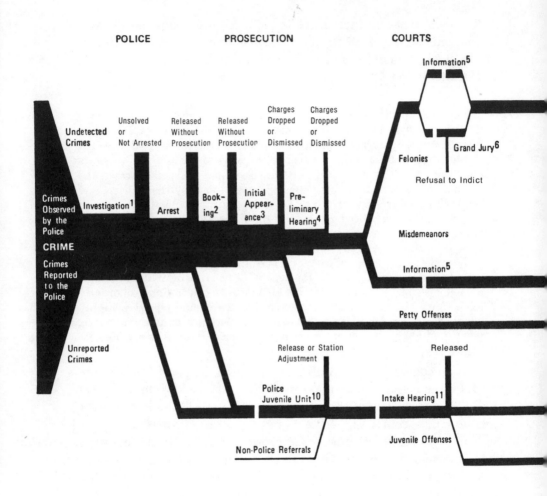

**POLICE**  **PROSECUTION**  **COURTS**

Information[5]

Undetected Crimes

Unsolved or Not Arrested

Released Without Prosecution

Released Without Prosecution

Charges Dropped or Dismissed

Charges Dropped or Dismissed

Grand Jury[6]

Felonies

Refusal to Indict

Crimes Observed by the Police

Investigation[1]

Arrest

Booking[2]

Initial Appearance[3]

Preliminary Hearing[4]

**CRIME**

Crimes Reported to the Police

Misdemeanors

Information[5]

Petty Offenses

Unreported Crimes

Release or Station Adjustment

Released

Police Juvenile Unit[10]

Intake Hearing[11]

Non-Police Referrals

Juvenile Offenses

[1] May continue until trial.

[2] Administrative record of arrest. First step at which temporary release on bail may be available.

[3] Before magistrate, commissioner, or justice of peace. Formal notice of charge, advice of rights. Bail set. Summary trials for petty offenses usually conducted here without further processing.

[4] Preliminary testing of evidence against defendant. Charge may be reduced. No separate preliminary hearing for misdemeanors in some systems.

[5] Charge filed by prosecutor on basis of information submitted by police or citizens. Alternative to grand jury indictment; often used in felonies, almost always in misdemeanors.

# THE CRIMINAL JUSTICE SYSTEM*

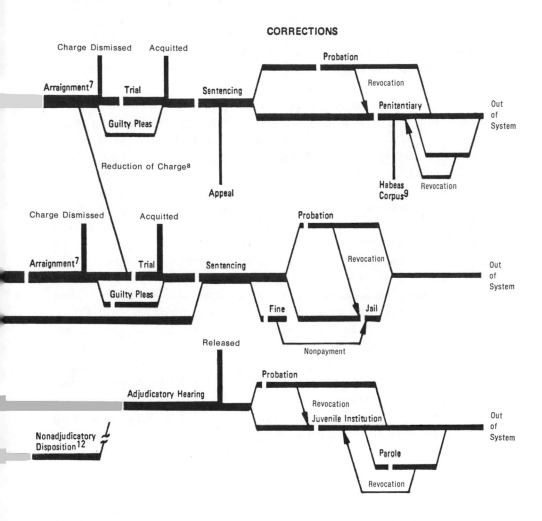

**CORRECTIONS**

Charge Dismissed    Acquitted

Arraignment[7]    Trial    Sentencing    Probation    Revocation    Penitentiary    Out of System

Guilty Pleas

Reduction of Charge[8]

Appeal    Habeas Corpus[9]    Revocation

Charge Dismissed    Acquitted    Probation

Arraignment[7]    Trial    Sentencing    Revocation    Out of System

Guilty Pleas    Fine    Jail

Released    Nonpayment

Probation

Adjudicatory Hearing    Revocation    Juvenile Institution    Out of System

Nonadjudicatory Disposition[12]    Parole

Revocation

---

[6]Reviews whether government evidence is sufficient to justify trial. Some states have no grand-jury system; others seldom use it.

[7]Appearance for plea; defendant elects trial by judge or jury (if available); counsel for indigent usually appointed here in felonies. often not at all in other cases.

[8]Charge may be reduced at any time prior to trial in return for plea of guilty or for other reasons.

[9]Challenge on constitutional grounds to legality of detention. May be sought at any point in process.

[10]Police often hold informal hearings and dismiss or adjust many cases without further processing.

[11]Probation officer decides desirability of further court action.

[12]Welfare agency, social services, counseling, medical care, etc., for cases not requiring adjudicatory handling.

either reports to or observations by a law enforcement agency or official. The police, as such, represent the frontline agency which determines, in the majority of instances, whether the criminal justice
process should be invoked. In circumstances where crimes have been
reported, investigation includes an examination of the scene of the
crime, a search for physical evidence, interviews of the victim and
possible witnesses, a determination if a crime has actually been committed, and if so, the initial quest for the perpetrator. In the case of
public order or "victimless crimes"—disorderly conduct, vagrancy,
drunkenness, and varieties of prostitution and drug law violations—the
offenses are often witnessed directly by the police and the investigation
phase becomes compacted into the observers' on-the-spot determination as to whether the law has been broken. In certain categories of
crime like vice, gambling, and illicit drug sales, investigative techniques involving informers, surveillance, and undercover personnel
may be utilized prior to the commission of a suspected offense, for the
purpose of observing the offender during the criminal activity. In addition there are law enforcement agencies at the local, state, and federal
levels which become involved in long-term investigations when
"crime" is not necessarily known, but strongly suspected. This is most
typical, for example, of enforcement bodies of the federal government
such as the Federal Bureau of Investigation (FBI), the Drug Enforcement Administration (DEA), the Internal Revenue Service (IRS), the
Customs Service, and the Postal Inspection Service. Investigation of this
order has been common in the strike force activities of the Organized
Crime and Racketeering Section (OCR) of the United States Department
of Justice.[18] Finally, in all types of investigative process, the operations
of investigation can continue beyond the point at which the preliminary evidence necessary for an arrest has been gathered.

   *Arrest.* When the investigation reveals that a crime has been committed, an arrest may be made. The arrest is simply the action of taking
an individual into custody, and it represents the initial step towards
prosecution. In most jurisdictions, an arrest warrant is necessary in
misdemeanor cases, unless the crime has been observed by the police
officer. The warrant is a written order giving authorization to arrest,
and is typically issued by a magistrate. Felony arrests can be made in
the absence of a warrant if the officer has "reasonable" certainty that
the person being arrested is indeed the offender.

   This notion of reasonable certainty provides police with a considerably wide latitude in arrest practices. It designates law enforcement

agents as the chief interpreters of the law and allows them wide-ranging discretionary powers. Yet police, within this circumstance, must nevertheless be cognizant of due process of law—an aspect of law enforcement that has been traditionally ignored in many arrest situations.[19] The neglect of due process on the part of police has generally been in the areas of unlawful arrest, illegal search and seizure, unlawful detention, and inadmissible confessions.

Unlawful arrests occur when police take individuals into custody on "suspicion," in the absence of a specific charge or when they cannot relate the arrest to a specific crime. This phenomenon often involves the mass arrest of individuals with prior criminal records (with the hope of finding evidence of crimes in the possession of those detained), and it has occurred with those who actively support political causes with which the police may not agree or with certain minority groups that are deemed as symbolic lawbreakers. In one San Francisco study, for example, it was found that members of juvenile gangs were often arrested for "disrespectful behavior" rather than for specific crimes.[20] When the youths reacted with defiance and hostility, they were repeatedly arrested for such vague and minor offenses as loitering, suspicion of rape, or disturbing the peace.

Illegal search and seizure, a common police activity in drug cases[21] and other crimes, is in direct violation of the Fourth Amendment to the Constitution of the United States, which reads:

> ... the right of the people to be secure in their persons, houses, papers, and effects, against unreasonable searches and seizures, shall not be violated, and no warrants shall issue, but upon probable cause, supported by oath or affirmation, and particularly describing the place to be searched, and the persons or things to be seized.

Under the law, police may search a suspect during the course of an arrest, but search and seizure not incident to an arrest requires a search warrant. Search and seizure of an illegal nature was extremely widespread at the state and local levels until the case involving *Mapp* v. *Ohio* in 1961 brought the issue into public focus.[22] In the *Mapp* case, the defendant was *suspected* of possessing "lewd and lascivious books, pictures, and photographs." Police officers arrived at Mapp's home demanding entrance, but after telephoning her attorney, she refused to admit them without a search warrant. Three hours later, after additional enforcement agents arrived on the scene, the house was forcibly entered. Mapp's attorney arrived, but the police refused to allow him either to enter the house or to see his client. After the officers had entered her home, the defendant asked to see the warrant. One of the officers produced a paper which he claimed was a warrant and which Mapp grabbed and tucked in her clothing. A struggle ensued, during which the "warrant" was forcibly taken from her. The house was then searched, and the obscene materials were found. Mapp was convicted on the basis of the seized evidence since a prior ruling maintained that the Fourth Amendment guarantee was applicable only in the federal courts. Under appeal, however, the Supreme Court reexamined the issue and held that all evidence obtained by illegal searches and seizures would be inadmissable in state courts as well.

Since police rely heavily on admissions and confessions in the clearing of cases, they often engage in prolonged and persuasive interrogations of their suspects in an effort to obtain evidence, admissions against the interest of the accused, and, if possible, confessions. This can result in unreasonably long detention, without the benefit of counsel, and in the use of brutality. In *Brown* v. *Mississippi* the Supreme Court ruled that confessions elicited through the use of brutality were not admissible as evidence,[23] but it was the case of *Miranda* v. *Arizona* in 1966 that more firmly established the legal rights of the accused.[24] In the *Miranda* case the defendant was arrested on charges of kidnapping and rape, identified by the complaining witnesses, and interrogated, after which he confessed to the crimes. He was convicted on the basis of his confession, but in an appeal he maintained that his civil rights had been violated since the police failed to advise him that he had a right to have an attorney present during the interrogation. Miranda's conviction was set aside, and the Supreme Court handed down the "Miranda warning," rules which required that as soon as a person was placed in custody, and before any interrogation, the police must advise the accused that:

—he has the right to remain silent;
—anything he says may be used against him in a court of law;
—he has the right to speak to an attorney and to have his attorney present during his questioning; and,
—if he desires counsel and cannot provide his own, one will be provided him without charge before questioning.

*Booking.* Booking is the administrative record of an arrest and may occur before or after questioning. In the actual booking process, the accused's name, time and place of arrest, and the arrest charge are entered into a police log. Booking can also include fingerprinting and photographing of the suspect. At this point the law requires that the accused be taken before some judicial authority for temporary release consideration. *Bail,* the most common mechanism of temporary release, involves the posting of financial security by the accused, or by someone acting in his behalf, guaranteeing that he will appear for trial. At the bail hearing, a decision is reached as to whether the suspect is likely to flee the jurisdiction or otherwise fail to appear at future proceedings. The level of bail, if granted, is determined according to the severity of the crime.

The Eighth Amendment to the Constitution provides that "... *excessive bail shall not be required ...,"* but despite this constitutional guarantee, there have been recurring criticisms of the system of bail administration. There has been no consistent mechanism of setting bail amounts from one jurisdiction to another; the reliance upon money as a means of insuring appearance created a multi-million dollar business subject to numerous abuses; and, since bail has a monetary base, it discriminates against the indigent causing their detention in substandard facilities.[25] Commenting on a number of these difficulties, former Attorney General Ramsey Clark noted:

> ... Over the years we have deprived hundreds of thousands of people, never convicted of any crime, of their liberty because they were poor. The rich, the mobster, the well-connected—they all made bail. Only the poor remained in jail, and as a result jobs were lost, families separated, and the best—sometimes only—chance to obtain evidence, find witnesses and prepare a defense was gone.
> ... Hundreds of thousands were released after weeks or more in jail without trial. As to some, formal charges were never filed and later dismissed. Many prisoners served longer awaiting trial than the maximum sentence provided for the crime with which they were charged.[26]

In 1961, as an alternative to bail, the Vera Institute of Justice initiated a *release on recognizance* (ROR) program in New York City. Known as the Manhattan Bail Project, it recommended the release of an individual on personal recognizance (obligation), when satisfied that there was no substantial risk that the accused would fail to appear for trial. There was no cash bail involved. As of August 31, 1965, more than 3,500 persons had been released on the program, and of these, some 98.4 percent returned to court when required.[27] Subsequent projects have demonstrated the benefits of the ROR concept, and it has widely replaced bail in many jurisdictions.

*Initial Appearance.* Due process of law requires that within a "reasonable" (not extreme, arbitrary, or capricious) time after arrest, a suspect must be brought before a magistrate to be given a formal notice of the charge for which he is being held. At this initial appearance, such notice is made, and the accused is advised of his rights. Although temporary release can occur in some cases at the booking phase, release on recognizance or bail is generally established at this point. In extremely minor offenses, such as "drunk and disorderly," summary trials and sentencing are conducted at the initial appearance, with no further court processing. In all cases, regardless of the level of their severity, the charges can be dropped or dismissed at this appearance if the presiding magistrate determines that there is not sufficient cause to warrant continued processing.

*Preliminary Hearing.* Many jurisdictions have abolished the initial appearance and proceed directly to a preliminary hearing. At this procedural step, the accused is advised of the charges against him and the formal complaint is read. The purposes of this hearing are to:

—determine whether a crime has been committed;
—determine whether the evidence establishes probable cause to believe that the defendant committed it;
—determine the existence of probable cause for which a warrant was issued for the defendant's arrest;
—inquire into the reasonableness of the arrest and search and the compliance of the executing officer with the requirements of the warrant; and,
—determine the appropriate bail or temporary release if not already addressed.

Since this preliminary hearing is not a trial to determine innocence or guilt, the defendant will not be asked to make a plea. However, since this phase does involve a preliminary testing of evidence, the charges can be reduced, dropped, or dismissed. The defendant is advised of his right to counsel, and if he decides to exercise this right, the proceedings will likely not continue until legal assistance has been obtained or appointed. Finally, a defendant may waive his right to the preliminary hearing and proceed directly to the next phase of judicial processing. However, most defense attorneys will insist on the use of this hearing as a tactic for gaining insight into the strengths and weaknesses of the state's case.

*Information or Indictment.* Information or indictment relates to the formal legal mechanism that can send a suspect to trial. The difference between the two is a procedural one—an information may be filed by a prosecutor, based on an investigation conducted by his office, while an indictment requires the concurrence of a *grand jury.*

The grand jury originated in twelfth-century England to determine whether the evidence available to the prosecution warranted the trial of an accused,[28] and it evolved into an instrument for the protection of the people against arbitrary accusation by the state. Grand juries are currently required in the United States in most jurisdictions east of the Mississippi River, and they range in size from five to twenty-three members. Following the early English concept, American grand juries make a determination, based on evidence submitted by the prosecution, as to whether there is sufficient indication to warrant a trial. The decisions of a grand jury need not be unanimous, but in most jurisdictions a two-thirds or three-fourths majority is required to return or refuse an indictment. If the majority decision is reached, a "true bill" is signed and the indictment would contain the following information:

—the type and nature of the offense;
—the specific statute alleged to have been violated;
—the nature and elements of the offense charged;
—the time and place of the occurrence of the crime;
—the name and address of the accused, or if not known, a description
  sufficient to identify the accused with reasonable certainty;
—the signature of the foreman of the grand jury showing that it has been
  returned as a true bill; and,
—the names of all codefendants in the offense charged, as well as the
  number of counts against them.[29]

Since the grand jury does not weigh the evidence presented, its finding is by no means equivalent to a conviction. Should this tribunal return a "no bill," that is, should it fail to reach the required majority vote and thus refuse an indictment, the accused would be released.

In recent years there have been some severe criticisms of the grand jury system in America. While it was originally established some seven centuries ago as a citizens' tribunal to protect civil liberties and prevent arbitrary accusation by the state, it has been reformed in some cases into a mechanism for the expedient prosecution of criminal and political behavior:

The nationwide grand jury network is emerging as a "chosen instrument" of an Administration strategy to curb dissent and to intimidate and demoralize radicals. This strategy is so effective because federal prosecuting officials—who themselves have no power of subpoena—are using the coercive powers of the grand jury for police and intelligence purposes.[30]

The subpoena is a writ or process issued by the clerk of a court compelling the attendance of a witness in a judicial proceeding, and from its use grand juries can indeed gather evidence and intelligence information through the testimony of witnesses. The major difficulty in this process emerges when, on the basis of testimony before a grand jury, without the protection of counsel, witnesses can be sentenced to prison for contempt, or they can be charged with a crime. Such a process is in violation of the Fifth Amendment to the Constitution which states that "*No person . . . shall be compelled in any criminal case to be a witness against himself,*" yet it is currently being employed in government inquiries into the activities of Patricia Hearst and the Symbionese Liberation Army.[31]

*Arraignment.* Following the return of an indictment as a "true bill" or the filing of an information by a prosecutor, the preliminary proceedings of the trial court begin. The first is the arraignment, at which the accused is taken before a judge, the formal information or indictment is read, and the defendant is asked to enter a plea—guilty, not guilty, *nolo contendere,* or he may stand mute. If a guilty plea is entered, the judge has the responsibility of determining if it was made voluntarily and if the defendant has a full understanding of the possible consequences of his decision. If the judge is satisfied, the defendant is scheduled for sentencing; if not, the judge can refuse to accept the plea and enter a not guilty plea into the record. When a not guilty plea is entered, the defendant is notified of his rights, a determination is made as to his competence to stand trial, counsel is appointed if indigency is apparent, and in some jurisdictions the defendant can elect for a trial by judge or a trial by jury. Should the defendant enter a plea of *nolo contendere*—literally "I do not wish to contend" or "no contest"—a plea of guilty is implied.[32] In some jurisdictions the *nolo contendere* option is not available to defendants, and in others, it must be approved by both the prosecutor and the judge. And while it has the same effect as a guilty plea, it also has considerable legal significance in that an admission of guilt is not present and cannot be introduced in later trials. It was this *nolo contendere* plea that the former Vice President Spiro T. Agnew entered when tried during the early 1970s for accepting illegal payoffs.[33] And finally, should the defendant remain mute, an automatic plea of not guilty is entered by the court. Its advantage rests in the fact that the accused is not waiving his right to protest any irregularities or defects which may have occurred in earlier phases of the criminal justice proceedings; by contrast, in some jurisdictions the entering of a plea may waive this right and imply the defendant's full acceptance of the jurisdiction of the trial court.[34]

*The Guilty Plea.* Lawyer-sociologist Abraham S. Blumberg has argued that negotiated guilty pleas have become common due to crowded court calendars, and from this has emerged a process that coerces defendants to plead guilty:

> ... the rational-instrumental goals of the court organization, in its urgent demand for guilty pleas, have produced a bargain-counter, assembly-line system of criminal justice which is incompatible with traditional due process. The dilemma is sharpened by the fact that the concern for the individual envisioned and postulated by the rules of due process in determining guilt or innocence, is no longer present at this crucial level. Instead, the concern, if any, appears to be the post-guilt, pre-sentence stage, while the actual determination of guilt is arrived at through perfunctory ministerial procedures which have become the hallmark of the criminal court's rationality.[35]

What Blumberg was referencing is *plea-bargaining* or "copping-a-plea." In plea-bargaining, the prosecutor and defense attorney discuss the case and work out a "deal" that will be offered to the judge for consideration. The prosecutor may agree to drop the charges if the defendant will inform on other criminals, or there will be a promise of leniency in sentencing if the accused pleads guilty to a charge less serious than the original. It has advantages in that courts do not have the resources to try all cases. From the perspective of a defendant who is knowingly guilty of the offense, it affords him the opportunity of being convicted and sentenced on a less serious crime—manslaughter, for example, reduced to assault. By contrast, however, plea negotiation can coerce an unsophisticated and perhaps innocent defendant into pleading guilty, it can extend inadequate sentencing to dangerous offenders, and it can result in unnecessarily heavier sentences for those who reject the bargaining process.[36] Currently, approximately 90 percent of all persons who are accused of criminal offenses plead guilty after the decision is made to prosecute.[37] This suggests that in the majority of criminal cases, the prosecutor makes most of the decisions regarding innocence or guilt and hence, acts as de facto judge.

*Trial.* In the small percentage of cases that actually go to trial, whether a trial by judge or by judge and jury, the accused can be found guilty only if the evidence proves, "beyond a reasonable doubt," that he actually committed the specific offense in question. And there are rules as to what kinds of evidence can be presented, how it can be obtained, and the way it may be interpreted.[38] Yet there is much that occurs even before the trial actually begins. The defendant may employ a number of *motions* in an effort to have the case dismissed or to gain a particular advantage in the preparation of the case or the introduction of evidence at the trial. A motion is an application made to a court or judge for the purpose of obtaining an order or rule directing something to be done in the favor of the applicant.[39] There are many kinds of motions, but the more common ones that appear in criminal proceedings include:

—*motion for a bill of particulars*—a motion by the defense requesting that the state provide additional facts in the indictment or information so that the accused can develop his defense;[40]
—*motion to suppress or quash evidence*—a motion by the defense attempting to have evidence gathered by the state excluded from consideration;[41]
—*motion for change of venue*—a motion requesting to move the trial to another jurisdiction, generally based on a defendant's contention that due to prejudice of some type, a fair trial could not be obtained in the particular locale of the court;[42]
—*motion for continuance*—a motion requesting that the trial be postponed for a given length of time.[43]

In the event that the defendant elects for a trial by jury, the pretrial activities also include the process of jury selection. The trial by jury is the best known feature of American justice, despite its limited use. Surprisingly, however, although a jury trial is a fundamental constitutional right, it was only as recent as 1968 that the U. S. Supreme Court extended this right to proceedings in state courts.[44] The selection of jurors must satisfy the minimum standards of due process—they must be a representative sample of the community drawn without discrimination based on race, sex, religion, or national origin, and they must meet specific requirements laid down by the particular jurisdiction. Both the defense and the prosecution are then given an opportunity to examine each prospective juror to determine if any may have already formed an opinion as to guilt or innocence, or be prejudiced, biased, or otherwise unable to fairly and impartially perform their duties. Jurors may be excluded by a *challenge for cause,* where the prosecution or defense indicates the specific reason for exclusion, or by a *peremptory challenge,* which requires no reason or explanation.[45]

After a jury has been selected, or in the case of a trial by judge, the trial proceeds as follows:

1. *Opening statements by prosecution.* The prosecutor outlines the state's case, how the state will introduce witnesses, and physical evidence to prove the guilt of the accused.
2. *Opening statements by defense.* The defense, if it elects to do so, explains how it plans to introduce witnesses and evidence in its own behalf.
3. *Presentation of state's case.* The state calls its witnesses to establish the elements of the crime and to introduce physical evidence; the prosecutor accomplishes this through *direct examination* of the witnesses, followed by their *cross-examination* by the defense.
4. *Presentation of the defense's case.* The defense may open with a *motion for dismissal* on the grounds that the state failed to prove the defendant guilty "beyond a reasonable doubt"; if the judge concurs, the case is dismissed, and the accused is released; if the judge rejects the motion, the defense case proceeds in the same manner as the state's presentation.
5. *Prosecutor's rebuttal.* The prosecutor may elect to present new witnesses and evidence, following the format of the state's original presentation.
6. Defense surrebuttal. The defense may again make a motion for dismissal; if denied, it, too, can introduce new evidence and witnesses.
7. *Closing statements.* The prosecutor, followed by the defense attorney, make closing arguments which sum up their cases and the deductions that can be made from the evidence and testimony.
8. *Charging the jury.* In jury trials, the judge instructs the jury as to possible verdicts and charges them to retire to the jury room to consider the facts of the case, to deliberate on the testimony, and to return a just verdict.
9. *Return of the verdict.* Once the jury has reached a decision, they return to the courtroom with a verdict which is read aloud by a member of the court. The jury may be *polled,* at the request of either the defense or the prosecution, whereby each member is asked individually as to whether the verdict announced is his or her individual verdict.[46]

*Post-Trial Motions.* Should the defendant be *acquitted,* that is, found not guilty, he is immediately released and the case drops out of the system. If a guilty verdict has been returned, most jurisdictions allow the accused to file a motion for a new trial or to set the judgment of the jury aside. This motion is generally filed by the defense on the grounds that:

—the state failed to charge an offense in the indictment;
—the court lacked proper jurisdiction in the case;
—the jury was guilty of misconduct in its deliberation;
—the court made some judgmental error in the presentation of evidence, examination of witnesses, or in overruling objections; or,
—the instructions to the jury were inappropriate or improper.[47]

The trial judge has the option to grant or deny the post-trial motions. In the majority of cases such motions are denied, but new trials have been granted at this level of the criminal justice process.

*Sentencing.* Prior to actual sentencing, a *presentence investigation* may be conducted. Such investigations are mandatory in many states for felony cases and are conducted in some misdemeanor actions. They are undertaken by the jurisdiction's probation department, and they represent a summary of the defendant's present offense, previous criminal record, family situation, neighborhood environment, school and educational history, employment record, physical and mental health, habits, and associates and participational activities.[48] The report of the investigation may also contain comments about the offender's remorse and recommendations for sentencing by the victim, the prosecutor, the district attorney, and the officer who conducted the investigation.[49]

Although presentence investigations are not mandatory in all jurisdictions, they have become widely used due to the many purposes they serve:

—by providing a detailed description of the offender and his social circumstances they aid the court in determining an appropriate sentence;
—they aid probation and parole officers in their supervision of offenders;
—they assist correctional personnel in their classification, treatment, and release programs;
—they furnish parole boards with useful information for release decision-making; and,
—they can serve as a data base for systematic research.[50]

The alternatives for sentencing are numerous, ranging from fines or suspended sentences for minor offenses, to probation, imprisonment, or even death as the cases become more serious. The two most common sentences, however, are probation and incarceration. Probation is a sentence, not involving confinement, which imposes conditions and retains authority in the sentencing court to modify the conditions of sentence, or to resentence the offender if he violates the conditions.[51] The probationer serves a determined period of time in the community under the supervision of a probation officer and subject to a series of conditions. These conditions can include mandates to report to the officer at specified intervals, maintain steady employment, attend a counseling or therapy program, and perhaps pay restitution to the victim of the crime. The violation of these or other conditions can result in a revocation of probation, and the offender is then resentenced to a period of incarceration.

Sentencing to a penitentiary can take the form of a *definite sentence,* which is for a stated period of time, e.g. 20 years. The *indeterminate sentence,* which most states employ, has a stated minimum and maximum length, e.g. five to ten years. Some indeterminate sentences, often referred to as *indefinite sentences,* have no minimum or maximum length. In New York, for example, under the sexual psychopath laws, an offender can receive the indefinite sentence of one day to life.

The most severe form of sentencing is, of course, the *death penalty,* and it is perhaps the most highly debated issue in correctional processing. The arguments in its favor have been ones of retribution, economy, protection, and deterrence. Those opposed to the death penalty have maintained that it is cruel and unusual punishment, and that capital punishment does not deter others from committing crimes. Much of the debate has circumscribed philosophical and moral issues, and currently, the controversy continues in the courts and legislature.[52]

In addition to the controversy over the death penalty, there has been much discussion of sentencing practices in general. The arguments have focused on the inappropriateness of incarceration as a correctional tool, the disparities in sentence length, and the ineffectiveness of correctional treatment.[53]

*Appeal.* Defendants found guilty in a criminal trial may appeal their conviction to some higher court. The appeal process is generally regarded as a continuation of the original case rather than as the inception of a new action. It is normally confined to a consideration of the record which comes from the court of original jurisdiction, with no new testimony taken. Appeals are based on claims that the rules of procedure (due process) were not properly followed, that the statute proscribing the behavior that resulted in the charge was unconstitutional, or that the sentence imposed was cruel and unusual.

*Parole.* Offenders sentenced to a correctional institution become eligible for parole after a portion of their sentence has been served. Parole can be defined as the release of an offender from the institutional setting, after he has served a part of his term, under the continued custody of the state and under conditions that permit his reincarceration in the event of their violation.[54] Parole might be considered as an extension of the rehabilitative aspect of the prison and as a method of reintegrating the offender into the community. It is also a mechanism for protecting the community since it continues the supervision of the offender after his release from the institution. Yet there are many difficulties with parole. Parole policies have been accused of being unfair and discriminating, parole decision-making is often arbitrary and haphazard, and parole supervision is readily deemed ineffective. And finally, since parole officers in many jurisdictions have been undertrained yet required to supervise large numbers of parolees and with inadequate resources, the utility of parole in many circumstances has been brought into serious question. The majority of offenders in institutions are paroled, however, and a significant portion of these finish their maximum sentence while in the community, at which point they exit from the criminal justice process.[55]

*Pardon.* The majority of convicted offenders exit from criminal justice processing and management through the payment of a fine or the expiration of their sentence. Termination can also come from a pardon, which is a "forgiveness" for the crime committed and serves to bar subsequent prosecution. The power to pardon is limited to the President of the United States and to state governors. These chief executives also have the authority to *commute* a sentence to a less severe one, or to delay the execution of a sentence by *reprieve.*

## THE RISE OF CRIMINAL JUSTICE

The President's Commission's conceptualization of the criminal justice process as a "system" was only the beginning of the movement that gave substance and growth to criminal justice. In 1965 the Office of Law Enforcement Assistance (OLEA) was created within the Justice Department to make federal funds available to states, localities, and private organizations to improve methods of law enforcement, court administration, and prison operations.[56] The act creating this agency was the first federal law to provide local government with funds for the improvement of criminal justice; yet funding for all practical purposes was limited. In 1968, however, the Omnibus Crime Control and Safe Streets Act became effective. The new act was severely condemned by many, for its Title III gave federal and local officials the right to place wiretaps and "bugs" on anyone who had committed, was committing, or was about to commit a crime punishable by a year or more in prison.[57] Title I of the Act, however, replaced the OLEA with the Law Enforcement Assistance Administration (LEAA)—the largest criminal justice bureaucracy in the nation. At the outset, the purpose of LEAA was made clear:

> The mission of LEAA is to reduce crime and delinquency by channeling federal financial aid to state and local governments, to conduct research in methods of improving law enforcement and criminal justice, to fund efforts to upgrade the educational level of law enforcement personnel, to develop applications of statistical research and applied systems analysis in law enforcement, and to develop broad policy guidelines for both the short- and long-range improvement of the nation's criminal justice system as a whole.[58]

This was a considerable departure from past policies, for state and local law enforcement and justice administration had traditionally not been part of the federal government's sphere of interest. Under the provisions of the Omnibus Crime Control and Safe Streets Act, as administered by LEAA, a number of funding programs became available to all 50 states, the District of Columbia, Puerto Rico, Guam, the Virgin Islands, and American Samoa. LEAA required states to develop centralized state planning agencies (SPAs) which were responsible for allocating the government funds to local agencies.

The concept of criminal justice in America grew further with the establishment of the National Institute of Law Enforcement and Criminal Justice, the research arm of LEAA. And finally, criminal justice as an academic structure emerged with LEAA's authorization to provide funds for educational purposes. The major program in this behalf was called the Law Enforcement Education Program (LEEP), and it has channeled funds to academic institutions for the educational support of persons employed in law enforcement, the courts, corrections, and other criminal justice agencies.

Since the establishment of LEAA, criminal justice in America has grown substantially. The LEAA budget increased from $60 million in 1969 to $880 million in 1977, with total federal expenditures on criminal justice exceeding $15 billion in 1976.[59] Yet as a final note, with these federal efforts at crime control, LEAA funds have been granted to law enforcement agencies at the expense of other components of the criminal justice system, and much of this funding has been used for police "hardware"—riot equipment, communications, automobiles—to the neglect of the research, education, and social programs which might more effectively reduce the crime problem. Furthermore, with the new emphasis on crime prevention, control, criminal justice, and treatment and rehabilitation, the criminal justice system continues to be criticized as being no more organized, efficient, or effective than it was a decade ago.[60]

## SUGGESTED READINGS

BEDAU, HUGO ADAM, (ed.), *The Death Penalty in America* (Chicago: Aldine, 1964).

BLUMBERG, ABRAHAM S., *Criminal Justice* (Chicago: Quadrangle, 1970).

CHEVIGNY, PAUL, *Police Power* (New York: Random House, 1969).

CLARK, RAMSEY, *Crime in America: Observations on Its Nature, Causes, Prevention and Control* (New York: Simon and Schuster, 1970).

FOSDICK, RAYMOND B., *American Police Systems* (New York: Century, 1920).

HARRIS, RICHARD, *Justice: The Crisis of Law, Order, and Freedom in America* (New York: Dutton, 1970).

von HIRSCH, ANDREW, *Doing Justice: The Choice of Punishments* (New York: Hill and Wang, 1976).

IVES, GEORGE, *A History of Penal Methods* (Montclair, N.J.: Patterson Smith, 1972).

JACOB, HERBERT, *Justice in America: Courts, Lawyers, and the Judicial Process* (Boston: Little, Brown, 1972).

KALVEN, HARRY and ZEISEL, HANS, *The American Jury* (Boston: Little, Brown, 1966).

LeGRANDE, JAMES L., *The Basic Processes of Criminal Justice* (Beverly Hills: Glencoe, 1973).

President's Commission on Law Enforcement and Administration of Justice, *The Challenge of Crime in a Free Society* (Washington, D.C.: U.S. Government Printing Office, 1967).

QUINNEY, RICHARD, *Class, State and Crime: On the Theory and Practice of Criminal Justice* (New York: McKay, 1977).

# POSTSCRIPT:

# The Pursuit of Knowledge in Criminology and Criminal Justice

The preceding chapters have offered an outline of the subject matter of criminology and criminal justice and have presented a glimpse of a number of the critical issues and problems confronting these two inter-related areas of study. Both disciplines have grown significantly during recent decades. Criminology, emerging as an independent science a century ago within the intellectual climates of positivism and determinism, has gone well beyond the basic ideas offered by its founders. It began with Lombroso's "born criminal," and although the notions of biological crime continue to persist in some quarters, the more social reality of crime has become an accepted idea. Theory construction and research endeavors have become conscious of the relative nature of crime, the role of crime in organized society, and the interface between crime and social behavior. And, too, it has been fully recognized that crime in many ways can be normal behavior, and that it emerges through an interactive process that serves to designate certain behaviors as nonconforming, deviant, and ultimately, *criminal.*

Criminal justice is a relatively new discipline. While the concepts of law, justice, and crime are as old as civilization, and while the enforcement of law and the administration of justice emerged with the growth of organized society, criminal justice as an integration of ideas and procedures was given observable form only a decade ago. It grew from the nation's "war on crime" during the 1960s, and it continues to flourish as an independent area of study. The new discipline of criminal justice has begun to deal with the many aspects of law enforcement and justice administration in an attempt to develop an orderly, efficient, and just mechanism for the processing and managing of crime in society.

Yet given the accumulated knowledge of both criminology and criminal justice regarding the concept and definition of crime and the mechanisms for its reduction and control, the tasks of the two disciplines have only just begun. In criminology we still know little about crime and how it comes into being. Much of our knowledge base remains contaminated by myth, prejudice, and stereotype. We have only minimal insight into the causes of crime despite our recognition of its social generation and definition. Furthermore, our methods and strategies for measuring, locating, and identifying crime remain at the most primitive levels. And finally, there are varieties of criminal behavior about which we know little. Theory and research have traditionally focused on those areas of law violation that are the most visible, or that cause the greatest social response, to the neglect of other types which may indeed have the widest social impact.

In criminal justice, like criminology, our knowledge is at best elementary. We have studied the processes of law enforcement, justice administration, and corrections, but our accomplishments are only ones of basic problem identification. This may indeed represent the necessary first step in the evolution of an efficient justice model, but it has also opened a Pandora's box compacted with a host of ills and deficiencies that previously remained unknown.

The task at hand, then, for both criminology and criminal justice, is the continued pursuit of knowledge. But such a quest must be both pragmatic and humanistic. It must be pragmatic in that it has to be appropriate and practical for dealing with the current and future goals of a dynamic and orderly social system. And it must be humanistic in that it must delineate its tasks, serve its purposes, and strive for its goals within an orientation that is dedicated to the protection of fundamental human rights.

# References

## Chapter 1

1. Raffaele Garofalo, *Criminology* (Boston: Little, Brown, 1914), p. 5
2. Hermann Mannheim, *Comparative Criminology* (Boston: Houghton Mifflin, 1965), p. 47.
3. Paul W. Tappan, *Crime, Justice, and Correction* (New York: McGraw-Hill, 1960), p. 10.
4. Sue Titus Reid, *Crime and Criminology* (Hinsdale, Ill.: Dryden, 1976), p. 11.
5. William S. Anderson (ed.), *Ballentine's Law Dictionary* (Rochester, N.Y.: Lawyers Cooperative, 1969).
6. Edwin H. Sutherland, *White Collar Crime* (New York: Dryden, 1949), p. 31.
7. Edwin H. Sutherland, *Principles of Criminology* (Chicago: Lippincott, 1939), p. 17.
8. Robert C. Bensing, "A Comparative Study of American Sex Statutes," *Journal of Criminal Law, Criminology, and Police Science,* 42 (May–June, 1951), pp. 57–72.
9. Harry Elmer Barnes, *The Repression of Crime: Studies in Historical Penology* (New York: George H. Doran, 1926), pp. 43–45.
10. William J. Bowers, *Executions in America* (Lexington, Mass.: D. C. Heath, 1974), p. 43. It might be noted here that Bowers' volume represents a fine source book on the death penalty, including a case by case inventory of the 5,355 executions in America under state authority from 1864 through 1967, as prepared by Negley K. Teeters and Charles J. Zibulka.
11. Curiously, of some 5,355 executions in America under state authority from January 20, 1864 through August 10, 1967 (excluding Alaska and Hawaii), none have occurred in the states of Delaware, Montana, New Mexico, Ohio, and Rhode Island, while some 40 percent (2,108) have occurred in the southern and border states of Florida, Georgia, Kentucky, North Carolina, South Carolina, Tennessee, Texas, and Virginia. See Bowers, op cit., pp. 200–401.

12. Emile Durkheim, *The Division of Labor in Society* (New York: Free Press, 1947).
13. Richard Quinney, *The Social Reality of Crime* (Boston: Little, Brown, 1970), p. v.
14. Howard S. Becker, *Outsiders: Studies in the Sociology of Deviance* (New York: Free Press, 1963), p. 9. Earlier statements of this view can be found in Frank Tannenbaum, *Crime and the Community* (New York: Columbia University Press, 1938), and Edwin M. Lemert, *Social Pathology* (New York: McGraw-Hill, 1951).
15. Kai T. Erikson, *Wayward Puritans: A Study in the Sociology of Deviance* (New York: Wiley, 1966), p. 6.
16. Becker, op. cit., pp. 147–63.
17. Quinney, op. cit., p. 16.
18. Andrew Sinclair, *Era of Excess: A Social History of the Prohibition Movement* (New York: Harper & Row, 1964), p. 10.
19. Richard Hofstadter, *The Age of Reform* (New York: Random House, 1955), p. 24.
20. Ibid., p. 25.
21. Sinclair, op. cit., pp. 9–22.
22. Frances E. Willard, *Woman and Temperance: or, the Work and Workers of the Woman's Christian Temperance Movement* (Hartford, Conn.: Park, 1883). For a further discussion of the WCTU and an excellent view of the Prohibition movement, see Joseph R. Gusfield, "Social Structure and Moral Reform: A Study of the Woman's Christian Temperance Union," *American Journal of Sociology,* LXI (November 1955), pp. 223–30. The most complete historical analysis of the Prohibition movement has been presented by Sinclair, op. cit.
23. Raymond G. McCarthy (ed.), *Drinking and Intoxication* (New Haven and New York: Yale Center of Alcohol Studies and The Free Press of Glencoe, 1959), pp. 395–96.
24. Jerome Michael and Mortimer J. Adler, *Crime, Law and Social Science* (New York: Harcourt, Brace, 1933), p. 5.
25. Tappan, op. cit., pp. 20–22.
26. Robert G. Caldwell, *Criminology* (New York: Ronald Press, 1965), p. 97.
27. Reid, op. cit., p. 16.
28. While the vast majority of known prostitutes are under 30 years of age, FBI data suggest that each year arrests for prostitution include persons over age 65. For a description of prostitution in the United States, see Charles Winick and Paul M. Kinsie, *The Lively Commerce* (Chicago: Quadrangle Books, 1971).
29. Maria Leach and Jerome Fried (eds.), *Funk & Wagnalls Dictionary of Folklore, Mythology and Legend* (New York: Funk & Wagnalls, 1972), p. 778.
30. Ibid.
31. Jan Harold Brunvand, *Folklore: A Study and Research Guide* (New York: St. Martin's Press, 1976), p. 139.
32. G. S. Kirk, *Myth: Its Meaning and Functions in Ancient and Other Cultures* (London: Cambridge University Press, 1973), p. 28.

33. James A. Inciardi, "Drugs, Drug-Taking and Drug-Seeking: Notations on the Dynamics of Myth, Change, and Reality," in James A. Inciardi and Carl D. Chambers (eds.), *Drugs and the Criminal Justice System* (Beverly Hills: Sage, 1974), pp. 203–20.

34. C. T. Onions, *The Oxford Dictionary of English Etymology* (New York: Oxford University Press, 1974), p. 601.

35. Kirk, op. cit., p. 8.

36. See, for example, Henry A. Murray (ed.), *Myth and Mythmaking* (New York: Braziller, 1960).

37. For a detailed examination of contemporary drug mythology, see Inciardi, op. cit. For an earlier statement on this topic, see Alfred R. Lindesmith, " 'Dope Fiend' Mythology," *Journal of Criminal Law and Criminology,* 31 (July–August 1940), pp. 199–208.

38. For an elaboration of some of these issues, the reader may wish to consult the following: John C. Ball and Carl D. Chambers (eds.), *The Epidemiology of Opiate Addiction in the United States* (Springfield, Ill.: Charles C. Thomas, 1970); Lawrence Kolb, *Drug Addiction: A Medical Problem* (Springfield, Ill.: Charles C. Thomas, 1962); Edward M. Brecker, *Licit and Illicit Drugs: The Consumers Union Report* (Boston: Little, Brown, 1972); Rufus King, *The Drug Hang-Up* (New York: Norton, 1972); David Musto, *Narcotics and America* (New Haven: Yale University Press, 1972).

39. Inciardi, op. cit.

40. Becker, op. cit., pp. 135–46.

41. Harry J. Anslinger, with Courtney Riley Cooper, "Marihuana: Assassin of Youth," *American Magazine,* CXXIV (July 1937), p. 19, 150; cited by Becker, op. cit., p. 142. Interestingly, it would appear that during the 1930s and 1940s *American Magazine* was a forum for numerous U. S. Department of Justice issues. In addition to the Anslinger-Cooper articles for the Bureau of Narcotics, the magazine also published sensationalized reports on the topic of gun control, written under the byline of J. Edgar Hoover but prepared by journalist Courtney Riley Cooper. See Sanford J. Ungar, *FBI* (Boston: Little, Brown, 1976), pp. 259–60.

42. William M. Hammel, *The Popular Arts in America: A Reader* (New York: Harcourt, Brace, Jovanovich, 1972), p. 1.

43. See Russel Nye, "The Popular Arts and the Popular Audience," in Hammel, op. cit., pp. 7–13.

44. Nye, op. cit., p. 8.

45. For a further discussion of popular culture, see Bernard Rosenberg and David M. White (eds.), *Mass Culture: The Popular Arts in America* (Glencoe, Ill.: Free Press, 1957); Henry Nash Smith (ed.), *Popular Culture and Industrialism, 1865–1890* (New York: New York University Press, 1967); Harold Rosenberg, *Discovering the Present: Three Decades in Art, Culture, and Politics* (Chicago: University of Chicago Press, 1973); Eric Larrabee and Rolf Meyersohn (eds.), *Mass Leisure* (Glencoe, Ill.: Free Press, 1958).

46. Ron Goulart, *Cheap Thrills: An Informal History of the Pulp Magazines* (New Rochelle, N. Y.: Arlington House, 1972), p. 10.

47. Charles Van Doren (ed.), *Webster's American Biographies* (Springfield, Mass.: G. & C. Merriam, 1974), pp. 753–54.

48. For a discussion of this period of publishing history, see Frank L. Schick, *The Paperbound Book in America* (New York: Bowker, 1958).

49. Goulart, op. cit., pp. 114–15.

50. Les Daniels, *Comix: A History of Comic Books in America* (New York: Bonanza Books, 1971), p. 2.

51. *The Yellow Kid* has a curious history. It first appeared as a color panel called *At the Circus in Hogan's Alley* which was one of several "slum kid" panels Outcault drew for the *New York World* during 1895. The Kid himself wore a blue nightshirt and had only subordinate roles in the strip, which usually had the running title of *Hogan's Alley.* On January 5, 1896 he began appearing in a yellow nightshirt, and with more prominent roles. His messages were saucy and irreverent, and the reading public gave the title of "Yellow Kid" to the nameless child. When Outcault left the *World* for William Randolph Hearst's *New York Journal,* the strip received the new name of *The Yellow Kid. (Hogan's Alley* continued in the *World* without the Kid's yellow nightshirt.) The "better people" in New York were opposed to the "sensational" journalism of both the *World* and the *Journal,* and they also regarded the Kid as a public disgrace. And it was from *The Yellow Kid* that these newspapers, and others like them, earned the label of *yellow journalism.* See Stephen Becker, *Comic Art in America* (New York: Simon and Schuster, 1959).

52. See Daniels, op. cit.; Maurice Horn (ed.), *The World Encyclopedia of Comics* (New York: Chelsea House, 1976).

53. Arthur Asa Berger, *The Comic-Stripped American* (Baltimore: Penguin Books, 1974), pp. 112–32.

54. Ibid.

55. Horn, op. cit., p. 207.

56. For a further discussion of comics, and their heroes and villains, see Robert H. Abel and David M. White (eds.), *The Funnies: An American Idiom* (New York: Free Press of Glencoe, 1963); Reinhold Reitberger and Wolfgang Fuchs, *Comics: Anatomy of a Mass Medium* (Boston: Little, Brown, 1972); Martin Sheridan, *Comics and Their Creators* (Boston: Hale, Cushman and Flint, 1942); Coulton Waugh, *The Comics* (New York: Macmillan, 1947).

57. See John Baxter, *The Gangster Film* (New York: Barnes, 1970); Andrew Sarris, *The American Cinema* (New York: Dutton, 1968); John M. Smith and Tim Cawkwell, *The World Encyclopedia of Film* (New York: Galahad Books, 1972).

58. John Gabree, *Gangsters: From Little Caesar to the Godfather* (New York: Pyramid, 1973), pp. 22–23.

59. Harry Hossent, *Gangster Movies* (London: Octopus Books, 1974), pp. 7–22.

60. Gabree, op. cit., p. 47.

61. Additional materials on the gangster film appear in Lawrence Alloway, *Violent America: The Movies 1946–1964* (New York: Museum of Modern Art, 1971); Andrew Bergman, *We're in the Money* (New York: Harper &

Row, 1972); Colin McArthur, *Underworld U.S.A.* (New York: Viking Press, 1972).

62. See John Dunning, *Tune in Yesterday: The Ultimate Encyclopedia of Old-Time Radio, 1925–1976* (Englewood Cliffs, N.J.: Prentice-Hall, 1976).

63. Horace Newcomb, *TV: The Most Popular Art* (Garden City, N.Y.: Double-day, 1974), pp. 100–8.

64. See Alan Dundes, "The American Concept of Folklore," in Alan Dundes (ed.) *Analytic Essays in Folklore* (The Hague: Mouton, 1975), pp. 3–16.

65. Brunvand, op. cit., p. 138.

66. The content of folklore is discussed in Richard Dorson (ed.), *Folklore and Folklife* (Chicago: University of Chicago Press, 1972); Jan Vansina, *Oral Tradition* (Chicago: Aldine, 1965).

67. For a description of banditry and the bandit-hero, see Eric Hobsbawm, *Primitive Rebels* (New York: Norton, 1959), and his *Bandits* (Harmonds-worth, England: Werdenfeld & Nicolson, 1969).

68. For example, Henry Dale, *Adventures and Exploits of the Younger Brothers; Missouri's Most Daring Outlaws, and Companions of Jesse James* (New York: Street & Smith, 1890).

69. See Jay Monaghan, *The Great Rascal: The Life and Adventures of Ned Buntline* (Boston: Little, Brown, 1952). It is interesting to note that with respect to the exploits of Buffalo Bill (William F. Cody), Buntline's novels were so inaccurate and contained so many falsehoods that Cody himself admitted that many of the reported "adventures" had never actually oc-curred. See Ramon F. Adams, *Six Guns and Saddle Leather* (Norman: University of Oklahoma Press, 1969), p. 98.

70. For example, Clarence E. Ray, *The Border Outlaws, Frank & Jesse James* (Chicago: J. Regan, n. d.); Clarence E. Ray, *The Dalton Brothers and Their Oklahoma Cave* (Chicago: J. Regan, n. d.); Clarence E. Ray, *The Oklahoma Bandits* (Chicago: J. Regan, n. d.). In all, Ray is responsible for writing some 15 of these books, all of which had little historical value.

71. Jesse James Benton's *Cow By the Tail* (Boston: Little, Brown, 1943), for example, which describes the adventures of Billy the Kid, should be com-pared with Thomas F. Daggett, *Billy Le Roy, the Colorado Bandit; or, the King of the American Highwaymen* (New York: Richard K. Fox, Police Gazette, 1881).

72. Walter Noble Burns, *The Saga of Billy the Kid* (Garden City, N. Y.: Double-day, Page, 1926).

73. Compare Walter Noble Burns, *The Robin Hood of El Dorado; The Saga of Joaquín Murieta* (New York: Coward-McCann, 1932), with John Rollin Ridge, *The Life and Adventures of Joaquín Murieta, the Celebrated California Bandit* (San Francisco: W. B. Cook, 1854).

74. For an examination of this phenomenon, see Joseph L. Albini, *The American Mafia: Genesis of a Legend* (New York: Appleton-Century-Crofts, 1971).

75. For a detailed examination of the historical view and the historical method as it relates to crime, see James A. Inciardi, Alan A. Block and Lyle Hal-lowell, *Historical Approaches to Crime: Research Strategies and Issues* (Beverly Hills: Sage, 1977).

# Chapter 2

1. U. S. Bureau of the Census, *Historical Statistics of the United States, Colonial Times to 1957* (Washington, D. C.: U. S. Government Printing Office, 1960), p. 756.
2. See Raphael Semmes, *Crime and Punishment in Early Maryland* (Baltimore: Johns Hopkins Press, 1938), pp. 41–49.
3. Carl Bridenbaugh, *Cities in the Wilderness: Urban Life in America, 1625–1742* (New York: Capricorn, 1964), pp. 68–71.
4. Ibid.
5. Kai T. Erikson, *Wayward Puritans: A Study in the Sociology of Deviance* (New York: Wiley, 1966), pp. 163–81.
6. Ibid., p. 174.
7. For a description of crime and punishment in early New York, see James F. Richardson, *The New York Police: Colonial Times to 1901* (New York: Oxford University Press, 1970), pp. 3–22; Bridenbaugh, op. cit.; Alice Morse Earle, *Colonial Days in Old New York* (New York: Scribner's, 1915), pp. 227–60.
8. Bridenbaugh, op. cit., p. 73.
9. Ibid., pp. 226–27.
10. The lower tip of Manhattan Island became known as the Battery shortly before the turn of the eighteenth century. The Battery earned its name from its designation as an artillery emplacement immediately prior to the Queen Anne's War when, from 1683 to 1688, 92 cannons were mounted in firing position along its sandy beach and rocky shore, thus commanding the approach to the Hudson River. The Battery later became the seaside resort where Jenny Lind gave her first American concert and P. T. Barnum exhibited his once well-known Cardiff Giant. Today, as Battery Park, it shares little with the past, standing as a ravaged wasteland at the entrance of the nation's busiest metropolis. See Rodman Gilder, *The Battery* (Boston: Houghton Mifflin, 1936); Robert Shackleton, *The Book of New York* (Philadelphia: Penn Publishing Company, 1917).
11. Bridenbaugh, op. cit., pp. 220–23.
12. Carl Bridenbaugh, *Cities in Revolt: Urban Life in America, 1743–1776* (New York: Knopf, 1965), p. 122.
13. This comment was offered by Patrick M'Robert, a Scotchman of some means who visited New York City in August, 1774. His letters, published in Edinburgh (1776) as *A Tour Through Part of the North Provinces of America: Being a Series of Letters Wrote on the Spot, in the Years 1774 and 1775,* may be found, edited by Carl Bridenbaugh, in *The Pennsylvania Magazine of History and Biography,* LIX (April 1935), pp. 134–75. See also, Bayrd Still, *Mirror for Gotham: New York as Seen by Contemporaries from Dutch Days to the Present* (New York: New York University Press, 1956), pp. 34–35, 342–43.
14. For a description of the Revolutionary War Years and their effects on the City of New York, see Thomas Jefferson Wertenbaker, *Father Knickerbocker Rebels: New York City During the Revolution* (New York: Scrib-

ner's, 1948); Division of Archives and History, *The American Revolution in New York: Its Political, Social and Economic Significance* (Albany: University of the State of New York, 1926); Edward Robb Ellis, *The Epic of New York City* (New York: Coward-McCann, 1966), pp. 157–75; Still, op. cit., pp. 37–53.

15. Bridenbaugh, op. cit., pp. 302–3.
16. Wertenbaker, op. cit., p. 216.
17. Bridenbaugh, op. cit.
18. Bridenbaugh, *Cities in the Wilderness,* op. cit., p. 380.
19. See Brinley Thomas, *Migration and Economic Growth* (Cambridge: Cambridge University Press, 1954); David M. Schneider, *The History of Public Welfare in New York State, 1609–1866* (Chicago: University of Chicago Press, 1938).
20. Oscar Handlin, *The Uprooted* (New York: Grosset and Dunlap, 1955), p. 155.
21. The original Five Points area was situated northeast of the present New York Courthouse. Today, of the five intersecting streets, only Mulberry retains its original name—Anthony is now Worth Street, Orange is Baxter Street, Cross is Park Street, and Little Water Street has totally vanished. For a more detailed history of the Five Points area, see Ellis, op. cit., pp. 230–46; Alvin F. Harlow, *Old Bowery Days* (New York: D. Appleton, 1931), pp. 80–98; Ladies of the Mission, *The Old Brewery and the New Mission House at the Five Points* (New York: Stringer and Townsend, 1854).
22. The genesis and evolution of the New York street gangs have been discussed at length in Herbert Asbury, "The Old-Time Gangs of New York," *The American Mercury,* XI (August 1927), pp. 478–86, and his *The Gangs of New York* (Garden City, N.Y.: Garden City Publishing Company, 1929); Craig Thompson and Allen Raymond, *Gang Rule in New York* (New York: Dial Press, 1940); Alfred Henry Lewis, *The Apaches of New York* (Chicago: M. A. Donohue, 1912); Richard O'Connor, *Hell's Kitchen* (New York: Lippincott, 1958); Courtney Terrett, *Only Saps Work* (New York: Vanguard Press, 1930); Jacob Riis, *How the Other Half Lives* (New York: Macmillan, 1890), his *The Making of an American* (New York: Macmillan, 1901), and his *The Battle with the Slum* (New York: Macmillan, 1902).
23. Asbury, op. cit., pp. 65–66.
24. Ibid., pp. 66–86; Charles Sutton, *The New York Tombs; Its Secrets and Mysteries* (New York: United States Publishing Company, 1874), pp. 467–81.
25. See Herbert Asbury, *Gem of the Prairie: An Informal History of the Chicago Underworld* (New York: Knopf, 1940); Clifton R. Wooldridge, *Hands Up! In the World of Crime, or Twelve Years a Detective* (Chicago: Thompson, 1901); Frederic M. Thrasher, *The Gang* (Chicago: University of Chicago Press, 1927).
26. See Frank Soule, John H. Gilran, and James Nisbet, *The Annals of San Francisco* (New York: D. Appleton, 1855); John S. Hittell, *A History of the City of San Francisco* (San Francisco: A. L. Bancroft, 1878); Walton Bean, *California: An Interpretive History* (New York: McGraw-Hill, 1968).
27. Henry Collins Brown, *Brownstone Fronts and Saratoga Trunks* (New York: Dutton, 1935), p. 126; Still, op. cit., pp. 167–204; Ellis, op. cit., pp. 317–19.

28. The Tenderloin and other vice districts are discussed at length in Charles H. Parkhurst, *Our Fight With Tammany* (New York: Scribner's, 1895), and his *My Forty Years in New York* (New York: Macmillan, 1923), pp. 106–45; Lloyd Morris, *Incredible New York* (New York: Bonanza Books, 1951), pp. 215–33.

29. See M. R. Werner, *Tammany Hall* (Garden City, N.Y.: Doubleday, Doran, 1928); Alfred Henry Lewis, *Richard Croker* (New York: Life Publishing Company, 1901); Charles N. Glaab and A. Theodore Brown, *A History of Urban America* (New York: Macmillan, 1967), pp. 201–27; Daniel J. Boorstin, *The Americans: The Democratic Experience* (New York: Random House, 1973), pp. 256–61.

30. See Harold Zink, *City Bosses in the U. S.* (Durham, N.C.: Duke University Press, 1930); Alfred Steinberg, *The Bosses* (New York: Macmillan, 1972).

31. See Edwin H. Sutherland, *The Professional Thief* (Chicago: University of Chicago Press, 1937); James A. Inciardi, *Careers in Crime* (Chicago: Rand McNally, 1975).

32. Ibid. For extensive data descriptive of professional criminal operations in New York City during the post-Civil War period, see Thomas Byrnes, *Professional Criminals of America* (New York: G. W. Dillingham, 1895); Edward Crapsey, *The Nether Side of New York* (New York: Sheldon, 1872); Edward Winslow Martin, *Secrets of the Great City* (Philadelphia: National, 1868); Helen Campbell, Thomas W. Knox, and Thomas Byrnes, *Darkness and Daylight; or, Lights and Shadows of New York Life* (Hartford, Conn.: A. D. Worthington, 1892).

33. See Phil Farley, *Criminals of America* (New York: Author's Edition, 1876); Byrnes, op. cit.

34. Harry Sinclair Drago, *Notorious Ladies of the Frontier* (New York: Dodd, Mead, 1969), pp. 156–57; Charles Kelly, *The Outlaw Trail* (New York: Bonanza Books, 1958), pp. 75–76.

35. Ralph Moody, *The Old Trails West* (New York: Crowell, 1963), p. 101; Glenn Shirley, *Law West of Fort Smith* (New York: Henry Holt, 1957).

36. D. J. Cook, *Hands Up!* (Norman: University of Oklahoma Press, 1958), pp. 155–64.

37. Robert M. Coates, *The Outlaw Years* (New York: Literary Guild, 1930).

38. Alvin F. Harlow, *Old Waybills* (New York: Appleton-Century, 1934), pp. 331–37.

39. See Stewart H. Holbrook, *The Story of American Railroads* (New York: Bonanza Books, 1962); Edward Hungerford, *Wells Fargo* (New York: Bonanza Books, 1949); William A. Settle, *Jesse James Was His Name* (Columbia: University of Missouri Press, 1966).

40. Nathaniel Pitt Langford, *Vigilante Days and Ways* (Chicago: A. C. McClurg, 1923).

41. See Roger Lane, "Criminal Violence in America: The First Hundred Years," *The Annals of the American Academy of Political and Social Science,* 423, (January 1976), pp. 1–13; James Elbert Cutler, *Lynch-Law: An Investigation into the History of Lynching in the United States* (New York: Longmans, Green, 1905).

42. Inciardi, op. cit., pp. 92–94.

43. Coates, op. cit., p. 301.
44. See Richard Hofstadter, *The Age of Reform* (New York: Random House, 1955); New York State Senate, *Report and Proceedings of the Senate Committee Appointed to Investigate the Police Department of the City of New York* (New York: Arno Press, 1971, reprinted from the 1895 Senate Committee Report); New York State Chamber of Commerce, *Papers and Proceedings of the Committee on the Police Problem, City of New York* (New York: Arno Press, 1971, reprinted from the 1905 Chamber of Commerce edition); Walter C. Reckless, *Vice in Chicago* (Chicago: University of Chicago Press, 1933).
45. History has suggested that the professional underworld endured for centuries in spite of the efforts of social coercion and control and the influences of social and technological change. See Inciardi, op. cit.; James A. Inciardi, "Visibility, Societal Reaction, and Criminal Behavior," *Criminology: An Interdisciplinary Journal*, 10 (August 1972), pp. 217–33.
46. Thompson and Raymond, op. cit., pp. 3–30; Asbury, *The Gangs of New York*, pp. 361–66.
47. The notion that Black Hand extortion was initiated on American soil at the turn of the century by individuals or limited groups of Italian criminals has been well documented. See, for example, James A. Inciardi, "Vocational Crime," in Daniel Glaser (ed.), *The Handbook of Criminology* (Chicago: Rand-McNally, 1974), pp. 369–70; Inciardi, *Careers in Crime*, op. cit.; Luigi Barzini, *From Caesar to the Mafia* (New York: Library Press, 1971), pp. 322–35; Illinois Association for Criminal Justice, *The Illinois Crime Survey* (Chicago: Illinois Association for Criminal Justice, 1929), pp. 943–44.
48. Humbert S. Nelli, "Italians and Crime in Chicago: The Formative Years, 1890–1920," *American Journal of Sociology*, LXIV (January 1969), pp. 373–91; Inciardi, op. cit., pp. 365–76.
49. Boorstin, op. cit., p. 81.
50. See Wayne C. Rohrer and Louis H. Douglas, *The Agrarian Transition in America: Dualism and Change* (Indianapolis: Bobbs-Merrill, 1969); Andrew Sinclair, *Era of Excess: A Social History of the Prohibition Movement* (New York: Harper and Row, 1964).
51. See Special Committee of the Senate to Investigate Organized Crime in Interstate Commerce (Kefauver Committee), Reports on Crime Investigations, Senate Reports, 82nd Cong., 1st sess., 1951; Nelli, op. cit.
52. The chronology of the Castellammarese War as well as the events that initiated it are detailed in Peter Maas, *The Valachi Papers* (New York: Putnam, 1968); John Kobler, *Capone: The Life and World of Al Capone* (New York: Putnam, 1971).
53. It might be stressed here that while descendants of the Sicilian Mafia had been active in the Italian-American underworld during the early decades of the twentieth century, the Mafia never became active outside of western Sicily. As such, the Mafia never existed as a criminal organization in the United States. For a complete account of the relationships between the Mafia, the Neapolitan Camorra, the Black Hand, *L'Unione siciliana*, the Cosa Nostra, and the Italian-American underworld, see Inciardi, *Careers in Crime*, op. cit., pp. 112–21.

54. In 1940–41, Murder, Inc. was exposed by Burton Turkus of the Kings County District Attorney's Office in Brooklyn. Testimony offered by Abe Reles, a top executioner and field commander in this underworld marketing service, suggested that some one thousand killings had been engineered by the organization since its inception less than a decade before. The unexplained death of Reles on November 12, 1941—his alleged jump from the sixth floor of Coney Island's Half Moon Hotel while under the guardianship of six New York City police officers—thwarted the full impact of the investigation. Without Reles, indictments could not be secured against Joe Adonis and Albert Anastasia, the reigning directors of Murder, Inc., and they were left free to continue their vocation. See Burton B. Turkus and Sid Feder, *Murder, Inc.: The Story of the Syndicate* (New York: Permabooks, 1951).

55. This point has been discussed at length in a number of places. See, for example, Joseph L. Albini, *The American Mafia: Genesis of a Legend* (New York: Appleton-Century-Crofts, 1971).

56. See Estes Kefauver, *Crime in America* (New York: Greenwood Press, 1968); Special Committee of the Senate to Investigate Organized Crime in Interstate Commerce, op. cit.

57. See John L. McClellan, *Crime Without Punishment* (New York: Duell, Sloan and Pearch, 1962); Walter Sheridan, *The Rise and Fall of Jimmy Hoffa* (New York: Saturday Review Press, 1972).

58. Jay Robert Nash, *Bloodletters and Badmen: A Narrative Encyclopedia of American Criminals from the Pilgrims to the Present* (New York: M. Evans, 1973), p. 55.

59. See Richard Hofstadter and Michael Wallace (eds.), *American Violence: A Documentary History* (New York: Random House, 1970).

60. Federal Bureau of Investigation, *Crime in the United States: 1975* (Washington, D. C.: U. S. Government Printing Office, 1976), p. 49.

61. Missouri Association for Criminal Justice, *The Missouri Crime Survey* (New York: Macmillan, 1926), p. 20.

62. Federal Bureau of Investigation, op. cit., pp. 77, 114.

63. Some excellent collections of historical materials relating to specific areas in criminal justice are easily available. See, for example, Julius Goebel and T. Raymond Naughton, *Law Enforcement in Colonial New York: A Study in Criminal Procedure* (New York: Commonwealth Fund, 1944; Montclair, N.J.: Patterson Smith, 1970); The Citizens Police Committee, *Chicago Police Problems* (Chicago: University of Chicago Press, 1931; Montclair, N.J.: Patterson Smith, 1969).

## Chapter 3

1. Harry Best, *Crime and the Criminal Law in the United States* (New York: Macmillan, 1930), p. 134.

2. See, for example, Edwin H. Sutherland, *Principles of Criminology* (Chicago: Lippincott, 1939), p. 29; Donald R. Taft, *Criminology* (New York:

Macmillan, 1956), p. 61; Herbert A. Bloch and Gilbert Geis, *Man, Crime, and Society* (New York: Random House, 1962), p. 141; Richard Quinney, *Criminology: Analysis and Critique of Crime in America* (Boston: Little, Brown, 1975), p. 17.

3. Federal Bureau of Investigation, *Crime in the United States: 1975* (Washington, D.C.: U.S. Government Printing Office, 1976), p. 233. For the balance of this chapter, this publication will be referenced as *Uniform Crime Reports–1975;* corresponding reports for previous years will be similarly cited by year.

4. Theodore N. Ferdinand, "The Criminal Patterns of Boston Since 1849," *American Journal of Sociology,* 73 (July 1967), pp. 84–99.

5. Leon Radzinowicz, *Ideology and Crime* (New York: Columbia University Press, 1966), p. 31.

6. Louis Newton Robinson, *History and Organization of Criminal Statistics in the United States* (New York: Hart, Schaffner & Marx, 1911), p. 40.

7. *Revised Statutes of 1929,* part iv, title 6, secs. 5, 6, 7, 8.

8. *Law of 1832,* ch. 130, secs. 8 and 9.

9. *Law of 1839,* ch. 408.

10. Robinson, op. cit., p. 90.

11. Social Science Research Council, *The Statistical History of the United States from Colonial Times to the Present* (Stanford: Fairfield Publishers, 1965), p. 215.

12. Albert Morris, *What Are the Sources of Knowledge about Crime in the U.S.A.?* Bulletin No. 15, United Prison Association of Massachusetts, November, 1965.

13. *Uniform Crime Reports–1975,* p. 6.

14. Ibid., pp. 6–7.

15. Carolyn J. Inciardi, "An Analysis of Crime Rates by City, Metropolitan Area, and State, 1971–1975," *Unpublished Statistical Report,* Division of Addiction Sciences, University of Miami School of Medicine, 1976.

16. *Initiatives Oriented Technical Assistance Diagnosis: St. Petersburg and Pinellas County, Florida,* Unpublished Research Report, Law Enforcement Assistance Administration and Resource Planning Corporation, Washington, D.C., 1975.

17. See Harry Manuel Shulman, "The Measurement of Crime in the United States," *Journal of Criminal Law, Criminology and Police Science,* 57 (1966), pp. 483–92; Donald R. Cressey, "The State of Criminal Statistics," *National Probation and Parole Association Journal,* 3 (July 1957), pp. 230–41; Ronald H. Beattie, "Criminal Statistics in the United States—1960," *Journal of Criminal Law, Criminology and Police Science,* 51 (1960), pp. 49–65.

18. See D. Seidman and M. Couzens, "Getting the Crime Rate Down: Political Pressure and Crime Reporting," *Law and Society Review,* 8 (1974), pp. 457–93; C. C. VanVechten, "Differential Case Mortality in Select Jurisdictions," *American Sociological Review,* 7 (1942), pp. 833–39.

19. President's Commission on Law Enforcement and Administration of Justice, *Crime and Its Impact: An Assessment* (Washington, D.C.: U.S. Government Printing Office, 1967).

20. Institute of Public Administration, *Crime Records in Police Management* (New York: Institute of Public Administration, 1952), p. 4.
21. D. I. Black, "Production of Crime Rates," *American Sociological Review,* 35 (1970), pp. 735–39.
22. Robinson, op. cit.
23. U.S. National Commission of Law Observance and Enforcement, *Report on Criminal Statistics* (Washington, D.C.: U.S. Government Printing Office, 1931).
24. President's Commission on Law Enforcement and Administration of Justice, op. cit., pp. 123–37.
25. National Advisory Commission on Criminal Justice Standards and Goals, *A National Strategy to Reduce Crime* (Washington, D.C.: U.S. Government Printing Office, 1973).
26. Philip H. Ennis, *Criminal Victimization in the United States: A Report of a National Survey* (Washington, D.C.: U.S. Government Printing Office, 1967).
27. Albert D. Biderman, "An Overview of Victim Survey Research," *Paper Presented at the Annual Meeting of the American Sociological Association,* Washington, D.C., 1967.
28. United States Department of Justice, Law Enforcement Assistance Administration, *Crimes and Victims: A Report on the Dayton—San Jose Pilot Survey of Victimization* (Washington, D.C.: U.S. Government Printing Office, 1974).
29. *LEAA News Release,* April, 1974; U.S. Department of Justice, Law Enforcement Assistance Administration, *Crime in the Nation's Five Largest Cities* (Washington, D.C.: U.S. Department of Justice, 1974).
30. United States Department of Justice, Law Enforcement Assistance Administration, National Criminal Justice Information and Statistics Service, *Criminal Victimization in the United States, January–June 1973* (Washington, D.C.: U.S. Department of Justice, 1974).
31. E. L. Willoughby and James A. Inciardi, "Estimating the Incidence of Crime: A Survey of Crime Victimization in Pueblo, Colorado," *Police Chief* (August 1975), pp. 69–70.
32. James A. Inciardi and Duane C. McBride, "Victim Survey Research: Implications for Criminal Justice Planning," *Journal of Criminal Justice,* 4 (1976), pp. 147–51; James A. Inciardi, "Criminal Statistics and Victim Survey Research for Effective Law Enforcement Planning," in Emilio C. Viano (ed.), *Victims and Society* (Washington, D.C.: Visage Press, 1976), pp. 177–89.
33. Ennis, op. cit.
34. Willoughby and Inciardi, op. cit.
35. Ibid.
36. Ennis, op. cit.
37. Queen's Bench Foundation, *Rape Victimization Study* (San Francisco: Queen's Bench Foundation, 1975).
38. A study of department store shoplifting in 1933, for example, estimated that of 5,314 thefts known to three Philadelphia establishments more than 95 percent remained unknown to the police. See Thorsten Sellin, *Research*

*Memorandum on Crime in the Depression* (New York: Social Science Research Council, 1937).

39. J. S. Wallerstein and C. L. Wyle, "Our Law-abiding Lawbreakers," *National Probation,* (March–April 1947), pp. 107–12.

40. J. Andenaes, N. Christie, and S. Skirbekk, "A Study in Self-reported Crime," in Scandinavian Research Council on Criminology, *Scandinavian Studies in Criminology* (Oslo: Universitelsforloget, 1965), pp. 87–88.

41. Methodological issues of this order are examined in Roger Hood and Richard Sparks, *Key Issues in Criminology* (New York: McGraw-Hill, 1970), pp. 46–79; Eugene Doleschal, "Hidden Crime," *Crime and Delinquency Literature,* 2 (October 1970), pp. 546–72.

42. James A. Inciardi and Carl D. Chambers, "Unreported Criminal Involvement of Narcotic Addicts," *Journal of Drug Issues* (Spring 1972), pp. 57–64.

43. Leon Radzinowicz, "The Criminal in Society," *Journal of the Royal Society of Arts,* 62 (1964), pp. 916–29.

44. Doleschal, op. cit.

45. Panel on Drug Use and Criminal Behavior, *Drug Use and Crime* (Washington, D.C.: National Institute on Drug Abuse and Research Triangle Institute, 1976).

## Chapter 4

1. Nigel D. Walker, "Lost Causes in Criminology," in Roger Hood (ed.), *Crime, Criminology and Public Policy* (New York: Free Press, 1974), pp. 47–62.

2. James A. Inciardi and Harvey A. Siegal (eds.), *Crime: Emerging Issues* (New York: Praeger, 1977), pp. 2–3.

3. Robert K. Merton, *Social Theory and Social Structure* (New York: Free Press, 1968), p. 231.

4. See Marion L. Starkey, *The Devil in Massachusetts* (New York: Knopf, 1949); Montague Summers, *The History of Witchcraft* (New Hyde Park, N. Y.: University Books, 1956); George L. Burr (ed.), *Narratives of Witchcraft Cases, 1648–1706* (New York: Scribner's, 1914).

5. Peter Haining, *Witchcraft and Black Magic* (New York: Grosset & Dunlap, 1972), pp. 86–87.

6. Originally published in 1693, Cotton Mather's *Wonders of the Invisible World* appears in Samuel G. Drake (ed.), *The Witchcraft Delusion in New England* (Roxbury, Mass.: W. Elliot Woodward, 1866).

7. William R. Hunt, *Dictionary of Rogues* (New York: Philosophical Library, 1970), pp. 61–62.

8. George B. Vold, *Theoretical Criminology* (New York: Oxford University Press, 1958), pp. 14–18.

9. Ibid.

10. This summary of Beccaria's position was drawn from Leon Radzinowicz, *Ideology and Crime* (New York: Columbia University Press, 1966), pp. 6–14.

11. Vold, op. cit., pp. 24–26.

12. Arthur E. Fink, *The Causes of Crime: Biological Theories in the United States, 1800–1915* (Philadelphia: University of Pennsylvania Press, 1938), p. 1.

13. Havelock Ellis, *The Criminal* (New York: Scribner's, 1900), p. 27.
14. Hermann Mannheim, *Comparative Criminology* (New York: Houghton Mifflin, 1965), p. 213.
15. Vold, op. cit., pp. 44–49.
16. Leon Radzinowicz, *In Search of Criminology* (Cambridge: Harvard University Press, 1962), p. 3; Olof Kinberg, *Basic Problems of Criminology* (Copenhagen: Levin and Munkgaard, 1935), p. 70.
17. Richard Quinney, *The Problem of Crime* (New York: Dodd, Mead, 1970), pp. 56–57.
18. Yale Levin and Alfred R. Lindesmith, "English Ecology and Criminology of the Past Century," *Journal of Criminal Law and Criminology,* 27 (March–April 1937), pp. 801–16; Alfred R. Lindesmith and Yale Levin, "The Lombrosian Myth in Criminology," *American Journal of Sociology,* 42 (March 1937), pp. 653–71.
19. Patrick Colquhoun, *Treatise on the Police of the Metropolis* (London: J. Mawman, 1806); Charles Booth, *Life and Labour of the People of London* (London: Macmillan, 1892–1897).
20. Luke Owen Pike, *A History of Crime in England* (London: Smith, Elder, 1873–1876).
21. Quinney, op. cit., p. 57. Curiously, a case has also been made for Franz Joseph Gall, credited with the initial doctrine of phrenology, as the first criminologist. See Leonard Savitz and Stanley H. Turner, "The Origin of Scientific Criminology: Franz Joseph Gall as the First Criminologist," *Paper Presented at the 28th Annual Meeting of the American Society of Criminology,* November 4–7, 1976, Tucson, Arizona. Finally, the literature also reflects contradictions as to the spelling of Lombroso's given name. It has appeared as *Cesare* and *Caesare* in many recent works, and as *Cesare* and *Caesar* in Lombroso's own publications.
22. There has been considerable discussion as to how the theories of crime causation ought to be grouped. Yet for the purposes of this overview, they will be presented in only the broadest of categories. For those concerned with the more acute typological aspects of causation theory, see Vold, op. cit.; Stephen Schafer, *Theories in Criminology* (New York: Random House, 1969).
23. Gina Lombroso Ferrero, *Criminal Man According to the Classification of Cesare Lombroso* (New York: Putnam, 1911), pp. 10–24.
24. Caesar Lombroso and William Ferrero, *The Female Offender* (New York: D. Appleton, 1895), p. 101.
25. Cesare Lombroso, *Crime, Its Causes and Remedies* (Boston: Little, Brown, 1911).
26. Charles Goring, *The English Convict* (London: His Majesty's Stationery Office, 1913).
27. Richard L. Dugdale, *The Jukes* (New York: Putnam, 1910).
28. See Henry H. Goddard, *The Kallikaks* (New York: Macmillan, 1912); Arthur H. Estabrook and Charles P. Davenport, *The Nam Family* (Cold Spring Harbor, N. Y.: Eugenics Record Office, 1912); Arthur H. Estabrook, *The Jukes in 1915* (Washington, D. C.: Carnegie Institution, 1916).

29. These studies of heredity were strongly criticized years later by physical anthropologist Ashley Montagu who claimed that they were so full of prejudice and assumption that they were of no merit. See Ashley Montagu, *Human Heredity* (New York: World, 1959), p. 125. It can also be noted here that although Charles Goring's study of the English convict served to criticize the Lombrosian theory, it also put forth the notion that crime resulting from defective intelligence could be transmitted by heredity. See Goring, op. cit.

30. See Johannes Lange, *Crime and Destiny* (New York: Charles Boni, 1930).

31. Max G. Schlapp and Edward H. Smith, *The New Criminology: A Consideration of the Chemical Causation of Abnormal Behavior* (New York: Boni and Liveright, 1928).

32. Louis Berman, *New Creations in Human Beings* (New York: Doran, Doubleday, 1938).

33. Ernest A. Hooton, *The American Criminal: An Anthropological Study* (Cambridge: Harvard University Press, 1939).

34. Joseph Wilder, "Sugar Metabolism and its Relation to Criminal Behavior," in Robert M. Lindner and Robert V. Seliger (eds.), *Handbook of Correctional Psychology* (New York: Philosophical Library, 1947), pp. 98–129.

35. William H. Sheldon, *Varieties of Delinquent Youth* (New York: Harper, 1949).

36. Edward Podolsky, "The Chemical Brew of Criminal Behavior," *Journal of Criminal Law, Criminology and Police Science,* 45 (1955), pp. 676–79.

37. See D. J. West (ed.), *Criminological Implications of Chromosome Abnormalities* (Cambridge: University of Cambridge, Institute of Criminology, 1969).

38. "The XYY Syndrome: A Challenge to Our System of Criminal Responsibility," *New York Law Forum,* 16 (Spring 1970), p. 232.

39. Quinney, op. cit., p. 64.

40. See, for example, Kate Friedlander, *The Psychoanalytic Approach to Juvenile Delinquency* (London: Kegan Paul, Trench, Trubner, 1947).

41. The problem of circularity in the psychoanalytic approaches is discussed in Michael Hakeem, "A Critique of the Psychiatric Approach to Crime and Correction," *Law and Contemporary Problems,* 23 (Autumn 1958), pp. 650–82.

42. William Healy, *The Individual Delinquent* (Boston: Little, Brown, 1914).

43. Nathaniel Hirsch, *Dynamic Causes of Juvenile Crime* (Cambridge: Sci-Art, 1937).

44. Vold, op. cit., pp. 101–2.

45. Quinney, op. cit., p. 75.

46. Robert E. Park, Ernest W. Burgess, and Roderick D. MacKensie, *The City* (Chicago: University of Chicago Press, 1925).

47. Clifford R. Shaw and associates, *Delinquency Areas* (Chicago: University of Chicago Press, 1929).

48. Clifford R. Shaw, *The Jack Roller* (Chicago: University of Chicago Press, 1930), and his *Brothers in Crime* (Chicago: University of Chicago Press, 1938).

49. Donald R. Taft, *Criminology* (New York: Macmillan, 1956), pp. 336–49.
50. Ibid., pp. 338–39.
51. Robert K. Merton, *Social Theory and Social Structure* (New York: Basic Books, 1957), pp. 166–76.
52. See, for example, Mannheim, op. cit., pp. 419–68.
53. Jerome Michael and Mortimer J. Adler, *Crime, Law and Social Science* (New York: Harcourt, Brace, 1933), p. 5.
54. Edwin H. Sutherland, "Crime and the Conflict Process," *Journal of Juvenile Research,* 13 (January 1929), p. 41; cited by Quinney, op. cit., p. 88.
55. Thorsten Sellin, *Culture Conflict and Crime* (New York: Social Science Research Council, 1938), p. 21.
56. Albert K. Cohen, *Delinquent Boys: The Culture of the Gang* (Glencoe, Ill.: Free Press, 1955).
57. Walter B. Miller, "Lower Class Culture as a Generating Milieu for Gang Delinquency," *Journal of Social Issues,* 14 (1958), pp. 5–19.
58. Gabriel Tarde, *Les Lois de l'imitation* (Paris: Alcan, 1890).
59. Gabriel Tarde, *Penal Philosophy* (Boston: Little, Brown, 1912), p. 252.
60. Edwin H. Sutherland, *The Professional Thief* (Chicago: University of Chicago Press, 1937).
61. Edwin H. Sutherland, *Principles of Criminology* (Philadelphia: Lippincott, 1947), pp. 6–7.
62. Richard Quinney, *Criminology: Analysis and Critique of Crime in America* (Boston: Little, Brown, 1975), p. 110.
63. See Albert J. Reiss, Jr., and A. Lewis Rhodes, "An Empirical Test of Differential Association Theory," *Journal of Research in Crime and Delinquency,* 1 (January 1964), pp. 5–18; James F. Short, Jr., "Differential Association and Delinquency," *Social Problems,* 4 (January 1957), pp. 233–39.
64. James A. Inciardi, *Careers in Crime* (Chicago: Rand McNally, 1975).
65. Clayton A. Hartjen, *Crime and Criminalization* (New York: Praeger, 1974), p. 51.
66. Don C. Gibbons, "The Study of Crime Causation," *American Journal of Sociology,* LXXVII (September 1971), pp. 262–78.
67. For Sutherland's own critique of differential association, see Edwin H. Sutherland, "Critique of the Theory," in Karl Schuessler (ed.), *Edwin H. Sutherland: On Analyzing Crime* (Chicago: University of Chicago Press, 1973), pp. 30–41. This paper was originally written in 1944, six years prior to Sutherland's death. It was intended only for circulation among his associates and did not appear in print until almost three decades after its writing.
68. Daniel Glaser, "Criminality Theories and Behavioral Images," *American Journal of Sociology,* 61 (March 1956), pp. 433–44.
69. Hutchins Hapgood, *The Autobiography of a Thief* (New York: Fox, Duffield, 1903), pp. 27–28.
70. Donald R. Cressey, "Changing Criminals: The Application of the Theory of Differential Association," *American Journal of Sociology LXI* (September 1955), pp. 116–20.

71. Rita Volkman and Donald R. Cressey, "Differential Association and the Rehabilitation of Drug Addicits," in John A. O'Donnell and John C. Ball (eds.), *Narcotic Addiction* (New York: Harper & Row, 1966), pp. 209–33.
72. Vold, op. cit., p. 198.
73. Howard S. Becker, *Outsiders: Studies in the Sociology of Deviance* (New York: Free Press, 1963), p. 1.
74. Richard Quinney, *The Social Reality of Crime* (Boston: Little, Brown, 1970), pp. 15–25.
75. Frank Tannenbaum, *Crime and the Community* (New York: Columbia University Press, 1938), pp. 19–20.
76. Edwin M. Lemert, *Social Pathology* (New York: McGraw-Hill, 1951), pp. 56–59.
77. Vold, op. cit., p. 202.
78. Karl Marx, *A Contribution to the Critique of Political Economy* (New York: International Library, 1904), pp. 11–13. This edition is the English translation of the original work of 1859.
79. Marx's *A Contribution to the Critique of Political Economy* was the theoretical forerunner of *Das Kapital,* in which he explained the logic and philosophy behind his revolutionary propaganda document *The Communist Manifesto.* For a clear analysis and view of the Marxian view of society, see Rolf Dahrendorf, *Class and Class Conflict in Industrial Society* (Stanford: Stanford University Press, 1959), pp. 3–35.
80. Taft, op. cit.
81. Merton, op. cit.; Sellin, op. cit.
82. Quinney, op. cit.
83. Quinney, *Criminology: Analysis and Critique of Crime in America,* op. cit., p. 291.
84. Nicolas F. Hahn, "Crime and Intelligence: An Historical Look at the Low IQ Theory," *Paper Presented at the Annual Meeting of the American Society of Criminology,* Atlanta, Georgia, November 29, 1977. This excellent work reviews the emergence and growth of the low IQ theories of crime, pointing to their social impact during the twentieth century.
85. Richard J. Herrnstein, "I. Q.," *Atlantic Monthly,* (September 1971), p. 57.
86. By "phenotypical" the author is referring to the detectable expression of both genetic and environmental influences. See David Rosenthal, "Heredity and Criminality," *Criminal Justice and Behavior,* 2 (March 1975), p. 3.
87. Hahn, op. cit.

## Chapter 5

1. Howard Becker, *Through Values to Social Interpretation* (Durham, N.C.: Duke University Press, 1950), p. 97.
2. Edward A. Shils and H. A. Finch, *Max Weber on the Methodology of the Social Sciences* (Glencoe, Ill.: Free Press, 1949), p. 90.
3. See Becker, op. cit., pp. 93–127; A. D. Grimshaw, "Specification of Boundaries of Constructed Types Through Use of the Pattern Variables," *The*

*Sociological Quarterly,* 3 (July 1962), pp. 179–95; John C. McKinney, *Constructive Typology and Social Theory* (New York: Appleton-Century-Crofts, 1966).

4. See Enrico Ferri, *Criminal Sociology* (New York: D. Appleton, 1896); Raffaele Garofalo, *Criminology* (Boston: Little, Brown, 1916); C. Bernaldo de Quirós, *Modern Theories of Criminality* (Boston: Little, Brown, 1911).

5. Ernst Kretchmer, *Körperbau und Charakter* (Berlin: Springer–Verlag, 1921).

6. Emil Kraeplin, *Psychiatric* (Liepzig: J. A. Barth, 1883).

7. See the discussion offered by George B. Vold, *Theoretical Criminology* (New York: Oxford University Press, 1958).

8. For example, Edwin H. Sutherland and Donald R. Cressey, *Principles of Criminology* (Philadelphia: Lippincott, 1955, 1960, 1966, 1970, 1974). Richard R. Korn and Lloyd McCorkle, *Criminology and Penology* (New York: Holt, Rinehart and Winston, 1959); Herbert A. Bloch and Gilbert Geis, *Man, Crime and Society* (New York: Random House, 1962, 1970).

9. Edwin M. Lemert, "An Isolation and Closure Theory of Naive Check Forgery," *Journal of Criminal Law, Criminology and Police Science,* 44 (September–October 1953), pp. 296–307.

10. Edwin H. Sutherland, *White Collar Crime* (New York: Dryden, 1949).

11. Donald R. Cressey, *Other People's Money* (New York: Free Press of Glencoe, 1953).

12. Ruth Shonle Cavan, *Criminology* (New York: Crowell, 1955), pp. 20–29.

13. Clarence C. Schrag, "Some Foundations for a Theory of Correction," in Donald R. Cressey (ed.), *The Prison: Studies in Institutional Organization and Change* (New York: Holt, Rinehart and Winston, 1961), pp. 309–57; Clarence C. Schrag, "A Preliminary Criminal Typology," *Pacific Sociological Review,* 49 (Spring 1961), pp. 11–16.

14. Marshall B. Clinard and Richard Quinney, *Criminal Behavior Systems: A Typology* (New York: Holt, Rinehart and Winston, 1967), pp. 4–5.

15. Julian B. Roebuck, *Criminal Typology* (Springfield, Ill.: Charles C Thomas, 1967).

16. Clinard and Quinney, 1970, op. cit., pp. 14–15.

17. Source: Marshall B. Clinard and Richard Quinney, *Criminal Behavior Systems: A Typology* (New York: Holt, Rinehart and Winston, 1967), pp. 14–18. Copyright © 1967 by Holt, Rinehart and Winston, Inc. Reprinted by permission.

18. Clayton A. Hartjen, *Crime and Criminalization* (New York: Praeger, 1974), p. 66.

19. For a critical analysis of classifications and typologies in criminology, see Roger Hood and Richard Sparks, *Key Issues in Criminology* (New York: McGraw-Hill, 1970), pp. 110–40.

20. Marshall B. Clinard and Richard Quinney, *Criminal Behavior Systems: A Typology,* 2d ed. (New York: Holt, Rinehart and Winston, 1973), p. 17.

21. See Nolen D. C. Lewis and Helen Yarnell, *Pathological Firesetting* (New York: Nervous and Mental Disease Monographs, 1951).

22. Bloch and Geis, 1970, op. cit., p. 338.

23. James A. Inciardi, "The Adult Firesetter: A Typology," *Criminology: An Interdisciplinary Journal*, 8 (August 1970), pp. 145–55.
24. See Roy Moreland, *The Law of Homicide* (Indianapolis: Bobbs-Merrill, 1952).
25. *Uniform Crime Reports–1975*, p. 19.
26. Jerome Hall, "Analytic Philosophy and Jurisprudence," *Ethics*, 77 (October 1966), pp. 14–28.
27. Bloch and Geis, 1962, op. cit., p. 256.
28. John Katzenbach, "The Law and Mr. Jones," *The Miami News*, January 15, 1977, pp. 1, 4.
29. Marvin E. Wolfgang, *Patterns in Criminal Homicide* (Philadelphia: University of Pennsylvania Press, 1958).
30. Jay Robert Nash, *Bloodletters and Badmen* (New York: M. Evans, 1973), pp. 319–27.
31. Nathan F. Leopold, *Life Plus Ninety-Nine Years* (New York: Doubleday, 1958).
32. William S. Anderson (ed.), *Ballentine's Law Dictionary* (Rochester, N. Y.: Lawyers Co-operative, 1969), p. 98.
33. Ibid.
34. Ibid., p. 51.
35. Ibid., p. 1181.
36. National Commission on the Causes and Prevention of Violence, *To Establish Justice, To Insure Domestic Tranquility* (Washington, D. C.: U. S. Government Printing Office, 1969), pp. 25–26.
37. President's Commission on Law Enforcement and Administration of Justice, *The Challenge of Crime in a Free Society* (Washington, D. C.: U. S. Government Printing Office, 1967), p. 18.
38. *Uniform Crime Reports–1975*, p. 20.
39. Anderson, op. cit., p. 1054.
40. Ibid., p. 1214.
41. Menachem Amir, "Forcible Rape," *Federal Probation*, 31 (March 1967), pp. 51–58.
42. Ibid.; Menachem Amir, *Patterns in Forcible Rape* (Chicago: University of Chicago Press, 1971); F. H. McClintock, *Crimes of Violence* (New York: St. Martin's Press, 1963); President's Commission, op. cit., pp. 39–41.
43. Amir, "Forcible Rape," op. cit.
44. Norval Morris and Gordon Hawkins, "From Murder and Violence, Good God, Deliver Us," *Midway*, 10 (Summer 1969), p. 70.
45. Lynn A. Curtis, *Criminal Violence: National Patterns and Behavior* (Lexington, Mass.: D. C. Heath, 1974), p. 87.
46. J. B. Csida and J. Csida, *Rape: How To Avoid It and What To Do if You Can't* (Chatsworth, Calif.: Books for Better Living, 1974), p. 18.
47. Martha Weinman Lear, "Q. If You Rape a Woman and Steal Her TV, What Can They Get You for in New York? A. Stealing Her TV," *New York Times Magazine*, January 30, 1972, p. 10.
48. Dan T. Carter, *Scottsboro: A Tragedy of the American South* (New York: Oxford University Press, 1969).

49. David M. Petersen and Marcello Truzzi (eds.), *Criminal Life: Views from the Inside* (Englewood Cliffs, N. J.: Prentice-Hall, 1972), p. 165.
50. See Haywood Patterson and Earl Conrad, *Scottsboro Boy* (Garden City, N.Y.: Doubleday, 1950); Leon Radzinowicz and Marvin E. Wolfgang (eds.), *The Criminal in Confinement: Crime and Justice,* vol. 3 (New York: Basic Books, 1971).
51. See David A. Ward and Gene G. Kassebaum, *Women's Prison: Sex and Social Structure* (Chicago: Aldine, 1965); Rose Giallombardo, *Society of Women: A Study of a Women's Prison* (New York: Wiley, 1966); Dorothy West, "I Was Afraid to Shut My Eyes," *The Saturday Evening Post,* 241 (July 13, 1968), p. 23.
52. This listing represents an expansion and revision of the 17-point typology offered by Sorokin. See Pitirim A. Sorokin, *Social and Cultural Dynamics,* vol. 2 (New York: American, 1937), ch. 15.
53. Clinard and Quinney, op. cit., p. 60.
54. *Uniform Crime Reports–1975,* p. 34.
55. James A. Inciardi, "The Pickpocket and His Victim," *Victimology: An International Journal,* 1 (Fall 1976), pp. 446–53.
56. Lemert, op. cit.
57. Mary Owen Cameron, *The Booster and the Snitch: Department Store Shoplifting* (New York: Free Press, 1964). See also, Loren E. Edwards, *Shoplifting and Shrinkage Protection for Stores* (Springfield, Ill.: Charles C Thomas, 1958).
58. James A. Inciardi, "Vocational Crime," in Daniel Glaser (ed.), *Handbook of Criminology* (Chicago: Rand McNally, 1974), pp. 299–300.
59. Ibid., pp. 300–45; James A. Inciardi, *Careers in Crime* (Chicago: Rand McNally, 1975); Edwin H. Sutherland, *The Professional Thief* (Chicago: University of Chicago Press, 1937).
60. For a complete description of the rise and decline of professional crime, see Inciardi, op. cit., pp. 5–82.
61. Ibid., pp. 85–103.
62. Werner J. Einstadter, "The Social Organization of Armed Robbery," *Social Problems,* 17 (Summer 1969), pp. 64–83.
63. See Donald R. Cressey, *Theft of the Nation* (New York: Harper & Row, 1969); Thorsten Sellin, "Organized Crime: A Business Enterprise," *Annals of the American Academy of Political and Social Science,* 347 (May 1963), pp. 12–19; Clinard and Quinney, op. cit., p. 225.
64. President's Commission, op. cit., pp. 187–209.
65. See, for example, Cressey, op. cit.
66. Luigi Barzini, *From Caesar to the Mafia: Sketches of Italian Life* (New York: Library Press, 1971); Joseph L. Albini, *The American Mafia: Genesis of a Legend* (New York: Appleton-Century-Crofts, 1971); Norval Morris and Gordon Hawkins, *The Honest Politician's Guide to Crime Control* (Chicago: University of Chicago Press, 1970).
67. Inciardi, "Vocational Crime," op. cit., p. 379.
68. Edwin H. Sutherland, "White Collar Criminality," *American Sociological Review,* 5 (February 1940), pp. 1–12.

69. Donald J. Newman, "White Collar Crime," *Law and Contemporary Problems,* 23 (Autumn 1958), p. 737.

70. Marshall B. Clinard, *The Black Market: A Study of White Collar Crime* (New York: Holt, Rinehart and Winston, 1952).

71. Richard Quinney, "The Study of White Collar Crime: Toward a Reorientation in Theory and Research," *Journal of Criminal Law, Criminology and Police Science,* 55 (June 1964), pp. 208–14.

72. Clinard and Quinney, op. cit., pp. 206–23.

73. See Patrick J. McGarvey, *C.I.A.: The Myth and the Madness* (Baltimore: Penguin Books, 1973); Victor Marchetti and John D. Marks, *The C.I.A. and the Cult of Intelligence* (New York: Dell, 1974); David Wise, *The Politics of Lying: Government Deception, Secrecy, and Power* (New York: Random House, 1973).

74. Richard Quinney, *Criminology: Analysis and Critique of Crime in America* (Boston: Little, Brown, 1975), p. 159. For a detailed discussion of the Watergate eipsode, see Carl Bernstein and Bob Woodward, *All the President's Men* (New York: Warner, 1974).

75. This section is based on James A. Inciardi, "Visibility, Societal Reaction, and Criminal Behavior," *Criminology: An Interdisciplinary Journal,* 10 (August 1972), pp. 217–33.

76. Edwin M. Lemert, *Human Deviance, Social Problems, and Social Control* (Englewood Cliffs, N. J.: Prentice-Hall, 1967), p. 23.

77. Sutherland, *The Professional Thief,* op. cit., p. 217.

78. Howard S. Becker, *Outsiders: Studies in the Sociology of Deviance* (New York: Free Press, 1963), pp. 147–63.

79. Ibid., pp. 147–48.

80. Ibid., p. 9.

81. Sutherland, op. cit., p. 82.

82. Becker, op. cit.

83. Kai T. Erikson, "Notes on the Sociology of Deviance," *Social Problems,* 9 (Spring 1962), pp. 307–14.

## Chapter 6

1. Luke Owen Pike, *A History of Crime in England; vol. 2, from the Accession of Henry VII to the Present Time* (London: Smith, Elder, 1873–76), pp. 457–62; see also, C. T. Onions (ed.), *The Oxford Dictionary of English Etymology* (New York: Oxford University Press, 1966).

2. Luke Owen Pike, *A History of Crime in England; vol. 1, from the Roman Invasion to the Accession of Henry VII* (London: Smith, Elder, 1873–76), p. 218.

3. Pike, op. cit.

4. For a discussion of the emergence and growth of police systems in America, see James F. Richardson, *The New York Police: Colonial Times to 1901* (New York: Oxford University Press, 1970); Raymond B. Fosdick, *American Police Systems* (New York: Century, 1920).

5. See George Ives, *A History of Penal Methods* (Montclair, N. J.: Patterson Smith, 1972); Harry Elmer Barnes, *The Story of Punishment: A Record of Man's Inhumanity to Man* (Montclair, N. J.: Patterson Smith, 1972).
6. See Abraham S. Blumberg, *Criminal Justice* (Chicago: Quadrangle, 1970); G. Edward White, *The American Judicial Tradition: Profiles of Leading American Judges* (New York: Oxford University Press, 1976).
7. *Dartmouth College* v. *Woodward,* (US)4 Wheat 518, 4L Ed 629.
8. Jerome Michael and Mortimer J. Adler, *Crime, Law and Social Science* (New York: Harcourt, Brace, 1933), p. 242.
9. Ibid., pp. 20–21.
10. Sanford J. Unger, *FBI* (Boston: Little, Brown, 1976), p. 73.
11. See John Toland, *The Dillinger Days* (New York: Random House, 1963).
12. Lyndon B. Johnson, *Message to the Congress,* March 9, 1966.
13. President's Commission on Law Enforcement and Administration of Justice, *The Challenge of Crime in a Free Society* (Washington, D. C.: U. S. Government Printing Office, 1967).
14. Originally published in 1931 by the U. S. Government Printing Office, the *Wickersham Commission Reports* have been republished in their entirety by Patterson Smith Publishing Corporation, Montclair, New Jersey, 1968.
15. President's Commission, op. cit., p. 7.
16. Ibid.
17. American Bar Association, *New Perspectives on Urban Crime* (Washington, D. C.: ABA Special Committee on Crime Prevention and Control, 1972), p. 1.
18. See Clark R. Mollenhoff, *Strike Force: Organized Crime and the Government* (Englewood Cliffs, N. J.: Prentice-Hall, 1972).
19. Arthur Neiderhoffer, *Behind the Shield: The Police in Urban Society* (New York: Doubleday, 1967); Paul Chevigny, *Police Power* (New York: Random House, 1969).
20. Carl Werthman and Irving Piliavin, "Gang Members and the Police," in David Bordua (ed.), *The Police* (New York: Wiley, 1967), pp. 56–98.
21. Steven M. Greenberg, "Compounding a Felony: Drug Abuse and the American Legal System," in James A. Inciardi and Carl D. Chambers (eds.), *Drugs and the Criminal Justice System* (Beverly Hills: Sage, 1974), pp. 183–201.
22. *Mapp* v. *Ohio,* 367 U. S. 643 (1961).
23. See Alexander B. Smith and Harriet Pollack, *Crime and Justice in a Mass Society* (Waltham, Mass.: Xerox, 1972), p. 194.
24. *Miranda* v. *Arizona,* 384 U. S. 436 (1966).
25. James P. Hall, *Criminal Justice Administration: The American Plan* (Dubuque, Iowa: Kendall/Hunt, 1976), p. 163.
26. Ramsey Clark, *Crime in America: Observations on Its Nature, Causes, Prevention and Control* (New York: Simon and Schuster, 1970), p. 300.
27. Smith and Pollack, op. cit., pp. 148–49.
28. Martin R. Haskell and Lewis Yablonsky, *Crime and Delinquency* (Chicago: Rand McNally, 1974), p. 762.
29. M. Cherif Bassiouni, *Criminal Law and Its Process* (Springfield, Ill.: Charles C Thomas, 1969), p. 454.

30. Frank J. Donner and Eugene Cerruti, "The Grand Jury Network: How the Nixon Administration Has Secretly Perverted a Traditional Safeguard of Individual Rights," *The Nation,* 214 (January 3, 1972), p. 5.

31. *60 Minutes,* CBS-TV, April 3, 1977. See also Morton H. Halperin, Jerry J. Berman, Robert L. Borosage and Christine M. Marwick, *The Lawless State: The Crimes of the U.S. Intelligence Agencies* (New York: Penguin Books, 1976).

32. *United States* v. *Safeway Stores, Inc.* (DC Tex) 20 FRD 451.

33. For a discussion of the events which led to Agnew's resignation from the Vice Presidency and the road to Watergate, see Arthur M. Schlesinger, Jr., *The Imperial Presidency* (New York: Popular Library, 1974).

34. James L. LeGrande, *The Basic Processes of Criminal Justice* (Beverly Hills: Glencoe, 1973), p. 102.

35. Blumberg, op. cit., p. 5.

36. Ibid., p. 167.

37. Sue Titus Reid, *Crime and Criminology* (Hinsdale, Ill.: Dryden, 1976), p. 265. For an extended analysis of plea negotiation, see Donald J. Newman, *Conviction: The Determination of Guilt or Innocence Without Trial* (Boston: Little, Brown, 1966).

38. See Herbert Jacob, *Justice in America: Courts, Lawyers, and the Judicial Process* (Boston: Little, Brown, 1972).

39. William S. Anderson (ed.), *Ballentine's Law Dictionary* (Rochester, N. Y.: Lawyers Co-operative, 1969), p. 818.

40. Ibid., p. 146.

41. Ibid., p. 1037.

42. Ibid., p. 192.

43. Ibid., pp. 260–61.

44. *Duncan* v. *Louisiana,* 390 U. S. 145, 88 S. Ct. 1444 (1968).

45. Robert D. Pursley, *Introduction to Criminal Justice* (Encino, Calif.: Glencoe, 1977), p. 289.

46. The trial process is discussed at length in Jacob, op. cit.; LeGrande, op. cit.

47. Bassiouni, op. cit., pp. 506–7; Pursley, op. cit., p. 293.

48. Walter C. Reckless, *The Crime Problem* (New York: Appleton-Century-Crofts, 1967), pp. 673–74.

49. James A. Inciardi, "The Impact of Presentence Investigations on Subsequent Sentencing," *Paper Presented at the 1976 Annual Meeting of the American Sociological Association,* New York, N. Y., August, 1976.

50. Administrative Offices of the U. S. Courts, Division of Probation, "The Selective Presentence Investigation Report," *Federal Probation,* 38 (December 1974), p. 48.

51. American Bar Association Project for Standards for Criminal Justice, *Standards Relating to Probation* (New York: Institute of Judicial Administration, 1970), p. 9.

52. For a more detailed discussion of the death penalty, see Hugo Adam Bedau (ed.), *The Death Penalty in America* (Chicago: Aldine, 1964); William J. Bowers, *Executions in America* (Lexington, Mass.: D. C. Heath, 1974); Harry E. Allen and Clifford E. Simonsen, *Corrections in America: An Introduction* (Beverly Hills: Glencoe, 1975), pp. 243–64.

53. Franklin E. Zimring and Gordon J. Hawkins, *Deterrence: The Legal Threat in Crime Control* (Chicago: University of Chicago Press, 1973); Andrew von Hirsch, *Doing Justice: The Choice of Punishments* (New York: Hill and Wang, 1976).

54. Allen and Simonsen, op. cit., p. 167.

55. For a discussion of the history, philosophy, and issues relating to both parole and probation, see Daniel Glaser, *The Effectiveness of a Prison and Parole System* (Indianapolis: Bobbs-Merrill, 1964); Howard Abadinsky, *Probation and Parole: Theory and Practice* (Englewood Cliffs, N. J.: Prentice-Hall, 1977).

56. Vern F. Folley, *American Law Enforcement* (Boston: Holbrook Press, 1973), p. 83.

57. See Richard Harris, *The Fear of Crime* (New York: Praeger, 1969), and his *Justice: The Crisis of Law, Order, and Freedom in America* (New York: Dutton, 1970).

58. Law Enforcement Assistance Administration, *3rd Annual Report of the Law Enforcement Assistance Administration, Fiscal Year 1971* (Washington, D. C.: U. S. Government Printing Office, 1972), p. ii.

59. Office of Management and Budget, *Federal Expenditures on Criminal Justice, 1967–77.*

60. See Richard Quinney, *Class, State and Crime: On the Theory and Practice of Criminal Justice* (New York: McKay, 1977).

# INDEX

Abadinsky, Howard, 204
Abel, Robert H., 184
Abortion, illegal, 78
Adams, Ramon F., 185
Adler, Freda, 154
Adler, Mortimer J., 10, 25, 104, 114, 157–58, 182, 196, 202
Adonis, Joe, 190
Adversary system, 156
Agnew, Spiro T., 170, 203
Agrarian myth, 9
Albini, Joseph L., 53, 185, 190, 200
Alcohol abuse, 12
Alfred the Great, 155
Alger, Horatio, 19
Allen, Harry E., 203, 204
Alloway, Lawrence, 184
Ames, Dr. Albert, 40
Amir, Menachem, 134, 154, 199
Anastasia, Albert, 48, 190
Andenaes, J., 193
Anderson, William S., 181, 199, 203
Anglo-American law, 2
Anslinger, Harry J., 16, 183
Anti-Saloon League, 45
Appeal, 175
Arrest, 164–66
Arrest history typology, 120
Arson, 6, 28, 58, 60, 65, 127–28, 130, 141
Asbury, Herbert, 187, 189
Assault, 1, 6, 28, 31, 58, 60, 61, 63, 65, 72–73, 82, 87, 132–33, 139

Atavism, 98
Auto theft. *See* Vehicle theft

Bail, 167, 168
Ball, John C., 183, 197
Bandit-heroes, 23–24
Banditry, concept of, 141
Bank robbery, 41, 158
Barker, Kate Clark "Ma", 142, 158
Barnes, Harry Elmer, 181, 202
Barnum, P. T., 186
Barrow, Clyde, 24, 142, 158
Bart, Black, 42
Barzini, Luigi, 189, 200
Bass, Sam, 24, 42
Bassiouni, M. Cherif, 202, 203
Bastardy, 56, 58
Bates, Alfred L., 158
Bates, Ruby, 135
Battery, 132
Baxter, John, 184
Bean, Walton, 187
Beattie, Ronald H., 191
Beccaria, Cesare, 94–95, 193
Becker, Howard, 197
Becker, Howard S., 7, 8, 16, 25, 110, 150, 182, 183, 197, 201
Becker, Stephen, 184
Bedau, Hugo Adam, 178, 203
Behrman, Martin, 40
Bensing, Robert C., 181
Bentham, Jeremy, 95
Benton, Jesse James, 185

Berger, Arthur Asa, 25, 184
Bergman, Andrew, 184
Berman, Jerry J., 203
Berman, Louis, 99, 195
Bernstein, Carl, 154, 201
Best, Harry, 54, 190
Bestiality, 6
Biderman, Albert D., 80, 192
Bigamy, 56, 58
Billington, John, 49
Billy the Kid, 24
Biological determinism, 98–101
Biological criminal, 100
Black, D. I., 192
Blackbeard, 141
Black Hand, 44, 46, 189
Blackmail. *See* Extortion
Black market, 48
Blackstone, William, 95
Bloch, Herbert A., 191, 198, 199
Block, Alan A., 25, 185
Blumberg, Abraham S., 171, 178, 202, 203
Bogart, Humphrey, 21
Booking, 166–67
Boorstin, Daniel J., 188, 189
Booth, Charles, 194
Bootlegging, 46
Bordua, David, 202
Borosage, Robert L., 203
Bossism, urban, 38–40
Bowers, William J., 181, 203
Breaking and entering. *See* Burglary
Brecker, Edward M., 183
Bridenbaugh, Carl, 186, 187
Brown, A. Theodore, 188
Brown, Henry Collins, 187
*Brown v. Mississippi,* 166
Brunvand, Jan Harold, 25, 182, 185
Buchalter, Louis "Lepke", 46, 47
Buffalo Bill. *See* Cody, William F.
Buntline, Ned, 24, 185
Burgess, Ernest W., 195
Burglary, 1, 6, 28, 30, 31, 40, 58, 60, 63, 65, 73–74, 82, 83, 87, 136–38, 140, 141
Burns, Walter Noble, 24, 185
Burr, George L., 193
Butler, "Colonial" Edward, 40
Byrnes, Thomas, 188

Cagney, James, 21
Caldwell, Charles, 96

Caldwell, Robert G., 11, 182
Cameron, Mary Owen, 139, 200
Campbell, Helen, 188
Capital crimes. *See* Death penalty
Capone, Al, 46
Carter, Dan T., 199
Case fixing, 151–52
Case law, 4
Cassidy, "Butch," 142
Cattle rustling, 41, 142
Causation of crime, theories, 90–115
Cavan, Ruth Shonie, 119, 198
Cawkwell, Tim, 184
Cerruti, Eugene, 203
Chambers, Carl D., 87, 183, 193, 202
Chevigny, Paul, 178, 202
Christie, N., 193
Clark, Ramsey, 167, 178, 202
Classical school of criminology, 94–95
Clinard, Marshal B., 120, 126, 129, 137, 141, 146, 154, 198, 200, 201
Coates, Robert M., 188, 189
Cody, William F., 185
Cohen, Albert K., 105, 114, 196
Colonial criminal codes, 6
Colquhoun, Patrick, 194
Comics, 19–20, 184
Common law, 4
Conceptions of crime, 12–25, 29
Confidence games, 28, 40, 140
Conflict theories of crime, 103–6
Conrad, Earl, 200
*Conscience collective,* 7
Conventional crime, 121, 123, 125, 126
Cook, D. J., 188
Cooper, Courtney Riley, 183
Corporate crime, 126, 146
Coronado, Francisco Vásquez, 91
Corrections, 6, 156–57, 181
Corrientes, Diego, 24
Corruption, 12, 37–41
Cosa Nostra, 47, 48, 143, 144
Costello, A. E., 59
Costello, Frank, 46, 47, 48
Counterfeiting, 30, 31, 36, 40, 61, 65, 82, 136, 140
Couzens, M., 191
Cox, George "Old Boy," 40
Crapsey, Edward, 53, 188
Cressey, Donald R., 89, 109, 154, 191, 196, 197, 198, 200

Crime
  as career, 139–45
  causation theories of, 90–115
  and the cinema, 20–21
  in colonial America, 28–32
  and comics, 19–20
  concealment of, 78–79
  conceptions of, 12–25, 29
  definitions of, 3–5
  and degeneration, 99, 113–14
  extent of, 63–76
  fear of, 1
  and folklore, 23–24
  and history, 23–24, 25
  history of, 26–53
  and Marxism, 111–12
  measurement of, 54–89
  and myth, 13–14
  and pulp fiction, 18–19
  and radio, 21–22
  relativity of, 5–11
  as social construction, 8–11
  and television, 22–23
  on Western frontier, 41–42
  See also specific types and
    behavior systems
Crime Index, 62–64
Crime in the streets, 12
Crime rate, computation of, 62
"Crimes known to the police,"
  59
Criminal, definition of, 11–12
Criminal behavior systems, 120–53
Criminal districts, 32–37
Criminal intent, 3–4
Criminal justice
  concept of, 155, 157–58
  and criminology, vii, 179–80
  definition of, vii
  discovery of, 158–60
  history of, 155–64
  rise of, 176–78
  process, 160–76
  system, 162–63
Criminal mythology, 12–15, 23
Criminal statistics, 54–89
  evolution of, 55–59
  unreliability of, 76–79
Criminal syndicates, 31
Criminal typologies, 118–26
Criminal victimization, 80–86
Criminals, labeling of, 11–12
Criminogenic culture, 103–4, 110–11

Criminology
  classical school, 94–95
  and criminal justice, vii, 179–80
  definition of, vii
  and history, 26–27
  neo-classical school, 95–96
  positive school, 96–98
Croker, Richard, 39
Crump, Ed, 40
Csida, J., 199
Csida, J. B., 199
Curley, James, 40
Curtis, Lynn A., 154, 199
Cutler, James Elbert, 53, 188

Daggett, Thomas F., 185
Dahrendorf, Rolf, 197
Dale, Henry, 185
Daniels, Les, 184
Darwin, Charles, 97, 113
Davenport, Charles P., 99, 194
Death penalty, 6–7, 181, 203
Degeneration theory, 99, 113–14
Dehistorization, 24
Delancey, James, 31
Delinquent subcultures, 105
Demonology, 92–93
Determinism, 96, 97
Deviance, 7–11, 152
Diamond, Jack "Legs," 46
Differential association, 106–8
Differential identification, 108–9
Dillinger, John, 142, 158
Dime novels, 24
Disorderly conduct, 29, 56, 58, 61, 65,
  164
Doleschal, Eugene, 89, 193
Donner, Frank J., 203
Doolin, Bill, 42
Dorson, Richard, 185
Douglas, Louis H., 189
Drago, Harry Sinclair, 188
Drake, Samuel G., 193
Drug abuse, 12, 15–16
Drug distribution, 46, 142
Drug law violations, 61, 65, 164
Drunkenness, 61, 65, 164
Duca, Angelo, 24
Due process, 156, 168
Dugdale, Richard L., 99, 194
Dundes, Alan, 185
Dunning, John, 185
Durkheim, Emile, 7, 25, 182

Earle, Alice Morse, 186
Edwards, Loren E., 200
Einstadter, Werner J., 142, 200
Eliot, T. S., 17
Ellis, Edward Robb, 187
Ellis, Havelock, 194
Embezzlement, 12, 28, 58, 61, 65, 119
Ennis, Philip H., 89, 192
Environmental crime, 126
Erikson, Kai T., 7, 25, 29, 53, 182, 186, 201
Estabrook, Arthur H., 99, 194
Evans, Chris, 42
Extortion, 12, 40, 44, 46, 140, 150

Farley, Phil, 188
Feder, Sid, 190
Federal Bureau of Investigation, 51, 59, 64, 66, 77, 147, 158, 164, 182
Feeblemindedness, 99
Fee-splitting, 78
Fein, Benny, 43–44
Felony, 4, 161
Felony-murder doctrine, 129–30
Fencing, 78, 152–53
Ferdinard, Theodore H., 89, 191
Ferrero, Gina Lombroso, 194
Ferrero, William, 194
Ferri, Enrico, 97, 118, 198
Finch, H. A., 197
Fink, Arthur E., 114, 193
Fitzwaren, Fulk, 23
Flegenheimer, Arthur. See Schultz, Dutch
Fletcher, Joseph, 97
Floyd, Charles "Pretty Boy," 142
Folk-heroes, 23–24
Folklore, 23
Folley, Vern F., 204
Forgery, 40, 58, 61, 65, 78, 82, 119, 136, 138, 140
Fornication, 29, 78
Fosdick, Raymond B., 178, 201
Franks, Robert, 132
Fraud, 12, 58, 61, 65, 78, 82
Free will, 94–96
Fried, Jerome, 182
Friedlander, Kate, 195
Fuchs, Wolfgang, 184
Furman decision, 6

Gabree, John, 184
Gall, Franz Joseph, 96, 197, 194
Gambling, 12, 33, 39, 46, 48, 56, 58, 61, 65, 78, 142
Gangs, 32–37
Gangster films, 20–21
Gangsterism, 42–49
Gardner, Erle Stanley, 22
Garofalo, Baron Raffaele, 2–3, 97, 118, 181, 198
Geis, Gilbert, 191, 198, 199
Genovese, Vito, 46, 47, 48
Giallombardo, Rose, 200
Gibbons, Don C., 196
Gilder, Rodman, 186
Gilmore, Gary, 7
Gilran, John H., 187
Glaab, Charles N., 188
Glaser, Daniel, 108, 189, 196, 204
Goddard, Henry H., 99, 194
Goebel, Julius, 190
Goldwater, Barry, 159
Goring, Charles, 98, 194, 195
Goulart, Ron, 183, 184
Gould, Chester, 19
Governmental crime, 126, 147
Grand jury, 169–70
Greenberg, Steven M., 202
Grimshaw, A. D., 197
Gurrey, André-Michel, 56, 57
Guilty plea, 170–71
Gusfield, Joseph R., 182

Hague, Frank, 40
Hahn, Nicolas F., 197
Haining, Peter, 193
Hakeem, Michael, 195
Hall, James P., 202
Hall, Jerome, 199
Hallowell, Lyle A., 25, 185
Halperin, Morton H., 203
Hammel, William M., 183
Hancock, John, 36
Handlin, Oscar, 187
Hapgood, Hutchins, 196
Harlow, Alvin F., 187, 188
Harris, Richard, 178, 204
Hartjen, Clayton A., 108, 114, 196, 198
Haskell, Martin R., 202
Hawkins, Gordon J., 154, 199, 200, 204

Healy, William, 101, 195
Hearst, Patricia, 170
Hearst, William Randolph, 184
Heresy, 6
Herrnstein, Richard J., 113, 197
Highway robbery, 30, 31 (*see also* hijacking, robbery)
Hijacking, 141
Hirsch, Nathaniel, 101, 195
Hirsch, Andrew von, 178, 204
History
 and crime, 23–24, 25
 and criminology, 26–27
Hittell, John S., 187
Hobsbawm, Eric, 185
Hoffa, James, 48
Hofstadter, Richard, 53, 182, 189, 190
Holbrook, Stewart H., 188
Homicide, 1, 6, 12, 60, 62, 63, 64, 65, 68–70, 126, 128–32, 139
Homicide rates, 50–51
Homicide weapons, 130
Homosexuality, 6, 78
Hood, Roger, 89, 114, 193, 198
Hooton, Ernest A., 99, 195
Hoover, Herbert, 159
Hoover, J. Edgar, 183
Hopkins, Matthew, 93
Horn, Maurice, 184
Hossent, Harry, 184
Hugon, Daniel, 100
Hungerford, Edward, 188
Hunt, William R., 193
Hypocalcemia, 100
Hypoglycemia, 100

Ideal types, 117–18
Inciardi, Carolyn J., 191
Inciardi, James A., 25, 87, 154, 183, 185, 188, 189, 192, 193, 196, 199, 200, 201, 202, 203
Index of Crime. *See* Crime Index
Indictment, 168–70
Information, 168–70
Initial appearance, 168
Inquisitorial system, 156
International Association of Chiefs of Police, 57
Investigation, 161, 164
Italian underworld, 46–49
Ives, George, 178, 202

Jackson, Andrew, 9
Jacob, Herbert, 178, 203
James, Frank, 24, 42, 142
James, Jesse, 24, 42, 142
Jefferson, Thomas, 9
Johnson, Lyndon B., 159, 202
Joyce, James, 17
Judson, Edward Z. C., 24
Juke family, 99

Kalven, Harry, 178
Karpis, Alvin, 142, 158
Kassebaum, Gene G., 200
Katzenbach, John, 199
Kefauver Committee, 48, 189
Kefauver, Estes, 190
Kelly, Charles, 188
Kelly, George "Machine Gun," 142, 158
Kidnapping, 6, 132, 141, 158, 166
Kinberg, Olof, 194
King, Rufus, 183
Kinsie, Paul M., 182
Kirk, G. S., 14, 182, 183
Knox, Thomas W., 188
Kobler, John, 189
Kolb, Lawrence, 183
Korn, Richard R., 198
Kraeplin, Emil, 119, 198
Kretchmer, Ernst, 119, 198

Labeling, 7–11
Labor racketeering, 45, 48
Lane, Roger, 53, 188
Lange, Johannes, 195
Langford, Nathaniel Pitt, 188
Lansky, Meyer, 46, 47
Larceny, 1, 28, 58, 60, 63, 65, 74–75, 82, 87, 136–38
Larrabee, Eric, 183
Lavater, J. K., 96
"Law and order," 158–59
Law Enforcement Assistance Administration, 81–82, 176–77
Law Enforcement Education Program, 177
Leach, Maria, 182
Lear, Martha Weinman, 199
Le Grande, James L., 178, 203
Lemert, Edwin M., 110, 139, 148, 182, 197, 200, 201
Leopold, Nathan F., 132, 199

Levin, Yale, 194
Lewis, Alfred Henry, 187, 188
Lewis, Nolen D. C., 198
Lind, Jenny, 186
Lindbergh, Charles A., 158
Lindesmith, Alfred R., 183, 194
Lindner, Robert M., 195
Liquor law violations, 61, 65
Liquor syndication, 46
Loan-sharking, 78, 142
Loeb, Albert A., 132
Loeb, Richard A., 132
Lombroso, Cesare, 90–91, 97–98, 99,
    102, 113, 118, 179, 194
Long, Huey, 40
Luciano, Lucky, 46, 47
L'Unione Siciliana, 44, 46, 47, 189
Lynching, 6

McArthur, Colin, 185
McBride, Duane C., 192
McCarthy, Raymond G., 182
McClellan, John L., 48, 190
McClintock, F. H., 89, 199
McCorkle, Lloyd, 198
McGarvey, Patrick J., 201
McKinney, John C., 154, 198

Maas, Peter, 189
MacKensie, Roderick D., 195
Madden, Owney, 46
Mafia, 44, 47, 142, 189
Malthus, Thomas, 106
Manhattan Bail Project, 167
Mannheim, Hermann, 3, 25, 181,
    194, 196
Manslaughter, 28, 128 (see also
    homicide)
Mapp v. Ohio, 165–66
Maranzano, Salvatore, 47
Marijuana, 6, 16
Marchetti, Victor, 201
Marks, John D., 201
Martin, Edward Winslow, 188
Marx, Karl, 106, 110–11, 197
Marwick, Christine M., 203
Masseria, Giuseppe "Joe, the Boss,"
    46, 47, 48
Mather, Cotton, 93, 193
Mather, Increase, 93
Merton, Robert K., 91–92, 104, 193,
    196, 197

Meyersohn, Rolf, 183
Michael, Jerome, 10, 25, 104, 114,
    157–58, 182, 196, 202
Miller, Walter B., 105, 196
Miranda v. Arizona, 166
Miranda warning rules, 166
Misdemeanor, 4, 161
Mob violence, 49
Mollenhoff, Clark R., 202
Monaghan, Jay, 185
Montagu, Ashley, 195
Moody, Ralph, 188
More, Thomas, 106
Moreland, Roy, 154, 199
Morgan, Henry, 141
Morris, Albert, 191
Morris, Lloyd, 188
Morris, Norval, 154, 199, 200
M'Robert, Patrick, 186
Motions, 172–74
Motion picture codes, 20–21
Munsey, Frank Andrew, 18
Murder, 31, 39, 58, 128 (see also
    homicide)
Murder, Inc., 47–48, 190
Murray, Henry A., 183
Musto, David F., 183
Murieta, Joaquín, 24
Myth, 13–16

Napoleon, 90
Narcotic addiction, 15–16
Narcotics traffic, 48
Nash, Jay Robert, 190, 199
National Advisory Commission on
    Criminal Justice Standards and
    Goals, 79
National Commission on Law
    Observance and Enforcement. See
    Wickersham Commission
National Opinion Research Center,
    79, 80, 84, 85
Natural law, 2–3, 7
Naughton, T. Raymond, 190
Neiderhoffer, Arthur, 202
Nelli, Humbert S., 53, 189
Neo-classical school of criminology,
    95–96
Newcomb, Horace, 185
Newman, Donald J., 146, 201, 203
Night watch, 156
Nisbet, James, 187

*Nolo contendere,* 171
Nominalism, 7
Nye, Russel, 183

Occasional property crime, 121, 122,
    124, 136–39 (*see also* property
    crime)
Occupational crime, 121, 122, 124,
    126, 146 (*see also* white collar
    crime)
O'Connor, Richard, 187
O'Donnell, John A., 197
"offenses", 5
Omnibus Crime Control and Safe
    Streets Act, 176, 177
Onions, C. T., 183, 201
Organized crime, 12, 45–49, 119, 121,
    123, 125, 126–27, 140, 142–45, 153
Orgen, Jacob "Little Augie," 46
Outcault, Richard, 19, 184

Pardon, 176
Park, Robert E., 102, 195
Parker, Bonnie, 24, 142, 158
Parkhurst, Charles H., 188
Parole, 175–76
Patterson, Haywood, 200
Pauperism, 33
Peel, Sir Robert, 156
Peers, Rosanna, 34, 35
Pendergast, Tom, 40
Perjury, 6
Petersen, David M., 154, 200
Perjury, 58
Phrenology, 96
Physiognomy, 96
Pickpocketing, 28, 87, 136, 138, 140
Pike, Luke Owen, 194, 201
Piliavin, Irving, 202
Piracy, 30, 36, 141 (*see also* river
    pirates)
Plato, 14
Plagiarism, 136
Plea-bargaining, 171
Podolsky, Edward, 100, 195
Police brutality, 12
Polk, James Knox, 9
Politicality of crime, 110–12
Political crime, 121, 122, 124, 126,
    147, 148, 149
Political machines, 38–40
Political patronage, 38–40

Pollack, Harriet, 202
Ponce de Léon, Juan, 91
Popular culture
    content of, 16–17
    and crime, 16–23
Positive school of criminology,
    96–98
Preliminary hearing, 168
President's Commission on Law
    Enforcement and Administration
    of Justice, 79, 133, 159, 160, 161,
    162–63, 176
Price fixing, 78
Price, Victoria, 135
Private detectives, 18–19
Probation, 174–75
Professional crime, 40–41, 43, 45, 121,
    123, 125, 140–41, 143, 145, 149–50,
    151–53
Professional "heavy" crime, 140,
    141–142, 143, 145, 151
Prohibition, 8–10, 43, 45–49
Property crime, 136–39, 148–49, 153
    (*see also* occasional property
    crime)
Prostitution, 12, 13, 29, 30, 31, 32, 39,
    46, 61, 65, 78, 142, 164, 182
Ptolemy Epiphanes, 90
Public order crime, 121, 122, 123,
    125, 148, 149, 153
Pulitzer, Joseph, 19
Pulp fiction, 18–19
Punishment, early forms, 94
Puritan Criminal Code, 6
Purse-snatching, 83, 87, 138
Pursley, Robert D., 203
Pyromania, 127

Quaker Criminal Codes, 6
Quetelet, Adolphe-Jacques, 56, 57
Quinney, Richard, 8, 25, 97, 101, 104,
    108, 110, 111–12, 114, 120, 126, 129,
    137, 141, 146, 154, 178, 182, 191,
    194, 195, 196, 197, 198, 200, 201,
    204
Quirós, C. Bernaldo de, 118–19, 198

Racial violence, 49
Radio, 21–22
Radzinowicz, Leon, 114, 191, 193,
    194, 200
Raleigh, Sir Walter, 91

Rape
  forcible, 1, 6, 31, 32, 60, 63, 65,
    70–71, 132, 133–36, 139, 166
  statutory, 78, 133
Rawson, R. W., 97
Ray, Clarence E., 24, 185
Raymond, Allen, 187, 189
Receiving stolen property, 61, 65, 78,
  152–53
Reckless, Walter C., 53, 189, 203
Reid, Sue Titus, 11, 181, 182, 203
Reiss, Albert J. Jr., 196
Reitberger, Reinhold, 184
Release on recognizance, 167
Reles, Abe, 190
Reno, John, 41
Reno, Simeon, 41
Revised Statutes of 1829, 57
Revolution, 6
Rhodes, A. Lewis, 196
Richardson, James F., 53, 186, 201
Ridge, John Rollin, 185
Riis, Jacob, 187
River pirates, 36, 39
Robbery, 1, 28, 30, 31, 32, 58, 60, 63,
  65, 71–72, 82, 83, 87, 132, 141–42
  (see also bank, stagecoach and
  train robbery)
Robin Hood, 23
Robinson, Edward G., 21
Robinson, Louis Newton, 79, 89, 191,
  192
Roebuck, Julian B., 120, 198
Rohrer, Wayne C., 189
Roman law, 2
Romilly, Samuel, 95
Rosenberg, Bernard, 183
Rosenberg, Harold, 183
Rosenthal, David, 113–14, 197
Ruef, Abe "Curly," 40
Rush, Benjamin, 91

Sabotage, 6
Sarris, Andrew, 184
Savitz, Leonard, 194
Scalise, Frank, 48
Schafer, Stephen, 114, 194
Schick, Frank L., 184
Schlapp, Max G., 99, 195
Schlesinger, Arthur M., 203
Schneider, David M., 187
Schrag, Clarence C., 119, 198

Schuessler, Karl, 114, 196
Schultz, Dutch, 46
Scottsboro Boys, 135
Search and seizure, 165–66
Seduction, 77
Seidman, D., 191
Self-reported criminal behavior,
  86–88, 89
Seliger, Robert V., 195
Sellin, Thorsten, 104, 114, 192, 196,
  197, 200
Semmes, Raphael, 53, 186
Sentencing, 174–76
Settle, William A., 53, 188
Sex offenses, 1, 61, 65, 82 (see also
  specific offenses)
Shackleton, Robert, 186
Shapiro, Jacob "Gurrah", 46
Shaw, Clifford R., 102–3, 114, 195
Sheldon, William H., 100, 195
Shepard, Jack, 24
Sheppard, Dr. Samuel, 11
Sheridan, Martin, 184
Sheridan, Walter, 190
Shils, Edward A., 197
Shirley, Glenn, 188
Shoplifting, 40, 78, 138, 139, 140
Short changing, 78
Short, James F. Jr., 196
Shulman, Harry Manuel, 89, 191
Siegal, Harvey A., 193
Siegal, Benjamin "Bugsy," 46, 47
Simonsen, Clifford E., 203, 204
Sinclair, Andrew, 53, 182, 189
Skirbekk, S., 193
Smith, Alexander B., 202
Smith, Edward H., 99, 195
Smith, Henry Nash, 183
Smith, John M., 184
Sneak theft, 40, 87, 140
Sociological theories of crime,
  102–9
Socrates, 96
Sodomy, 78
Sontag, John, 42
Sorokin, Pitirim A., 200
Soule, Frank, 187
Sparks, Richard, 89, 193, 198
Stagecoach robbery, 41, 142
Starkey, Marion L., 193
Starr, Henry, 42
Statutory law, 4

Steinberg, Alfred, 188
Still, Bayrd, 186, 187
Street gangs, 32–37
Strike breaking, 43
Subpoena, 170
Summers, Montague, 193
Sternberg, Josef von, 20
Sutherland, Edwin H., 5, 25, 104, 107–8, 114, 145–46, 154, 181, 188, 190, 196, 198, 200, 201
Sutton, Charles, 187
Swindling, 12, 40
Symbionese Liberation Army, 170
Synanon, 109

Taft, Donald R., 103, 111, 190, 196, 197
Tag-switching, 78
Talmadge, Gene, 40
Tammany Hall, 38–40
Tannenbaum, Frank, 110, 182, 197
Tappan, Paul W., 3–4, 181, 182
Tarde, Gabriel, 106–7, 196
Tax evasion, 12
Teamster Union, 48
Teeters, Negley K., 181
Television, 22–23
Terrett, Courtney, 187
Texas Rangers, 42
Theft, dollar losses from, 137
Theories of crime, 90–115
Thomas, Brinley, 187
Thompson, Craig, 187, 189
Thrasher, Frederic M., 187
Toland, John, 202
Tongs, 40
Torrio, John, 46
Tracy, Dick, 19–20, 22
Train, Arthur, 51
Train robbery, 41–42, 142
Treason, 6
Trial, 171–73
True bill, 169
Truzzi, Marcello, 154, 200
Turkus, Burton, 190
Turner, Stanley H., 194
Turpin, Dick, 24
Tweed, William, 39
Twins studies, 99
Tyler, John, 9

Ungar, Sanford J., 183, 202
Uniform Crime Reports, 59–79, 80, 81, 129, 130, 131
Urschel, Charles F., 158
U. S. Department of Justice, 164, 183
U. S. Supreme Court, 6, 156, 166

Vagrancy, 56, 59, 61, 65, 164
Vandalism, 61, 65, 127
Van Doren, Charles, 184
Vansina, Jan, 185
Van Vechten, C. C., 191
Vehicle theft, 1, 60, 63, 65, 75–76, 82, 87, 137, 138
Vera Institute of Justice, 167
Verri, Alessandro, 94
Viano, Emilio C., 89, 192
Vice, 30–32, 61, 65, 78
    areas, 37
    commercialization of, 37–41
Victimless crime, 56, 78, 164 (see also public order crime)
Victims of crime, 83–85
Victim survey research, 80–86, 88–89
Vigilantism, 42
Villa, Pancho, 24
"Violations", 5
Violence, 49–53
Violent personal crime, 121, 122, 124, 126, 128–36, 139, 148
Visibility of crime, 148–53
Vocational crime, 139–45
Vold, George B., 101–2, 110, 115, 193, 194, 195, 197, 198
Volkman, Rita, 197

Walker, Nigel D., 193
Wallace, Michael, 53, 190
Wallerstein, J. S., 193
Ward, David A., 200
Washington, George, 36
Waterfront racketeering, 48
Watergate, 147
Waugh, Coulton, 184
Weapons violations, 61, 65
Weber, Max, 117–8
Webster, Daniel, 156
Werner, M. R., 188
Wertenbaker, Thomas Jefferson, 186, 187
Werthman, Carl, 202
West, D. J., 115, 195

West, Dorothy, 200
Wheeler, Stanton, 89
White collar crime, 12, 78, 119,
  145–7, 149 (*see also* corporate
  and occupational crime)
White, David M., 183, 184
White, G. Edward, 202
Wickersham Commission, 79, 159
Wickersham, George W., 159
Wilder, Joseph, 100, 195
Willard, Frances E., 10, 182
Willoughby, E. L., 192
Winick, Charles, 182
Wise, David, 201
Witchcraft, 93
Wolfgang, Marvin E., 89, 131, 154,
  199, 200

Woman's Christian Temperance
  Union, 10, 182
Woodward, Bob, 154, 201
Wooldridge, Clifton R., 187
Wyle, C. L., 193

XYY chromosome, 100–1
Yablonsky, Lewis, 202
Yale, Frankie, 46
Yarnell, Helen, 198

Zeisel, Hans, 178
Zibulka, Charles J., 181
Zimring, Franklin E., 204
Zink, Harold, 53, 188
Zwillman, Abner "Longy," 47